I Shouldn't Have Done This:
A Heartfelt Love Story

Harmeet Singh

Chennai • Bangalore

CLEVER FOX PUBLISHING
Chennai, India

Published by CLEVER FOX PUBLISHING 2024
Copyright © Harmeet Singh 2024

All Rights Reserved.
ISBN: 978-93-56489-26-4

This book has been published with all reasonable efforts taken to make the material error-free after the consent of the author. No part of this book shall be used, reproduced in any manner whatsoever without written permission from the author, except in the case of brief quotations embodied in critical articles and reviews.

The Author of this book is solely responsible and liable for its content including but not limited to the views, representations, descriptions, statements, information, opinions and references ["Content"]. The Content of this book shall not constitute or be construed or deemed to reflect the opinion or expression of the Publisher or Editor. Neither the Publisher nor Editor endorse or approve the Content of this book or guarantee the reliability, accuracy or completeness of the Content published herein and do not make any representations or warranties of any kind, express or implied, including but not limited to the implied warranties of merchantability, fitness for a particular purpose. The Publisher and Editor shall not be liable whatsoever for any errors, omissions, whether such errors or omissions result from negligence, accident, or any other cause or claims for loss or damages of any kind, including without limitation, indirect or consequential loss or damage arising out of use, inability to use, or about the reliability, accuracy or sufficiency of the information contained in this book.

DISCLAIMER

The content within the pages of this novel, "I Shouldn't Have Done This: A Heartfelt Love Story," is crafted for entertainment purposes only. The author takes no responsibility for the accuracy or correction of facts presented herein. It is important to note that the characters, events, and scenarios depicted in this work are entirely fictitious and any resemblance to real persons, living or deceased, is purely coincidental.

Readers are encouraged to immerse themselves in the captivating narrative, understanding that the primary objective is to provide an engaging and enjoyable reading experience. While the storyline may evoke emotions and provoke thought, it is essential to recognize that the author's intent is to stimulate the imagination rather than convey historical or factual accuracy.

All rights reserved. No part of this publication may be reproduced, distributed, or transmitted in any form or by any means, including photocopying, recording, or other electronic or mechanical methods, without the prior written permission of the publisher, except in the case of brief quotations embodied in critical reviews and certain other noncommercial uses permitted by copyright law.

ACKNOWLEDGMENTS

I extend my deepest gratitude to all those who have contributed to the creation of "I Shouldn't Have Done This: A Heartfelt Love Story." This novel would not have been possible without the unwavering support and encouragement from my loved ones.

First and foremost, I thank the divine for guiding me throughout this journey and granting me the inspiration to weave this tale. To my family, your enduring love and belief in me have been my pillars of strength. Your patience, understanding, and unwavering support have fueled my determination to bring this story to life.

I am profoundly grateful to my friends and mentors who have stood by me with their invaluable advice, encouragement, and constructive feedback. Your perspectives have enriched the narrative and helped shape the characters within these pages.

To every individual who trusted in me and offered their assistance, whether big or small, I am deeply appreciative of your contributions. Your belief in this project has been a driving force behind its completion.

Special thanks are also due to Clever Fox Publication House for their partnership and support throughout the publishing process. Your expertise and dedication have been instrumental in bringing this book to fruition.

Lastly, to the readers who embark on this journey with an open heart, thank you for allowing me to share this story with you. It is my sincerest hope that it brings you moments of joy, reflection, and inspiration.

With heartfelt thanks,
Harmeet Singh

Chapter 1

Seated beside me was a young woman, emanating a blend of confidence and curiosity that belied her relative inexperience in her field. Dressed in elegant attire, her presence commanded attention, akin to a captivating blend of Jessica Alba's allure and Angelina Jolie's charm.

"How did you manage to achieve such remarkable success in just four years?" she inquired, her interest piqued by my journey from a middle-class background to becoming one of the city's top entrepreneurs.

Taking a moment to consider her question, I reflected on the countless hours spent refining my response. "Before I answer, may I pose a question of my own?" I offered politely.

"Of course," she replied, intrigued.

"Where is it written that only those born with a silver spoon will end up in a silver coffin?" I asked, raising an eyebrow.

Her eyes widened in realization. "Nowhere," she acknowledged.

"Precisely. While the world may allocate resources favoring the affluent, talent transcends such barriers. It emerges from unexpected corners, a testament to the impartiality of nature," I explained, a sense of enlightenment coloring my words.

Our conversation flowed effortlessly, transitioning from inquiries about my journey to discussions on the responsibilities accompanying success. I emphasized the profound impact of community support and the weight of expectation that comes with it.

"We admire your contributions to society," she assured me warmly.

I momentarily teased her in a playful exchange before steering the conversation back to the interview.

As our discussion progressed, I shared personal anecdotes and insights shaped by my upbringing and entrepreneurial endeavors. The interview evolved into a genuine exchange of ideas, punctuated by laughter and mutual understanding.

Finally, she led me to the editor's office, teeming with creative energy and vibrant personalities. Amidst the lively atmosphere, our conversation continued, enriched by the editor's perspective.

As the day progressed, the dream took an unexpected turn. The interview and the editor's cabin vanished into thin air, and I found myself back in my pajamas, lying in bed, jolted awake by the annoying alarm clock.

My heart still raced from the surreal experience, leaving me with a lingering sense of wonder and determination. The dream may have ended, but the aspiration to impact the world remained more vigorous than ever.

"Wow, it's already 6 pm," I exclaimed in shock, realizing I'd slept for four hours straight. Sunday afternoons always had this sneaky way of slipping away unnoticed. And now, with a pile of assignments looming over me, the pressure was palpable. It had only been two weeks since starting at this college, yet the workload seemed to have multiplied overnight.

Glancing over at Ankit, who was still blissfully asleep, I nudged him gently. "Wake up, it's already 6 pm." Ankit and I had been inseparable since sixth grade. He wasn't just a friend; he was my confidant, my partner in mischief, and my pillar of strength during tough times. With his sturdy frame and infectious smile, he effortlessly charmed everyone he met.

Our bond transcended materialistic pursuits like wealth or social status. It was forged through shared experiences, endless laughter, and unwavering understanding. Ankit had an uncanny ability to grasp my thoughts before I voiced them, and I could discern his emotions merely by looking into his eyes.

After freshening up, I dove headfirst into the sea of books on my desk. Unlike many of our friends who opted for the college hostel, we chose a PG for its freedom from strict rules and its edible food.

"Feeling hungry, I'm making some Maggi for myself. Do you want some?" Ankit inquired, heading to the kitchen without pausing for my response. Soon, his frustrated voice echoed from the kitchen, "The cooking pot is filthy. What should I do?"

"Use the frying pan instead. Just be cautious; its handle is loose," I retorted, my frustration mounting as I yearned for some peace to focus on my assignments.

After sometime Ankit returned with a bowl of steaming Maggi, breaking the silence of my vexed concentration with an unexpected question. "Have you heard?" he blurted out, his tone laden with intrigue.

"What?" I replied, already drowning in the pending assignments, tests, and lab reports that seemed determined to consume us for those dreaded credits. Ankit's interruptions only added to my mounting irritation.

"That Rahul Pradhan is hosting a fresher's party," he exclaimed. Rahul pradhan was our senior and apparently a cool guy who can play guitar.

"How do you even know? Shouldn't you be focusing on more important things?" I retorted, my annoyance palpable in my voice. College life was far from the exhilarating experience I had envisioned.

"Everyone's talking about it around campus, man. Maybe you need to lighten up a bit," he suggested, grabbing a beer from the fridge and tossing one to me.

"This college is such a letdown. It's nothing like the glamorous portrayal in movies. They should ban those films," I grumbled, closing my books and shoving them aside. Taking a swig of beer, I attempted to calm my nerves. Perhaps I was taking everything too seriously. I never imagined I'd end up like this.

As I stared at the clutter in my drawer, Ankit's words echoed. The drawer remained a mess, untouched since my arrival at this lackluster college.

"So, about the fresher's party..." I sighed, closing my eyes, sinking into the chair with my legs crossed on the bed, and trying to relax.

"Hey, I was just saying we should totally go. It's happening next Sunday at a club. I heard that students from every branch will be there. And guess what? Akshita might show up too," Ankit said, a grin spreading across his face. He always had that wide smile plastered on whenever her name came up. Akshita, a girl from the computer science department, had caught Ankit's eye. He joined the library committee to get closer to her—a choice he soon regretted.

"Alright, fine. Count me in," I replied, winking and downing the last sip of my beer.

* * * * *

The club, nestled in South Delhi, exuded an aura of sophistication that piqued my curiosity. I spotted a few familiar faces as students from various branches trickled in. With the party yet to commence, I stepped outside for a smoke, relishing the anticipation. Meanwhile, Ankit, brimming with excitement, ventured inside in search of Akshita.

As I neared the end of my cigarette, my phone buzzed. It was Ankit who informed me that the party was already underway.

"I'm on my way," I confirmed before hanging up. With a final drag, I stubbed out the cigarette and entered.

Entering the venue, I was greeted by an energetic atmosphere. People mingled, some swaying to the beat of complex rock music on the dance floor. Surveying the crowd, I searched for Ankit. Despite the moderate crowd, the dim lighting made it challenging to locate him. Eventually, I spotted him in a corner, nursing a drink with a clear expression of annoyance.

"What's up with this party?" he grumbled.

Intrigued, I asked, "What's the matter?"

"They're not serving any liquor here. Can you believe it? Feels like a little girl's birthday party," he complained.

I couldn't help but chuckle at his frustration. "That's quite the observation. By the way, have you seen Akshita? Any sign of her yet?" I diverted the conversation.

"She hasn't shown up. I spoke to her friend, who mentioned she had some urgent matters at home," he replied, irritation still evident. Suddenly, his earlier grievances made sense—he behaved like a sulky child.

"Let's go find something to drink," I suggested.

He waved off the mocktail in his hand. "I'm not interested in this nonsense."

With a mischievous smirk, I teased, "Who said I was referring to this stuff?"

"But they don't serve hard drinks here, and bringing our own is against the rules," he pointed out.

With a knowing grin, I replied, "Rules are meant to be broken?"

The mischievous glint in my eyes matched the excitement building between us.

* * * * *

"Thanks, buddy," I patted him on the shoulder. The waiter agreed to help us when I gave him a small tip.

"Now, let's really enjoy this party," I said, a grin spreading across my face as we clinked our glasses and savored the drinks.

Ankit and I found a spot near the dance floor, settling in for the night. The music paused, grabbing everyone's attention. "Ladies and gentlemen! Hope you're all having a blast," Pradhan's voice boomed through the speakers. "Now it's time for the moment you've all been waiting for—Mr. and Miss Fresher. So, gentlemen, clear the dance floor, and ladies, gather around!"

"Now, this won't be a cakewalk because..." she paused, "we're judging not just on looks, but wit too. So, if you think you've got what it takes, get ready. Otherwise, you might end up the butt of the joke." Priya Deshmukh, hailing from the second-year computer science department, took center stage as the host. Despite murmurs circulating about her rumored relationship with Rahul Pradhan since their first semester, that detail paled in comparison to Priya's presence. Dressed in a striking red outfit, her heels adding to her allure, she commanded attention under the club's subdued lighting.

The announcement disheartened some girls, but a few bold souls stepped up. "Let's hear it for our contestants," Pradhan cheered. "Now, let's keep it simple: three rounds—Screening, Talent Showcase, and Q&A. Screening's done, thanks to Priya's idea." The crowd applauded Priya's wit, though some non-participants felt slighted, maybe even nursing a grudge.

"Now, onto the Talent Showcase. One minute each, ladies. Ready?"

Growing disinterested, I returned to the waiter with whom I had made prior arrangements. As he accepted the cash, a ripple of cheers erupted for Priya Deshmukh. Scanning the room, a girl with luscious black curls seated a few stools away caught my eye. Flashing her a smile, I noted her brief reciprocation before a guy's arm encircled her, extinguishing any possibility of further interaction. What a pity—I wouldn't have minded playing with those curls. Nevertheless, her loss.

The talent round droned on, followed by the Q&A session, but I found myself increasingly bored, succumbing to a sense of ennui. Glancing at the waiter, he understood my silent request and handed me another drink without accepting a tip. Perhaps someone from the senior staff had their eye on him, but I didn't dwell on it. Raising my glass, I took a sip, casually surveying the room. The gathering of so-called college kids fascinated me—ambitious, yet naïve; miles from home, yet emotionally inept. Just the way I preferred them.

Amidst my musings, I found myself pondering which of these girls would be the fortunate one tonight. Suddenly, the girl with the captivating curls approached and settled beside me. Introducing herself as Akriti, her almond-shaped eyes held my gaze, sparking a newfound interest. "Hi, I'm Meet. Drink?" I offered.

"Sure, I'll have what you're having," she replied, catching on to my arrangement with the waiter. She took my glass hesitantly took a sip, grimacing at the taste.

"Weren't you participating?" I asked, intrigued by her absence from the stage.

"Yes, I'll be next after this girl," she replied, nodding toward the girl onstage. I couldn't recall her name; it had been a while. The alcohol was doing its job, and the investment I made was paying off. It was time for Priya to pose some questions.

"It can't be seen, felt, heard, or smelt. It lies behind stars and under hills, filling empty holes. It comes first and follows after, ending life and killing laughter." The riddle caught my attention. The girl onstage, dressed in white, appeared bewildered and requested clarification. The crowd chuckled, and I felt a twinge of sympathy for her.

Priya moved on to another question, but the girl struggled again. Priya thanked her for her time. From her reaction, I could tell she wouldn't be winning. The next contestant to take the stage was hard to forget; she introduced herself as Kritika Merchant, likely the daughter of a wealthy businessman. Her black dress and pearl earrings matched her pearl locket, hinting at her affluence. She seemed trying to downplay it, perhaps to fit in with her new peers.

"You're traveling down a country lane to a distant village. You reach a fork in the road and find a pair of identical twin sisters standing there—one on the road to the village and the other on the road to Neverland. You don't know where each road leads; one sister always tells the truth while the other always lies. Both sisters know where the roads go. If you're allowed to ask only one question to one of the sisters to find the correct road to the village, what would you ask?" Priya posed a challenging riddle, prompting laughter from the crowd even before Kritika could respond.

"That's simple. I would ask, 'Hello, beautiful lady, what would your sister say if I asked her which road leads to the village?' And then I would take the opposite road," she confidently replied. Applause erupted at her clever response.

"Here's another one," Priya continued, firing another question. "Only one color, but not one size, stuck at the bottom, yet easily flies. Present in the sun, but not in rain, doing no harm and feeling no pain. What is it?" This time, Kritika swiftly answered, "It's a shadow."

The crowd cheered for her. "Impressive. You're sharp," Priya commended from her judge's seat alongside Pradhan and his cohort.

"Apparently, I stumbled upon the same website you copied all these questions from," Kritika remarked boldly, provoking Priya. I could see the frustration on Priya's face, but she maintained her composure and continued, "So, you're a pretty honest girl. Let me ask you some questions, honestly." People were enjoying the exchange, and so was I. Akriti, seated next to me, seemed a bit concerned, but we continued to share the same glass.

Priya launched into a rapid-fire interrogation to avenge the insult from a freshie.

"Do you sing in the shower?"

"Occasionally," Kritika admitted.

"Do you pick your nose?"

"No," she hesitated, then admitted, "Well, sometimes. Who doesn't?"

"Ever peed in a pool?"

Kritika smirked. "Absolutely. It's practically a tradition."

"What's the last thing you searched on your phone?"

I Shouldn't Have Done This

"The website where you got these questions," Kritika fired back, a playful gleam in her eye. This pissed off Priya even more.

"Practiced kissing in front of a mirror?" I can sense the frustration in Priya's voice

"Why bother when you're a natural?" Kritika replied confidently, and the crowd cheered for her.

"Caught your parents doing it?" Priya almost lost it and crossed the line.

"Nope, we have a strict 'knock before entering' policy at home," she quipped, drawing laughter from the crowd. She would definitely snap if someone else were in her place, but Kritika handled it like a pro.

"Worst habit?" Priya asked without giving Kritika any time to think.

"Honestly? Being too honest," Kritika winked, earning cheers from the audience.

"If you could trade lives with someone here, who?"

"Definitely not you," Kritika shot back, her words a bold declaration that visibly rattled Priya. With an air of defiance, she kept her microphone down and left the stage without glancing at Priya. The crowd erupted into wild cheers, swept up in admiration for her fearless attitude.

"Thank you for your time," Priya managed through gritted teeth, clearly irked by Kritika's responses. The Q&A session had become the talk of the party, and Kritika was now the center of attention. Despite five contestants remaining, it was evident that none could top her performance.

After Kritika, it was Akriti's turn on stage. I cheered her on, and she glanced at me, returning the smile.

After all the contestants finished with Q&A the judges reached a unanimous decision for this year's Miss Fresher, and the announcement met with anticipation rippling through the air. "The winner of the title is none other than Akriti," declared one

9

I Shouldn't Have Done This

of Pradhan's enthusiastic sidekicks. As the news sank in, a mix of emotions filled the crowd. Some applauded, but many faces betrayed their disappointment, convinced Kritika deserved the crown. Akriti had showcased talent, yet she couldn't match the captivating presence and charm that Kritika possessed. Nevertheless, a distinctive quality about Akriti couldn't be overlooked—she refrained from publicly insulting Priya, setting her apart from the Kritika.

"Now it's time to choose Mr. Fresher," announced the sidekick, his voice laced with intrigue. "We will adhere to the same three rounds: Screening, Talent Showcase, and Question-Answer. But here's an interesting twist. As we have the esteemed Miss Fresher amongst us, she will participate in the screening process and personally select five contestants who will proceed to the next round." A chair was placed beside the judges, symbolizing Akriti's authority. "Gentlemen, take your seats and witness Miss Fresher perform her duty."

Amidst the anticipation, I spotted the first guy Akriti chose; he was the same person who had confidently wrapped his arm around her earlier in the evening when I attempted to approach her. Curiosity sparked within me. Did they share a prior connection? And then, to my astonishment, Akriti's gaze swept across the room and locked onto mine. It felt like time had frozen, and our eyes engaged in a silent conversation for that fleeting moment. At that moment, she extended an invitation, summoning me to join the selected contestants on the stage. The crowd erupted in cheers, fueling my hesitant steps.

"Now, it's time for you, Meet, to showcase your talent," Priya's voice resonated through the microphone, carrying an undertone of excitement.

Confidence surged within me, influenced by the intoxicating spirits coursing through my veins. "I possess a multitude of talents. Which one would you like to witness?" I responded, emboldened by the Chivas.

Pradhan interjected, his curiosity piqued. "Then show us your very best," he urged, eager for a captivating display.

"I have a deep passion for photography, and my portfolio can be explored on my blog. If you wish, feel free to take a glimpse. It's the true essence of my talent," I explained, hoping they would perceive the artistry behind my chosen medium.

Pradhan called me over, and his interest piqued. He requested that I open my blog on his laptop. As I complied, an internal mix of assurance and uncertainty wrestled within me. I believed in the power of my photographs, but I remained unsure of how the judges would perceive them as a talent.

"These pictures are exquisite, deserving to be witnessed by all," Pradhan proclaimed as he connected his laptop to the club's main screen. All four screens illuminated, showcasing an array of photographs from my blog. While the majority depicted breathtaking landscapes captured during my past vacations, one particular image bewitched everyone's gaze. It portrayed a scene from my daily commute to college—a captivating moment frozen in time. It captured children dancing in the rain, their innocent faces beaming with joy, unburdened by the weight of life's challenges. They embodied a vibrant sense of ambition and happiness, unafraid of the uncertainties ahead and unburdened by past regrets.

"Those are truly remarkable pictures, Meet. I insist that everyone present should have the privilege of witnessing your artistry," Pradhan declared, eliciting a round of applause from the enthralled audience. "We shall undoubtedly consider this for the competition. However, you still need to entertain our esteemed guests," Priya interjected, her words softly spoken, bearing a touch of sincerity yet constrained by the rules of the event.

"No need to worry. I shall dance for you all, or rather, for the guests," I teased, provoking laughter to ripple through the crowd. "So, DJ, please play a lively Punjabi track."

The DJ promptly obliged, filling the air with the infectious beats of "3 Pegg," a renowned Punjabi number and a personal favorite of mine. A surge of energy coursed through me as I flawlessly executed the dance steps, guided by the spirit of the alcohol within me. The joyous atmosphere infected everyone, with even Ankit unable to resist whistling his approval from amidst the crowd. Enthusiasm overpowered the limitations of the one-minute rule, and the song continued to echo through the club. In the grand finale, I concluded with a signature spinning move, leaving the audience awestruck and culminating in Priya's standing ovation.

"You were absolutely right, Meet. Your talent knows no bounds," Priya complimented, her voice resonating with genuine admiration as the crowd gradually settled.

"I told you so," I responded, acknowledging the support and applause with gratitude before retreating to my stool. Ankit approached me, exclaiming, "You nailed it, man," as he savored the last sip of his drink.

The night progressed with other contestants showcasing their talents, building up to the long-awaited announcement of the winner. Priya gracefully ascended the stage, clutching an envelope in her hand, her poised demeanor enveloping the room. "We have unanimously decided who shall claim the title of this year's Mr. Fresher. And to reveal the result, I humbly request Miss Fresher herself to join me," she announced, modulating her voice to enhance the suspense.

Akriti joined Priya on the stage, her presence radiating elegance and anticipation. With bated breath, she proclaimed my name as the winner. Surprised and overcome with a blend of emotions, I handed my glass to Ankit, who offered a congratulatory smile and made my way to the stage amidst the resounding cheers and applause from the ecstatic crowd.

"Now it's time for Mr. and Miss Fresher to grace us with their dance," Priya announced, her tone filled with familiarity and

I Shouldn't Have Done This

excitement. Akriti drew closer, and together, we swayed to the rhythm of the music. Given my limited dance skills, it proved to be a challenging moment for me, but Akriti's understanding and guidance allowed me to navigate the steps gracefully, ensuring our performance remained captivating. As the song reached its crescendo, the dance floor became a bustling haven of celebration, and I excused myself momentarily, seeking solace in a quiet corner to indulge in a smoke. Retrieving the car keys from Ankit, I invited him to accompany me, but he declined, wholly absorbed in the revelry.

Outside, the cold night air enveloped me, a sensation that invigorated my senses. I extracted a cigarette from the car and ignited it, savoring each drag with a tranquil appreciation. Lost in contemplation, I observed Kritika stepping out of the club and engaging in a fervent phone conversation. Her expressions painted a vivid tale of dissatisfaction, with muttered curses punctuating her words as she strode by.

As she returned, a tinge of worry etched across her features. An impulse stirred within me, urging me to inquire about her well-being. Yet, the memory of her ruthless confrontation with Priya on stage stifled my courage, apprehensive of her sharp tongue. Thus, I chose silence over inquiry, allowing the moment to pass in silence.

She approached me, standing nearby as if wrestling with her thoughts. I sensed her hesitation, but I remained uncharacteristically silent. After a brief pause, she finally asked, "Do you mind if I have one?" gesturing towards my cigarette.

Caught off guard, I momentarily failed to comprehend her request, still lost in my musings. "Sorry?" I replied, reminiscent of the girl I encountered on stage.

"A cigarette," she clarified, extending her hand. I then noticed a pearl ring adorning her finger, a detail that had eluded me earlier.

"Sure," I handed her a cigarette, watching as she took a long puff before passing it back to me.

I Shouldn't Have Done This

"Is everything alright? You seem somewhat troubled," I gathered the courage to inquire, sensing an opportunity for connection.

"Yeah, it's just that my roommate was supposed to pick me up, but she abandoned me at the last moment," she responded, her voice laced with a hint of disappointment.

"I see," recognizing the insignificance of her concern, yet choosing to remain silent. Inhaling deeply, I sighed, leaning against the wall and casting my gaze heavenward. Absently, I extended the cigarette to her, offering a momentary respite from the cold. "You were quite ruthless with Priya earlier. It was akin to a cold-blooded murder," I interjected, seeking a topic of discussion amidst our shared silence.

She took another drag, flicking the ash to the ground. Disregarding my comment, she posed a different question. "Do you have any more?" she inquired, her curiosity overriding my remark.

"Yes," I tossed her the keys, saying, "In the glove compartment." She grabbed the keys, opened the car door, and began searching. When she pulled back, she hit her head on the top of the door, uttering a curse.

"Shit," she rubbed the back of her head.

"Are you okay?" I asked, concerned.

She slowly lifted her chin, meeting my eyes. Her gaze widened, and her jaw dropped. She lowered her hands from the back of her head.

"I... " She glanced at her phone in her other hand and slipped it inside her brown leopard print purse. "I'm fine. I just..." She closed the car door. "I just hit my head. But it's not a big deal. It's not like it's the first time."

I raised my eyebrows. "So, it happens all the time?"

Her jaw dropped again. "No, I... It's happened before, but not all the time. I'm not clumsy. It was just an accident."

I Shouldn't Have Done This

I felt relieved that she hadn't read my mind or heard my thoughts out loud. "You're shivering," I pointed out, noticing her trembling in the cold. Her dress was doing a poor job of protecting her.

Her eyebrows furrowed. "No, I'm not... shivering. I..."

I waited for her to finish her sentence.

She wrapped her arms around herself and rubbed her arms. "Okay, fine. It's cold, alright? I shiver when it's cold," she sarcastically retorted.

"I think I can do something about that..." I took another puff while she rolled her eyes. "I mean, about the cold."

I reached into Ankit's car and pulled out my jacket. "I can lend you my jacket," I offered.

"No," she stepped back, still rubbing her arms. "I mean, no thanks. I'm heading back inside anyway."

"What will you do inside? The party is about to end," I pointed out.

She pondered for a moment, seeming to consider my words. She wanted to accept my chivalry but hesitated. Sensing her dilemma, I made it easier for her. "Take it, don't worry about returning it now. You can return it to me tomorrow when we're at college."

She was shivering uncontrollably, her crimson lips trembling. She eventually accepted my jacket and promised to return it the next day. It wasn't a perfect fit, but she looked cute wearing it.

Looking at herself in the car's rearview mirror, she laughed. "I must look like a slob."

"No, I think you look cute," I blurted out.

"Really?" She furrowed her eyebrows, surprised by my compliment.

Feeling embarrassed, I didn't respond. Instead, I lit another cigarette, handed it to her, and then lit one for myself.

"So, how's the girls' hostel?" I asked, trying to initiate conversation.

I Shouldn't Have Done This

"How would I know?" she responded, reverting to her usual direct and straightforward manner. "I don't live in the hostel. I'm staying in a PG nearby."

"Where is it?" I inquired.

She took a puff and glanced at me. I thought I had asked the wrong question. She exhaled the smoke and replied, "It's near the college."

"That's good. I live near the college too. If you want, I can drop you off," I suggested.

"No thanks, I'm fine," she declined my offer. "I'll just book a cab."

"Cabs aren't safe at this hour in Delhi. Moreover, Delhi is already so polluted. Why add more to it?" I looked at her. "Let's pool cars and save Delhi."

She laughed for the first time, finding my comment amusing.

Chapter 2

"*H*i, gotta go, kind of an emergency. See you at home. Book a cab, sorry," I quickly texted Ankit on my way back, though "home" was actually Kritika's place now. She had agreed to my proposal to drop her home, and in return, she asked how she could return the favor. Shamelessly, I asked her to cook Maggi for me, as I hadn't eaten anything all day and wasn't in the mood to go home and cook for myself. Surprisingly, she agreed, mentioning she was feeling hungry too.

"Are you still feeling cold?" I asked, concerned.

"No, I'm fine, but I'd prefer to keep wearing your jacket," she replied.

"I... I didn't mean that," I quickly clarified, realizing she had misunderstood my words.

"Oh, don't worry, I was just kidding," she said, surprising me with her lightheartedness.

"So?" I asked, making a left turn onto the road.

"So what?" she replied.

"Nothing," I blurted out while accelerating. The roads were empty, with hardly any traffic at this hour.

"I'm fine. Don't be uncomfortable," Kritika assured, almost as if she could read my thoughts. "Miss, you are the one making me uncomfortable," I wanted to retort, but instead, all I managed to say was, "Do you want to listen to some music?"

"No, I'm not in the mood," she replied, wanting to maintain the silence.

"How far is your home..." I began to ask but was swiftly interrupted by her sharp exclamation.

"Wait, wait, wait. Did you just jump a red light?" she exclaimed.

"Yeah, so what? No traffic on the roads, and no cops are around to give you tickets. It's obvious that nobody stops at a red signal now," I tried to reason with her.

"Just don't do it again," she said firmly, gazing out the window, clearly unimpressed by my reasoning.

"Okay," I responded, realizing that no matter how reasonable I sounded, it didn't seem much to her.

"Okay, we're here. Have a good night," I dropped her off at her home and hesitated about going inside, considering the recent events.

"What? Aren't you coming?" she asked, sounding surprised.

"No, I was just kidding," I lied, opting for a small lie to avoid potential complications.

"What? I messaged my roommate that I was coming with a friend. She has arranged the whole apartment and must have made Maggi by now. And now you're telling me that you were just kidding?" Her tone carried a hint of frustration.

"I don't think it's a good idea," I hesitated, unsure how to proceed.

"Okay, thanks for dropping me home. Now go to hell," she snapped, her frustration evident. I knew I had inadvertently upset her, so I quickly apologized and agreed to come inside. It seemed like the only diplomatic option available.

Her apartment was on the third floor of the building, and we climbed the stairs together. Upon reaching her door, she removed her keys from her bag and unlocked the metal door. Inside, another wooden door remained unlocked. The apartment appeared decent but not as well-prepared as she had indicated. There was no sign of her roommate, who was supposed to have arranged everything. The kitchen was cluttered with dirty dishes, and the living room was

I Shouldn't Have Done This

strewn with clothes. She casually picked up a top from the floor and placed it on the sofa.

"Have a seat," she gestured, scanning the room to clear a spot. I glanced around but couldn't find a clean place to sit. Sensing my dilemma, she quickly gathered all the clothes from a nearby chair and piled them on the sofa.

"My roommate must have done laundry today. I'll be right back," she said, disappearing into her room. I could hear her calling out for Seerat, her roommate.

Left with nothing to do, I checked my phone and noticed three missed calls from Ankit, along with a message that read, "I know which emergency you had, you dickhead. Anyways, take advantage of the situation. Good luck." That's just like Ankit, always ready with a sarcastic comment. I couldn't help but smile at his message before tucking my phone back into my pocket and surveying the apartment again.

Three walls were painted pink, while the fourth wall boasted a bold tomato-red hue. A sizeable 52-inch TV adorned the red wall, flanked by wooden shelves. Atop the shelves sat an array of trophies, undoubtedly earned by Kritika herself. Seeing her achievements displayed so prominently made me feel a twinge of insecurity. She was clearly accomplished and intelligent, and I couldn't help but wonder if I could measure up.

Beneath the trophies, a laughing Buddha figurine occupied the top shelf, symbolling prosperity and joy. It reminded me of a similar gift I had given to my sister on her birthday. Below, a collection of photographs drew my attention. One depicted Kritika posing with her family, her resemblance to the woman beside her suggesting it was her mother.

In another photograph, Kritika was captured alongside another girl whose identity eluded me; she appeared to be a close friend or perhaps a cousin. Kritika donned a stylish ensemble of black jeans paired with a vibrant red top, exuding confidence and charm. Beside her stood the mystery girl, dressed in a striking knee-length off-shoulder dress adorned with shades of blue, emanating a sense of elegance and grace. Around her neck, she wore a pendant fashioned from a captivating green stone, adding a touch of sophistication to her ensemble. The two friends stood shoulder to shoulder, their bodies playfully leaning towards each other, both sporting endearing pouts that conveyed a sense of camaraderie and affection captured in that moment.

Yet another photo caught my eye—a girl adorned in a vibrant red and green Patiala suit with Phulkari embroidery. Her natural beauty radiated from the image, her round face and fair complexion accentuated by her captivating smile. It was a candid moment frozen in time that seemed to hold an inexplicable allure.

It took a moment for me to realize that the girl in the second and third photographs was the same person. Although her appearance differed between the Western and traditional attire, her distinctive charm remained constant. "That must be her roommate, Seerat," I surmised, noting the ease with which she transitioned between styles.

"Sorry, would you like some water?" Kritika's interruption snapped me out of my reverie.

"Yes, sure," I responded, glancing at her. She had changed into red pajamas adorned with white polka dots and a matching t-shirt. As she moved, I noticed her roommate approaching from behind. The roommate was dressed in pink shorts adorned with tiny hearts and a simple white t-shirt. It was indeed the same girl from the photograph, confirming my earlier suspicion.

"That's my roommate, Seerat," Kritika introduced her to me, but Seerat didn't seem to care; she was too sleepy to pay attention to any guests in her home. Rubbing her eyes with her hands, she mumbled a half-hearted greeting.

"Hi, would you like some coffee with Maggie," she said, showing little interest in engaging in conversation or formalities.

I Shouldn't Have Done This

"No, I'm fine," I replied, not wanting to disturb the sleepy Seerat.

"Yes, make some, please. It's cold outside. Coffee would be good," Kritika said, expressing her desire for warm refreshment.

Without a word, Seerat shuffled towards the kitchen, her eyes still heavy with sleep. I couldn't help but feel a pang of regret for accepting the offer, not wanting to disturb the drowsy figure.

"Let me tidy up a bit," Kritika offered, gathering the scattered clothes from the sofa, table, and chair. Carrying the bundle to her room, she returned and settled into a chair opposite me.

"Sorry for the mess. I messaged Seerat to let her know I was bringing a friend and asked her to straighten up," Kritika explained, pouring water for me before taking a sip herself. "She just replied 'okay' and went back to sleep," she added, clarifying the situation.

"I'm sorry. If I had known your roommate was here, I would never have disturbed you or asked for Maggi. I didn't want to intrude," I expressed genuine remorse for my unintended disruption.

"Don't worry about it. Let me help her," Kritika said, heading back to the kitchen.

After a while, they both returned with coffee and Maggi.

"I'm going back to sleep," Seerat announced, placing the tray on the table, her eyes still half-lidded. She disappeared into her room, the door closing with a soft thud.

"Alright," Kritika responded without much ceremony. Settling back into her seat, she picked up her bowl of Maggi and ate.

"Thanks for dropping me home," she said between spoonfuls.

"Oh, it's no trouble," I replied.

"No, really, thank you. It's a nice neighborhood, but not very safe. A few weeks ago, a girl who lives in the C-wing of this complex went missing. She works in Sarita Vihar and got held up due to urgent work. She called home before leaving the office, but when she didn't arrive after two hours, her father tried calling her back, only to find her phone switched off. Two days later, her body was

21

I Shouldn't Have Done This

discovered in a jungle near the Delhi-Haryana border, about 20 kilometers from here. She was found partially clothed and badly bruised. So when Seerat said she couldn't pick me up, I got worried," Kritika shared, pausing to take another bite of Maggi. "I didn't want to risk taking a cab, so I agreed to come with you when you offered."

I wasn't sure how to respond, so I nodded in agreement.

"Do you want to smoke?" she asked, retrieving a pack of cigarettes from the bottom drawer of her study table. She lit her cigarette and passed it to me without waiting for my response.

"Yes, I suppose," I shrugged, and she couldn't help but notice the casualness of her gesture. We shared a chuckle.

"So, you weren't afraid of me," I remarked, taking a drag.

"Well, I was. That's why I messaged Seerat your name, major, and even a snapshot of your car's number plate," she revealed, a mischievous glint in her eye.

"What? Seriously? When did you snap a picture of my car's number plate?" I inquired, surprised by her resourcefulness.

"A magician never reveals her secrets," she teased, laughter filling the room.

"And how did you know my major?" I pressed, curious about her knowledge.

"Your reputation precedes you. You were the talk of the party last night. A classmate of mine, whose name I won't disclose, had some flattering things to say about you," she explained cryptically.

"Is that so? And what exactly did this mystery classmate say?" I leaned in eagerly, eager for some insider information.

"Sorry, but that's classified information according to the girl code. I can't spill the beans. But I will admit, even I was impressed by your photography skills," she admitted, a playful grin tugging at her lips.

"My photography skills? Are you stalking me now?" I joked, feigning suspicion.

I Shouldn't Have Done This

"No, not at all. I meant the photos you've shared on your blog," Kritika clarified, laughing with me.

"Well, I should probably be on my way," I said after finishing my cigarette. "Thanks for everything." I rose from my seat, preparing to leave.

"Thank you for dropping me home," she replied graciously. As I made my way towards the door, she called out my name. I turned back, and she handed me my jacket before closing the door behind me. It was a small gesture, but it left a lasting impression.

As I stepped out into the cool night air, I couldn't shake off the intrigue and curiosity that Kritika had sparked within me. This encounter unveiled layers of mystery and charm, leaving me eager to unravel more about the enigmatic girl who had unexpectedly captured my attention.

Chapter 3

"*H*ey buddy, is everything okay?" I asked Ankit, noticing his distant expression as he sat on his study chair, books open but untouched for the past two hours. It was evident he was lost in thought, brooding over something.

"Ankit?" I called his name, but he seemed to snap out of his thoughts without fully registering my words.

"Are you all right?" I inquired again, concern lacing my voice.

"Yeah... yeah, I'm fine," he replied, picking up his pen and feigning interest in his notebook.

"Look, if you don't like talking about it, that's okay. But please don't lie to me. I've known you since school time,"

"It's nothing like that," Ankit responded, attempting to brush off his troubles.

"Is everything fine at home? How are uncle and aunty?" I probed gently.

"They're fine. It's just that when I called home yesterday, Mom seemed a little upset. When I asked her about it, she didn't say anything," Ankit explained, his tone reflecting his worry.

"And then?" I encouraged him to continue.

"I tried to act normal, so I didn't press her too hard," he said, shifting to sit closer to me on the bed. "But then I called my sister. I asked her if everything was okay, and she said nothing." Ankit's voice grew tense as he recounted the events.

24

I Shouldn't Have Done This

"When I pushed her, she told me that Dad was upset. He was drinking alone in his study," Ankit continued, his worry evident in his tone.

"But Uncle never drinks," I remarked, surprised.

"He does when he's upset," Ankit replied, his expression troubled. "Do you remember I told you he was due for a promotion this year?

"Yeah, definitely; how could I forget that?" I recalled Ankit's excitement when he shared the news of his father's potential promotion. It seemed like yesterday when he messaged me to meet at Frisko bar to celebrate.

"So, he's not getting the promotion now," I summarized, shocked by the sudden turn of events.

"Yeah, that's what's happening," Ankit confirmed, his voice heavy with sadness. "Good cops don't get promoted around here."

As Ankit continued, I listened intently, feeling a mix of anger and disbelief at the injustice of the situation. "Last week, when he was on duty, he received a complaint about eve-teasing. When my father and a head constable reached the site, they found the girl in tears. She explained that a guy named Debashish and his friends from college had been harassing her. So, my father got their address from the college office and went to confront them. They were staying in a PG near western Delhi. When my dad questioned them, they started misbehaving. In response, he slapped Debashish and took them all to the police station. Later, he found out that one of the guys was the nephew of the district magistrate, Mr Sinha. My dad is not getting promoted, and they've even filed a case against him."

"That's terrible, man," I exclaimed, appalled by the blatant injustice of the situation.

"You're right," I nodded solemnly as Ankit expressed frustration. "What's truly terrible is that because of people like Sinha, my father has to endure this injustice. What's terrible is that guys like Debashish feel entitled to harass girls without consequences. And

I Shouldn't Have Done This

what's truly terrible is that because of them, girls like my sister don't feel safe outside their homes."

"But don't worry," I reassured him, handing him a glass of water. "Your father is smart; I'm sure he can handle this situation."

"Now, let's focus on your studies. We have mid-semester exams next week, and I bet your father wouldn't be pleased if you flunked them," I added with a hint of humor, trying to lighten the mood.

"I'm definitely going to fail. I can't seem to get a single correct answer," Ankit lamented, his frustration evident.

"Let me help you with that," I offered, pulling out my notes and textbooks.

After a few hours of studying together, Ankit seemed more focused on his exams and less weighed down by his worries about his father.

* * * * *

"Hey, I'm feeling pretty confident about the exams now," he said, pausing mid-sentence to glance at me. "But..."

"But what, Ankit?" I interjected, accustomed to his attention-seeking antics.

"But I'm worried about the computer section," he admitted with a grin.

I nodded understandingly. Computers were often a stumbling block for those more inclined towards mechanical subjects, primarily when they hadn't studied them extensively in high school. The gap between what was taught in class and what was expected in exams, particularly with the demanding C programming, only added to the challenge. And to top it off, our instructor—a retired gentleman from some government college—was brilliant but struggled to effectively convey his knowledge, exacerbated by his thick South Indian accent.

"Me too," I acknowledged with a brief nod.

I Shouldn't Have Done This

"Why don't you reach out to your friend Kritika for help? She's from the Computer Department, so teaching us those programs shouldn't be a big deal for her."

Ankit's suggestion to seek help from Kritika for our computer studies made sense, even though I felt hesitant about it. Despite our growing friendship since the fresher's party, I still didn't consider us close enough for me to comfortably ask her for academic assistance. Moreover, I was concerned about potentially tarnishing her image of me after the events at the fresher's party.

After the freshman meet-up, Kritika and I developed a good friendship. We'd often catch up in the college canteen for lunch or occasionally head out for movies, though never just the two of us— Ankit and some other friends always tagged along.

"I don't think it's a good idea," I hesitated, though secretly hoping to convey to Kritika that I wasn't finding the subject as easy as she might think. Since the freshman event, she seemed to hold me in higher regard, and I didn't want to tarnish that image over a subject I struggled with.

"Bro, it's the only way out. I don't want to fail in the first year," Ankit insisted, seemingly unfazed by the challenges ahead.

Taking a deep breath, I finally relented. "Alright, I'll ask Kritika. But I can't guarantee she'll have the time or inclination to help."

Ankit nodded in agreement, understanding my reservations. "It's worth a shot, at least. And if not her, perhaps someone else can help us."

But, Ankit's insistence and worries about failing in the first year pushed me to consider the idea more seriously. He was right; failing in our first year would set a negative precedent for the rest of our college journey.

I called her, but she didn't pick up. So, I decided I would ask her the next day in college. However, after about 15 minutes, she called me back.

"Hey, how are you?" she greeted.

I Shouldn't Have Done This

"I'm fine. How about you?" I replied.

"Nothing much, just struggling with these books," she said, her tone carrying a mix of frustration and exhaustion.

I couldn't help but chuckle. "What's so funny?" Kritika asked, clearly irritated.

"Oh, it's nothing. Just Ankit making funny faces," I lied, trying to divert the conversation away from the real reason I had called.

"Why's he making funny faces? Is he auditioning to be a clown at the Delhi circus?" she retorted sarcastically.

"Let's forget about him. What's going on?" I redirected, hoping to avoid further discussion about Ankit's antics.

"I'm just not getting this engineering drawing stuff. I signed up to be a computer engineer, not a draftsman," she complained.

I realized we faced similar struggles—being forced to study subjects outside our primary interests. It was a common issue among students, but unfortunately, the administration wasn't likely to change the curriculum to suit our preferences.

"I can help you with that," I offered.

"Can you?" she sounded surprised.

"Yes, of course. I'm a mechanical engineer," I insisted.

"No, you're not," she countered.

"Yes, I am," I insisted again.

"No, you're not," she repeated stubbornly.

"Do you want my help or not?" I pressed a hint of amusement in my voice at the playful banter.

"Yes, I do. When will you teach me?" Kritika's voice held a note of eagerness.

"Anytime you want," I replied, happy to assist her.

"How about 7 pm?" she suggested.

"That sounds perfect," I agreed.

"I'll be there in two hours. Bye," she said before hanging up the call.

I Shouldn't Have Done This

With Kritika arriving in two hours, I turned to Ankit, who was lounging in his boxers, scratching himself without a care. "You better take a shower," I advised, trying to maintain some level of decency.

Ankit groaned at my suggestion, dragging himself off the bed. "Fine, I'll go freshen up. But why do I have to wear something decent?"

I chuckled, shaking my head. "Because we're going to study with Kritika, not attend a pajama party."

Rolling his eyes, Ankit disappeared into the bathroom, grumbling about the inconvenience of unexpected guests. Meanwhile, I tidied up the room, stacking our books neatly on the desk and clearing any unnecessary clutter.

As the minutes ticked by, I found myself growing increasingly nervous. Despite my assurance to Kritika, I couldn't help but worry about my ability to teach engineering drawing effectively. It had been a while since I last reviewed the subject, and I hoped I wouldn't embarrass myself in front of her.

* * * * *

"That must be Kritika," I remarked, standing up from my chair and heading to the door as the doorbell rang. Remembering the state of her room the last time I visited, I made sure our place was tidy and changed into more presentable clothes.

"Hi, come in," I welcomed her as I opened the door. Kritika looked stylish in her blue denim jeans and black top, her blue glasses accentuating her sharp nose. Her hair tied back in a ponytail made her look different from the elegant image I had of her from the freshman party. In fact, it was the first time I had seen her with her hair up; in college, she always wore it down.

She smiled and entered without saying anything, placing her bag on the table and pulling out her book. Sensing her discomfort, I decided to engage in some small talk to lighten the mood. But before I could speak, she surprised me by asking, "Where is Ankit?"

I Shouldn't Have Done This

"He's in his room," I replied, finding her question unexpected, assuming she was just trying to break the ice. "Do you want me to call him here?"

"No, it's fine," she responded.

"Would you like something to drink?" I offered, but she declined, mentioning she had already eaten dinner, which struck me as odd, but I didn't dwell on it.

We started with the basics of engineering drawing, and it was evident that Kritika was struggling with the subject. However, she was a diligent student, quickly grasping concepts once explained. After some time, Ankit joined us, slightly disappointed to learn that Kritika wasn't here to teach us computers but to study engineering drawing. I reassured him that I would still ask her about computers later.

"Would you like to eat something?" I asked Kritika, not really caring whether she wanted it or not. It had been about two hours since I had started teaching her, and I was starving.

"I wouldn't mind having some Maggi," she replied.

I instructed her to continue practicing the drawing she was working on and told her to ask Ankit, who was sitting idly nearby, for help if needed.

In the kitchen, I reached for a cold beer from the fridge, seeking relief from the day's stress. With a pan already on the gas stove, I prepared to boil water for a quick meal of Maggi.

But as I poured the boiling water into the pan, disaster struck—the handle broke off under the pressure, sending scalding water cascading onto my right hand.

"Damn it!" I cried out in pain, the intensity of the burn searing through me. Instinctively, I clutched my injured hand with my left, trying to shield it from further harm. Within moments, the skin on my hand began to blister and peel, the searing sensation threatening to overwhelm my senses. It felt like the pain might just cause me to lose consciousness.

I Shouldn't Have Done This

Ankit and Kritika rushed into the kitchen, witnessing me sitting on the floor with my badly burned hand. Kritika quickly retrieved a water bottle from the fridge and poured it over my hand while Ankit, in his usual insensitive manner, suggested pouring the cold beer I had been drinking, claiming it would work as an antiseptic. I had warned you that he was an asshole.

"Come on, we need to get him to the hospital," Kritika instructed Ankit to bring his car. However, due to our society's parking arrangements, our car was parked half a mile away in the DDA market.

"I'll take him on my Scooty," Kritika declared as she helped me stand up.

By the time we reached the hospital, my hand was covered in blisters, a natural defense mechanism against burns. The doctor provided me with ointment, antibiotics, and some advice to be more careful in the future. I wanted to tell him that I hadn't done this on purpose, this time either.

Kritika visited me after college, visibly burdened with guilt over the incident with the boiling water. I lay on the bed, my hand throbbing from the burn.

"I'm sorry all this happened because of me," she apologized, her expression troubled.

"It's not your fault; I should have been more cautious. The handle of that pan was loose, and I should have replaced it ages ago."

I reassured her, grateful for her concern. Ankit assisted me with adjusting my pillow as I sat up. "The doctor said it will heal in a few days. There's nothing to worry about."

"What about the exams?" Kritika inquired, her concern shifting to my academic situation.

"I can't write them," I admitted, lifting my injured hand as a reminder.

"Yes, you can't write them, but someone can write them for you," she proposed.

I Shouldn't Have Done This

"But I don't have any friends outside of college here, and all my college friends will be busy with their exams," I lamented.

"Maybe I can help," Kritika suggested, surprising me with her offer.

"How? Are you going to write my exams?" I asked incredulously.

"No, but I can ask Seerat. She might be willing to help," she explained, offering hope.

Chapter 4

"Yes, I'm at the college gate. Where are you? Okay, stand there, I'm coming." It was Seerat. She had agreed to help me, even though she had to skip a few classes. I walked over to where she was waiting at a different gate and greeted her with a "Good morning." She seemed a bit puzzled, probably because she was half-asleep the last time we met and didn't recognize me. So I introduced myself, "I'm Meet."

"Oh, how are you? How is your hand?" she asked with concern. I showed her my hand, which was still in the process of healing. "It's not great, but it's getting better."

"Oh my god," she said, frowning and scrunching her nose. I could see the empathy in her eyes.

"It's fine; let's go to the classroom" Technically, we weren't supposed to sit in the classroom, but in the HOD's cabin so we wouldn't disturb other students during the exam. We entered the cabin and found it empty. Since we had some time before the exam started, we took a seat.

It was a computer exam, and I was feeling a bit nervous. I thought it would be a good idea to share my concern with Seerat. I gathered courage and said, "Due to this accident, I couldn't prepare well for the exams."

"I know," she replied. I wanted to ask her how she knew, but the HOD entered the cabin just then. I greeted him and introduced Seerat. He didn't pay much attention and handed me the question

33

I Shouldn't Have Done This

paper and answer sheet. He collected our cell phones and kept them in his locker before returning to his desk, engrossed in his laptop.

"Ahh, this is an interesting question paper," I sighed and started dictating whatever I knew. "Hey, what are you writing?" I asked her, noticing she wasn't transcribing as I dictated. I instructed her to stop and write down exactly what I was saying.

"I know what I'm writing," she whispered, putting a finger to her lips. Her eyes looked cold, and I trusted her and let her do her job.

* * * * *

"Thanks..." It was the seventh time I had thanked her for her help. The mid-semester exams were over, and the results were out. I scored well, and it wouldn't have been possible without her assistance.

To thank her, I planned to take her out for dinner. Because my hand was still healing, she had to drive. Although she was hesitant at first, she agreed when I insisted. I waited for her outside the society gates where she picked me up.

"If you say it one more time, I swear..." She stopped mid-sentence, her hand on the steering wheel.

"You will? What will you do, Seerat?" I teased her. She fell silent, the smile fading between her pursed lips. A blush tinged her cheeks as she returned her gaze to the road. Her hand delicately tucked strands of hair behind her ear.

She wore black skinny jeans and a white top, with her black hair cascading past her shoulders. A black jacket kept her warm at the onset of winter in Delhi. I loved Delhi's winter; it was one of the things I adored about the city.

"Never mind," she said, shifting the gear and avoiding my gaze. Soon, we reached Connaught Place, the heart of Delhi. The area was instantly recognizable on any map, with a big circle in the middle

34

I Shouldn't Have Done This

and radial roads spreading out in all directions. One wrong turn, and you'd be on the wrong path, miles away from your destination.

Once we reached the inner circle, we parked the car and headed to the restaurant. "Lord of the Drinks," she read the sign as we arrived. It was a good restaurant in the inner circle, my favorite place for dinner, not because of the food but because of its fantastic view.

We went straight to the roof, where I had reserved a table. It was a table near the edge, providing a view of the entire Connaught Circle. The design of Connaught Place was inspired by European Renaissance architecture, giving it a classical touch. The place was named after Prince Arthur, 1st Duke of Connaught, and has become one of Delhi's largest commercial and business centers.

As we sat down, I noticed the Indian tricolor flag waving proudly nearby. The flag, measuring 90 feet by 60 feet, was the most enormous known Indian national tricolor flag when it was first hoisted on March 7, 2014. The pole on which it stood measured 207 feet. It was a sight to behold.

Seerat was visiting this place for the first time, and I could see the amazement in her eyes. In my opinion, that was the second-best thing about Connaught Place—the mesmerizing view.

"It's a beautiful view from here," she remarked, taking a deep breath and hugging herself for warmth. Her jacket didn't seem to be doing the job.

"Are you alright? We can move inside if you're feeling cold," I suggested, pointing to a table in the monitored indoor area.

"No, I'm fine. I like it here," she replied, gazing toward me and offering a feeble smile.

"What would you like to have?" I handed her the menu. "Would you like a drink?"

"No, I have to drive back home," she replied with another smile, glancing at my hand and furrowing her brows.

I Shouldn't Have Done This

"Oh, yes, my hand," I said, looking at it. "It looks miserable, but believe me, it's fine." I showed her my hand and placed it on my lap instead of the table this time.

"I was just kidding. It's just that I'm not in the mood," she said, looking through the menu.

"Alright, then, how about some soup? It will warm you up a bit; it's a little chilly out here," I suggested.

"Okay, I'll have corn soup then," she decided, placing the menu down and reaching for her phone. "Ah, that was my aunt," she explained when she noticed me looking at her. She put her phone back in her pocket.

Unsure of how to respond, I asked, "How is she?" That was the first thing that came to my mind.

"She's good, just a little angry that I forgot to call her," she replied.

"You must be very close to your aunt."

"Yes, after my mom died, she was the one who was always there for me."

"I'm sorry," I said, realizing I didn't know about her mother's passing. We hadn't had many honest conversations before, just brief exchanges about my hand and her coming to college to help with my exams. I hadn't had a chance to get to know her.

"How is your dad?" I decided to seize the opportunity to learn more about her.

"He's no more," she replied, pausing while having her soup. She set her spoon back in the bowl, her eyes filled with sadness.

I felt like an idiot, unknowingly dampening her mood. I had to be more cautious in my choice of topics. But what could I do to rectify the mistake I had already made?

"I'm really sorry. I didn't mean to..."

"No, it's fine," she interrupted me. She spun her spoon in the bowl, lost in memories.

"He died last year in a car accident."

I Shouldn't Have Done This

"That's sad," I said, placing my right hand on hers. Seerat flinched, her gaze shifting from the bowl to my hand, but she didn't pull away.

"Everything will be alright," I assured her, wondering why fate always inflicted hardships on good people who deserved happiness.

She didn't say anything, only gave a faint smile and left her hand on mine. I shuddered, realizing it was the first time she had touched my hand. We hadn't even shaken hands before. The first time we met, she was sleepwalking and paid no attention to such formalities. And after that, my hand was burned, making it impossible for me to shake hands.

"It's really fine. Tell me something about your family," she suggested, attempting to change the topic.

I, too, didn't want to dampen her mood any further, so I began telling her about my family. Soon, she was laughing at the stories I shared about my mother. Her laughter had a hint of pain in her eyes. She had endured so much at such a young age.

* * * * *

"Thanks for the treat," she said as she dropped me off at the gate of my society. I told her I could take a cab back home, but she insisted it would only take her five minutes to drive back to her place. "That was a great evening, by the way," she added before rolling up the window, revving the engine, and disappearing from my sight. We went our separate ways at the society gate, and I made my way toward my PG. The journey felt arduous, but I stayed focused enough to reach my apartment. As soon as I stepped inside, I changed into fresh clothes and flopped face down onto the bed. I buried my face in a soft pillow and closed my eyes, allowing my thoughts to drift to the girl I had met that day—Seerat. She was beautiful. I remembered how innocent she looked when we first met, wearing shorts with her half-closed eyes. And today, she looked fantastic when she arrived in her black jeans and white top. The

I Shouldn't Have Done This

touch of her hand on mine still lingered, sending tingles down my spine. Memories of her brought a smile to my face. "Don't dwell on it, Meet," I repeated as I waited for sleep to wash over me. But I couldn't help but wonder what it would feel like to be someone like her. That was my last clear thought before everything became muddled and faded away.

Chapter 5

$\mathcal{P}$erched on my bike amidst the chatter of Ankit and other classmates lingering by the college gate, I was enveloped in the aftermath of a particularly long day. Our minds were still wrapped around the impending submission of our semester-end report, dissecting faculty feedback and brainstorming ideas. Amidst this academic haze, a figure caught my eye—a girl clad in blue jeans and a slightly lighter jacket. At first, I questioned whether I was merely lost in reverie, but as she drew closer, the realization dawned upon me—it was Seerat.

A flutter of anticipation swept through me as she made her approach. It had been nearly a week since our last encounter, a fleeting dinner that left little room for meaningful conversation. As she drew nearer, my heart quickened, adrenaline coursing through my veins, and my senses heightened to a feverish pitch. It felt as though my blood pressure had skyrocketed, my palms growing clammy with nerves. I watched her intently, hoping for a chance to reconnect, yet as she passed by without so much a glance in my direction, the realization struck—she wasn't here for me.

Desiring a private moment to gather my thoughts, I excused myself from the group without eliciting a second glance. Ignoring their obliviousness, I descended the familiar path, tracing the winding footpath flanked by trees and hedges. Casting a furtive glance over my shoulder to ensure I remained undetected, I quickened my pace, determined not to let this opportunity slip through my fingers.

I Shouldn't Have Done This

Drawing closer to her, I called out her name—Seerat. She paused, glancing over her shoulder, her face aglow with its customary innocence—a sight that never failed to captivate me.

"It's a pleasant surprise to see you here," I greeted, extending my hand in camaraderie.

Her warm smile greeted mine as she withdrew her hand from her pocket, its touch igniting a familiar sensation that sent shivers down my spine.

"I came here to meet Kritika," she explained, her words punctuated by a glance at her watch. "By now, she must be at her apartment."

A flicker of concern crossed my mind. "She wasn't there?" I queried, sensing a hint of tension in her demeanor.

"No, she wasn't," she confirmed, tucking a loose strand of hair behind her ear—an action that never failed to captivate me, rendering me momentarily speechless. "That's the problem," she continued, drawing me back into the conversation.

"Problem?" I echoed my focus solely on her.

"Yes, this morning I was running late and forgot to grab my keys before leaving for college," she elaborated. "When I realized, I called Kritika, and she told me to meet her here, to pick the keys. But on my way, I got stuck in traffic, and when I tried calling her, her phone was switched off. So..." Her voice trailed off, her expression tinged with apprehension.

"So what happened?" I prodded, concern furrowing my brow.

"She called to say she'd waited for me but had to leave for home," she confessed, her disappointment palpable. "Now, I have no choice but to head to my aunt's house. I just don't want to inconvenience her."

My heart ached at her distress, and a spontaneous offer slipped past my lips before I could second-guess it. "You could stay at my apartment."

I Shouldn't Have Done This

Her eyes widened in surprise, a delicate blush gracing her cheeks. "No, it's fine," she demurred, though her reaction hinted at a different sentiment.

"Would you like some coffee?" I offered, spotting Dabbu nearby. Known for his exceptional brew, his stall was a favorite among the college crowd, adorned with snippets from newspapers and blogs praising his concoctions.

"Yes, I guess so," Seerat replied, and we made our way to the stall, ordering two cups of his renowned brew. Perching ourselves on makeshift seats—cement rocks stacked one atop the other—we settled in as evening approached.

As Dabbu served us, the rich aroma enveloped us, enticing my senses as I tapped the surface of my coffee, watching the ripples cascade outward. Seerat, lost in her own thoughts, sipped her drink, her gaze fixed on the shifting hues of the horizon.

The sun, a fiery orb, dipped low, casting a warm glow across the sky. Clouds, resembling cotton candy, blushed at its touch as silhouettes of birds traversed the magenta sky. The landscape transformed with each passing moment, and the sun eventually disappeared beyond the horizon.

Seerat's demeanor remained serene, her lips curled into a gentle smile, lost in her contemplation of the fading daylight. "How's your coffee?" I interjected, attempting to draw her back to the present moment. She glanced at me, offering a smile before returning her focus to the mesmerizing vista before us.

"How will you go to your aunt's home?" I inquired as we strolled along the road, the college now nearly deserted save for a handful of students heading for coffee or the hostel.

"I'll probably take a cab or maybe the Metro," Seerat responded, her expression thoughtful.

"Where does she live?" I asked, seizing the opportunity to extend our time together.

"Chandni Chowk," she replied.

"That's not far from here. I can drop you," I offered eagerly, keen to prolong our conversation and deepen our connection. "If you take a cab now, you'll be stuck in traffic forever."

"I'm fine, I'll manage," she grinned.

Determined not to let this chance slip away, I persisted. "I can drop you on my bike. It won't take much time. You drove me to dinner the other day, so now it's my turn to return the favor."

Though I felt a twinge of apprehension, I knew I had to seize the moment. Finally, after some persuasion, she relented, and we returned to the college gate where my bike was parked. With her hand resting lightly on my shoulder for support, she settled in behind me—an experience sending anticipation shivers down my spine. This was a moment I had imagined countless times since our last meeting, and now it was unfolding even better than I had dared to hope.

Navigating through the crowded streets of Chandni Chowk, I opted for narrow lanes to circumvent the notorious traffic jams. As we approached her aunt's home, the cacophony of sounds and scents enveloped us—the mingling aromas of exhaust and street food, the clamor of vendors vying for attention, and the vibrant energy of the bustling streets. It was a sensory overload unlike anything I had experienced before, and I couldn't help but be captivated by the chaos and charm of Chandni Chowk.

"Here we are," I announced as I halted my bike at the corner of the street, the narrow lane preventing us from venturing any further. Seerat, once again leaning on my shoulder for support, dismounted from the bike.

"Thank you so much. That was such a nice ride," she expressed, her voice tinged with genuine happiness this time.

"My pleasure," I responded, securing my bike and meeting her gaze.

She appeared slightly puzzled, prompting me to inquire, "What's on your mind?"

I Shouldn't Have Done This

"I told you I'd drop you off at your aunt's home, so I can't just leave you here," I explained matter-of-factly. "I'll walk you to her house."

Seerat hesitated, insisting, "No, I'm fine. It's not far from here. I can walk."

"It might be fine for you, but not for me. I made a promise, and a gentleman always keeps his word," I declared sternly.

Her smile softened her features as she relented, "Okay, gentleman, you can walk me to her house."

"I didn't ask for your permission," I teased, and we laughed as we embarked on the short journey to her aunt's home.

* * * * *

As we meandered through the narrow streets of Chandni Chowk, the ancient heart of Delhi, the architecture whispered tales of bygone eras. Not far from our path stood the majestic Red Fort, a testament to the grandeur of the Mughal Empire, its silhouette casting a regal shadow over the bustling market below. Chandni Chowk wasn't merely a commercial hub; it was a tapestry of history, culture, and spirituality, boasting revered sites like the Gurudwara Sheesh Ganj Sahib, the Jama Masjid, and the Gauri Shankar Temple, each drawing devotees from all walks of life.

"Would you like some fruit cream?" Seerat pointed to a shop adorned with the sign "Punjab Fruit Cream." "His fruit cream is famous throughout Delhi," she informed me with a hint of excitement.

"Punjab Fruit Cream in Delhi? That's quite the paradox," I remarked, unable to suppress a chuckle. "I've heard of fruit and cream separately, but 'fruit cream' is new for me. And how famous can a shop be if I've never heard of it?"

"Are you serious?" Seerat shot me reproachfully as if I had committed a grave offense.

I Shouldn't Have Done This

"I've never tried it," I confessed sheepishly, feeling a pang of guilt for my culinary ignorance.

"You must try it," Seerat insisted, linking her arm with mine and guiding me towards the shop.

No matter how innocent, I couldn't deny the thrill I felt from her touch. It was as if an electric current surged through me at her slightest contact. Why did she have such an effect on me? Would I ever grow immune to her allure?

We ordered two cups of fruit cream. Seerat opted for a large scoop while I played it safe with a regular serving. The shop was tranquil, considering its purported fame.

"Quite a famous shop, I must say," I remarked, scanning the sparse surroundings.

"You..." Seerat began, then abruptly stopped, tapping my elbow gently. Though fleeting, the contact sent me a jolt of unfamiliar energy.

"Why are we here?" I questioned, puzzled by our visit.

"We're here to eat fruit cream," she declared with a hint of nostalgia. "When I was a child, visiting my aunt's home with my mother, I always begged for fruit cream. But my mother would say, 'It's winter, you can't have it, you'll get sick.' So, in the evening, my aunt and I would sneak out, and she'd buy me a big scoop. I loved it so much," she reminisced, her voice tinged with both fondness and sorrow as she brushed away a tear, turning her gaze away.

"Here it is; try this ingenious discovery," Seerat offered, attempting to mask her pain behind a facade of normalcy.

I understood that offering her comfort or sympathy might only exacerbate her distress, so I chose to act as if I hadn't noticed anything amiss. "It's great; I think we should come here more often," I replied diplomatically, though inwardly, I found the concoction somewhat underwhelming—just some chopped fruits mixed with whipped cream, as the name suggested. However, I couldn't voice my disappointment, knowing the sentimental value it held for Seerat.

Seerat's laughter rang out, tinged with a hint of hurt—a raw, unfiltered expression that reminded me of a child unburdened by social constraints. "What?" I inquired, genuinely perplexed by her sudden amusement.

"Your nose," she managed to choke out between fits of laughter, holding onto the table for support.

Confused, I reached for a mirror, only to find none. "What's wrong with my nose?" I asked, my curiosity piqued.

"Cream," she finally managed to articulate, still giggling.

Realizing the mishap, she grabbed a tissue and wiped away the cream, though the damage had been done. Her gaze lingered on me, causing my heart to race and my breath to hitch. Her presence had a way of unsettling me in the most exhilarating manner.

"You want some more?" Seerat interrupted my reverie, her words jolting me back to the present moment.

"I'm good," I replied, taking the last spoonful from my cup.

As we exited the shop, a sense of contentment washed over me, and I was grateful for the opportunity to spend time with her, however brief. Yet, I knew the inevitable farewell loomed ahead, and despite my reluctance to part ways, I found myself uttering, "It was a delight for your tongue," desperate to prolong our interaction for just a few more precious moments.

"Yes, that is why I love it," Seerat responded, her voice tinged with sadness, starkly contrasting to her previous laughter.

Concern gnawed at me as I observed her sudden change in demeanor. "What's wrong?" I finally asked, unable to contain my curiosity any longer.

She regarded me with a puzzled expression, unsure whether to confide in me.

"You can talk to me," I encouraged gently, sensing her hesitation.

She pursed her lips, weighing her words carefully. Knowing the power of emotional appeals, I played my card. "If you won't tell me, I would believe that you do not consider me your friend."

"It's nothing like that. It's just..." She trailed off, her gaze falling to a pebble on the ground, which she began idly playing with.

"I'm waiting," I prompted, focusing on her.

"It's just... I don't want to go to my aunt's home," she admitted, her tone laden with vulnerability.

"But I thought you loved being with her," I remarked, confusion creeping into my voice.

"Yes, I love her," she affirmed, meeting my gaze. "After my mom died, I felt so alone. She was the one who loved me and took care of me. If she weren't there, I would have been shattered after her death." Seerat tucked her hands into the pockets of her jeans, her stance reflective of her inner turmoil.

"So what's the problem?" I inquired, still puzzled by her distress.

"Her daughter," she revealed, her words tumbling out almost involuntarily. "She's at home."

As she shared her story, I struggled to piece together the puzzle. "When my mom died, my aunt asked me to live with her. My dad was busy working most of the time, and I felt horrible at home, so I decided to spend some time with her. She's a wonderful lady, she loves me so much. Certainly, no one can take my mother's place, but when I was with her, I had the feeling that someone out there loved me and could look after me. I felt secure, and life didn't feel like such a burden."

As we approached her aunt's house, the weight of the impending visit hung heavy between us. Seerat's hands remained buried in her pockets, her gaze fixed on the familiar façade of her aunt's home, yet her mind seemed miles away, lost in the depths of her own thoughts.

"But when her daughter came home from her college hostel, everything changed," Seerat's voice strained with emotion. "She didn't like that her mother and I were so close; she cared about me so much and loved me deeply. At first, she pretended to be nice and even feigned concern for me, but it soon became clear when her true feelings surfaced. She began hurling hurtful and cruel words at me for every little thing I did. I spent countless days drowning in despair, wishing for an escape, wishing to reunite with my mom."

A solitary tear escaped her eye, tracing a path down her cheek—a silent testament to the pain she had endured. Unable to bear her suffering, I reached out, gently grasping her elbow. She turned to me, her eyes searching mine for solace.

I cupped her cheek, brushing away the tear with my thumb. "You don't have to go there," I whispered softly, my heart aching at her distress.

Her gaze met mine, uncertainty clouding her expression. "Then where will I stay tonight?"

"I don't know," I admitted honestly, squeezing her hand reassuringly. "But we'll figure it out together." With that, I led her away from the oppressive confines of the narrow streets, determined to spare her from any further anguish.

* * * * *

"Okay, then it's final," I declared after numerous failed attempts to find a suitable accommodation for Seerat. Despite my offer for her to stay at my home being swiftly declined, we eventually settled on a plan: retrieve the keys from Kritika, who was at her home in Murthal, and then I would drop Seerat off at her place, with the condition that she treat me to dinner at one of the famous Murthal Dhabas.

It seemed like a win-win situation for both of us. Seerat avoided spending the night with her detested cousin, but I got to spend more time with her and enjoy a hearty meal at Murthal.

It had been a while since I last visited my home, so I eagerly anticipated indulging in various stuffed parathas.

"I estimate you should be home by 11 pm," I calculated aloud, to which Seerat simply nodded before hopping onto my bike. Despite spending most of the evening together, she maintained a cautious distance, even as she settled behind me on the bike.

As we left Delhi behind, the surroundings transformed drastically. The narrow, crowded lanes led to a six-lane highway flanked by sprawling farms. However, the absence of street lamps and the pitch darkness hinted at a power outage.

The wind howled fiercely, biting into our skin with an icy chill that penetrated the bone. I had underestimated its force, having grown accustomed to the milder winds of Delhi's congested streets. As I adjusted the gears to slow down, I felt Seerat's hands rest on my shoulders.

Gradually, the space between us diminished until I could feel her body pressed against mine. She enveloped me in a hug from behind, and instantly, my heartbeat quickened, drowning out the roar of the wind. Her touch emanated warmth, dispelling the biting cold and replacing it with the scent of damp earth.

For the remainder of the journey, she held me close, her presence a comforting shield against the elements. Perhaps she sensed my shivers, or maybe she felt the cold. Whatever the reason, it was a beautiful ride, made all the more special by her embrace.

After a while, we arrived in Murthal, where many Dhabas lined the roadside. While they may have started as humble establishments, many had evolved into sprawling complexes resembling four-star hotels. Seerat directed me to stop near Sukhdev Dhaba, a renowned spot that had become a staple for travelers along this highway. I had frequented Sukhdev Dhaba countless times before, as had most Delhiites, and its popularity had spawned numerous similar establishments in the area.

Pulling over near the Dhaba, I glanced at the time to ensure we were still on schedule. Seerat, with her arms folded across her chest, avoided making eye contact, but I couldn't help but observe her

I Shouldn't Have Done This

demeanor. Despite her initial reluctance, it didn't take long for her to crack. Although she didn't meet my gaze, a slow, heart-stopping smile curved her lips.

Unwilling to let her off the hook so quickly, I remained silent, maintaining my fixed gaze. She eventually laughed, her silvery voice ringing, "What?"

"Nothing," I grinned, playing along. "Where is Kritika?" I inquired, noting that Seerat had arranged for Kritika to meet us here rather than heading straight to her home, likely to save time, as she lived nearby.

"I don't know, let me call her," Seerat replied, retrieving her cell phone and placing a call. As it turned out, Kritika was already present, accompanied by her friend Roohdeep, waiting for us inside.

"It's been a while since we last met," Kritika remarked, rising to hug me. Though Seerat's expression briefly flickered when she saw Kritika embracing me, she seemed unaware of the reaction.

After introductions, we settled for a well-deserved dinner, with Kritika already placing our order. I expressed gratitude for her thoughtful gesture.

As we finished our meal, Seerat reached for the bill, but Roohdeep assured her there was no need to worry, as her father was friends with the owner.

Raising an eyebrow, I quipped, "In that case, you're my best friend from now onwards."

Kritika responded with a high-five, and we all shared a hearty laugh, enjoying the camaraderie and warmth of the moment.

Chapter **6**

*T*he ride back home wasn't as challenging. Although Seerat didn't hug me this time, she wasn't cautious about maintaining a distance either. I thought nothing could go wrong now, but fate seemed to have different plans for us. We were just a mile from her home when it started raining. The rain came suddenly without warning, falling in a chaotic and wild manner, carried by gusting winds. Puddles formed everywhere, and the temperature dropped dramatically within moments.

I wanted to stop the bike as the gusting wind made it difficult to maintain balance. We were only a few minutes away from her home, so I decided to slow down but stopped only when we reached her building. As soon as the bike stopped, Seerat ran towards her building. It was a tough call for me should I follow her inside the apartment or head back to my place?

Considering it was already midnight, I preferred to return to my home. However, the rain was pouring relentlessly. Water accumulated everywhere within minutes, and the wind was so strong that it could uproot trees. To call it wind would be an understatement; it was a tempest, a force of nature, unlike anything I had ever witnessed.

I started my bike to return home when she asked, "What are you doing there? Come fast." Seerat was utterly drenched, standing at the entrance of her building, waiting for me. She rubbed her hands together, trying to keep warm. Even from a distance, I could tell that she was shivering. Seerat stood there, kissed by the rain and glistening under the dim light.

50

I Shouldn't Have Done This

I was captivated by her beauty. "Come fast, Meet," she called out again, snapping me back to reality. I realized it was time to act. The temperature must have dropped to around 3 or 4 degrees Celsius, but with the wind, it felt like minus 5 degrees. By the time we reached her apartment, we were soaked and shivering.

"Can I take your jacket?" she asked, concern evident in her voice.

I looked at her, noticing she had removed her jacket and slung it over her arm. She stood in her blue jeans and a white deep-necked t-shirt, her thick, dark hair framing her breathtaking face and her eyes glistening a wild and dazzling black. Little drops of water fell from her hair, and she looked like a mermaid emerging from the water. Her wet top clung tightly to her body, accentuating her curves. In a word, she amazed me. I couldn't believe I was standing there with this marvelous girl.

"Meet?" she called out, raising an eyebrow as I stood in a daze.

"You are beautiful, Seerat," I blurted out, the words escaping without conscious thought.

Her brows lifted, and then softness came into her eyes as her mouth curved into a cute smile.

She hung our jackets on a hanger behind the door and motioned me to follow her. I was still standing at the entrance, confused and cursing myself for my impulsive words, but at least I was being honest.

Seerat returned with some clothes and a towel and handed them to me. "That's all I have," she said. Seerat showed me the way to the bathroom. "Go and change," she added in an authoritative yet calm tone.

I took the clothes from her and followed her instructions. I was still hypnotized by her beauty. A few moments later, I found myself in the bathroom, with cream-colored tiles blending perfectly with the attached room.

I Shouldn't Have Done This

"Give me your clothes, and I'll put them in the dryer," she offered.

Should I give her all my clothes or just a T-shirt and jeans? I wondered and ultimately decided to give her only jeans and a T-shirt. I opened the door slightly and handed her my clothes.

Feeling cold and tempted to have a hot shower, I couldn't help but wish that we could take a shower together. The mere thought of being in the shower with her sent shivers down my spine.

The shower provided some relief, but what followed became a horrible dream. Seerat gave me some shorts and a T-shirt. Judging by the size and little hearts all over the clothes, I could tell they belonged to her.

I could barely fit into those clothes. It felt like I was wearing a bikini. I considered going out without clothes, but I wasn't sure how she would react.

When I opened the bathroom door, she stood in a black cotton shirt covered in white umbrellas and similar shorts just above her thighs. She looked adorable in her bunny slippers and blue specs, her hair still wet.

She glanced at me and arched her brow. Before she could say anything, I cut her off. "Don't even think about it."

She pressed her lips together, trying hard to control herself, but it only took a few seconds before she burst into laughter. I couldn't resist and joined in.

"You look wonderful when you laugh," I thought in my head or maybe I said it out loud. I still wasn't sure.

I took a bedsheet and wrapped it around myself, trying to avoid any more embarrassment, and sat sulking on the sofa.

When she noticed me sulking on the sofa, she approached me, placing her left foot on the sofa and leaning closer. I could feel her breath on my face, and the scent of her fancy shampoo filled the air.

She cupped my face with her right hand and moved closer, her lips just an inch away from mine.

I Shouldn't Have Done This

"Meet," Seerat spoke my name in a decadent purr. Her voice was sensuous, and a strand of hair fell on her cheek as she leaned forward.

My heartbeat quickened with each passing second, and I could hear my heart pounding in my ears. I wanted to do the same to her: touch her cheeks with my fingers and tuck that strand of hair behind her ear. But I resisted the temptation and leaned in to touch my lips to hers.

"You were looking sexy in that bikini," she exclaimed, pushing me back and running away. I could hear the happiness in her laughter.

"If you like it, you'll get more," I said, throwing the bedsheet to the ground and chasing after her. She could barely escape from me in that small space. I caught hold of her elbow and pulled her towards me.

She lost her balance, and so did I. We both fell onto the sofa, and I shuddered at her touch, wondering if she had felt it too.

I readjusted myself on the sofa while she struggled to regain her balance. She ended up lying in my lap, one hand around my shoulder and the other on the table for support.

I held her left arm and cupped her cheek, looking straight into her eyes. They were brown, I noticed. I had always thought they were black.

A few moments passed, and she remained still, her eyes wide. Her chest rose and fell rapidly with each breath, and the only sound in the room was the raindrops falling on the windowpane.

I tucked that strand of hair behind her ear and whispered her name, "Ms. Seerat." My voice was low, audible only to her.

She didn't utter a word, her eyes still locked on mine. She didn't move an inch. I leaned closer to her, and she closed her eyes. "You find me sexy in these clothes, but what about you? Ever since I met you, I can hardly think of anything else."

With each word, I leaned in and pressed my lips against hers. Initially, Seerat didn't move, freezing like a statue and holding her breath. Then, slowly, her lips quivered and parted to let out a breath. I pressed my lips against hers, shocked by how soft and firm they were.

Heat coursed through my chest, making breathing difficult, and my skin tingled all over. Why? Why did her touch affect me so much?

Her lips parted further, and her tongue brushed against mine, causing her to shudder.

In the tiny corner of my brain that was still functioning, I heard a voice warning me to pull away, telling me I was making a mistake. But I couldn't resist the temptation, just as I couldn't resist touching her.

I let go of her arm and placed my right hand on her back for support. She regained her balance and sat on my lap, her hands entwined in my hair.

We both got lost in the moment, kissing each other and savoring every second.

I was losing control, my hand moving along her spine. Abruptly, she yanked herself away, struggling to regain her footing.

Reality crashed back down on me, and I realized that what I had experienced was too good to be true. She stood there, still and calm. I desperately wanted to know what she was thinking, but her expression was unreadable. Her breathing was short and shallow, and she turned and returned to her room before I could say anything.

"Fuck," I cursed myself, devastated by the mess I had created. I felt crushed. My brain rumbled with negative thoughts.

"But she was the one who teased you first; that's a fact," a voice in my head reminded me. That fact provided a small measure of relief.

"But facts won't improve things," I agreed, drowning in negativity.

I Shouldn't Have Done This

"Shh..." I hushed the chaos in my mind. All this negativity wouldn't help. The damage was done, and all I could do was control it. She was the best thing that had happened to me, and I couldn't afford to lose her over my foolishness.

I took a deep breath and let out a sigh. Should I go home, stay here, or go to her room and apologize? I mustered up some courage and again took the bedsheet to hide my shame. I walked towards her room, smacking my brain with a whirlwind of thoughts.

"You've screwed yourself," a voice in my head laughed at me.

I knocked on her door, but she didn't reply. I opened it slowly, scared that she might throw something at me. She was standing there, calm.

"I'm going home," I said, my voice low.

"Why? What happened? You can stay here tonight, or at least until the rain stops," she suggested, her tone laced with concern.

"Yes, I guess so," I replied, trying to keep a smile on my face. I wanted to talk things out, but I believed it wasn't the right time.

I sat on the sofa, both of my legs crossed over it. The warmth of the shawl she had given me felt comforting. I was lost in my thoughts when she came with a tray in her hands, carrying two coffee mugs.

Her picture was printed on one of the mugs with "Happy Birthday" written in red. I hadn't seen this picture before.

She placed the tray on the table. "Do you want something to eat?" she asked, focused on making coffee.

"No, coffee is fine," I replied, grabbing the mug with her picture on it before she could take it. I held the cup with both palms, feeling the warmth against my cold hands.

The vibrant aroma seemed to have escaped the thick cream coating on the surface, penetrating deep into my nose and making my mouth water. I took a sip, and it was marvelous. How could she be so perfect in everything she did?

I glanced at the TV screen, but my eyes were on her from the corner of my vision. She was enjoying her coffee, her hair still wet.

I Shouldn't Have Done This

She noticed me looking at her, and I turned my gaze instantly. "What?" she asked cheerfully, a mischievous smile on her face.

"Nothing," I replied, unable to contain my laughter.

I had been worried about everything that had happened that day, but the way she handled it all was a tremendous relief for me. I wanted to ask her how she felt, but I didn't want to make things awkward again.

"Can I ask you something?" I decided to break the ice and start a conversation.

"Yes, sure," she replied, sipping her coffee.

Before I could say anything, she interrupted, "Wait, let me bring some cookies first." She got up and went to the kitchen.

Damn, I cursed myself. I was worried and didn't want to jeopardize anything, but she only cared about coffee and cookies.

"Yes, tell me. What do you want to ask?" She returned with a pack of cookies and sat beside me. The awareness of her presence beside me sent a prickling sensation across my skin. A magnetic pull between us made me shift restlessly in my seat. I felt an inexplicable attraction to her once again.

I struggled to speak, but the words didn't appear as intended. I cleared my throat and tried again, "Nothing," that was all I could manage at that moment.

"Tell me," she demanded in a commanding tone.

"Why did you make that face when Kritika hugged me?" I finally asked, wanting to know the truth.

"No, I didn't make any face," she replied dismissively.

"Don't lie," I said firmly. "I saw you when you made that face."

"It's just..." she arched her brows and rolled her eyes. "I didn't know you and Kritika were such close friends."

"Did you feel jealous?" I asked, searching for a glimpse of honesty.

"Why would I feel jealous?" she snorted. "Do you want to watch TV?" She attempted to change the topic.

I Shouldn't Have Done This

On any other day, I wouldn't have allowed her to change the subject. But that day was different. I didn't want to push things further. "Yes, sure," I nodded with a smile.

I couldn't remember how the movie ended. Clearly, I had fallen asleep before it finished.

When I woke up, it was dark and silent. I was lying on the sofa, with my head in Seerat's lap. She was still sitting there, her eyes closed, her back leaning against the couch for support, and her legs crossed.

All the lights in the room were off. I checked the time on my phone and realized it was 3:30 in the morning. The rain had stopped. It was a perfect moment, and I didn't want to change it in any way. I adjusted myself and closed my eyes again, a smile on my face. Deep down, I knew this was the beginning of something new, something meaningful.

Chapter 7

"Can't you do anything right, Meet?" I gritted my teeth in frustration, pounding my fist into the back of the couch. Anger surged through me as I glanced at my phone once again. Seerat hadn't been answering my calls or responding to my messages. Exasperated, I sighed and ran my hands through my hair.

The day I spent with her was extraordinary. Every single moment we shared felt cherished. It was the first time we had spent such an extended period together. The longing I felt was intense as if she had become a drug to my body, the source of exhilarating highs.

I sank onto the couch and grabbed my bottle of beer, hoping the bitterness of the alcohol would wash away some of my turmoil. Damn it, why did that girl have to be so unpredictable?

After we kissed, she didn't show any signs of anger. She might regret it, be furious with me, or even throw things at me. But none of that happened. She remained calm and relaxed. I even got the feeling that she was pleased that we kissed. She asked me to stay, made coffee for me, we watched a movie together, and I even fell asleep with my head in her lap.

When I woke up, she wasn't there, but she had prepared a delicious breakfast for me and left a note explaining that she had to attend college and had to go. I finished my beer and grabbed another one from the fridge.

It has been three days since her phone has been out of reach. She must have blocked my number or perhaps changed her number. But why does she have to be so enigmatic? If she didn't like what

I Shouldn't Have Done This

happened, she could have simply told me. There's no reason to ignore me.

As I downed my beer, I tried to gather my thoughts to reach some conclusions. However, my thoughts scattered when Ankit arrived.

"You didn't come to college today?" he inquired.

"No, I didn't feel like doing anything," I replied, glancing at the empty bottles I had consumed. "That's quite evident," Ankit remarked.

Alcohol was meant to dull my senses so that I could forget everything, but it seemed to be failing in its task.

"What happened, buddy? Is everything alright?" Ankit sat beside me on the couch and touched my shoulder. Having someone there for me felt comforting when I was in need.

I poured out everything that had transpired between Seerat and me that day.

"So much has happened to you, and you're telling me now?" Ankit took a swig from a beer he grabbed from the fridge. I had expected him to be more concerned about my loss, or at least pretend to be.

"Have you called Kritika?" he asked simply.

"No," I responded, realizing I hadn't thought of that before. I cursed myself for the oversight. Perhaps alcohol had impaired my ability to think, or maybe it was the pain of losing her.

"Then call her and ask. She must know why Seerat isn't answering your calls," Ankit suggested.

I expressed my gratitude and retrieved my phone to call Kritika.

"Hey, it's Meet. How are you?" I greeted her in a calm voice, though I was eager to inquire about Seerat. I didn't want to come across as rude or reveal my frustration.

"I'm fine," she replied.

"Hey, I've been trying to reach Seerat, but she hasn't answered. Do you happen to know her whereabouts?" I rose from the couch

I Shouldn't Have Done This

and walked to the balcony, wanting to get straight to the point and not waste time on unnecessary small talk.

"She's in the hospital," Kritika revealed.

I couldn't believe what I was hearing. Those words hit me like a shockwave. My feet turned numb, and I collapsed onto a chair on the balcony.

"Hey, are you alright?" Kritika's voice brought me back to my senses. I swallowed a lump in my throat, struggling to regain composure. "Yes, what happened to her?"

"Stay calm. Seerat is fine," Kritika reassures me, sensing the tension in my voice. "Her aunt is in the hospital, and she's there taking care of her."

A wave of relief washes over me. I'm relieved that Seerat is unharmed and nothing serious has befallen her. But I suppress my happiness. After all, I'm not a sadist. Her aunt is still in the hospital, and that remains a cause for concern.

"Text me the details," I request before hanging up.

* * * * *

When I arrived at the hospital, I found Seerat standing in the corridor, conversing with a nurse. Her face looked worn out as if she hadn't slept in days.

I approached her slowly, unsure of what to say. Why did I even come here, I wondered. But I couldn't leave her alone in this state. So, I walked closer until I stood a short distance away. She kept talking to the nurse, and even though I couldn't hear them, her worry was evident.

I observed her closely, and when the nurse left, our eyes met. No words were spoken, but her eyes spoke volumes.

As I moved closer, I noticed tears glistening in her eyes. Unable to hold back any longer, she burst into sobs and threw herself into my arms, holding me tightly. This was the moment I had longed for, but I never imagined it would happen like this.

I Shouldn't Have Done This

I held her close, refusing to let go. "Shh," I gently patted her back. "Everything will be alright. Don't worry, I'm here now." My fingers ran through her hair as I kissed her head tenderly.

Gradually, she regained control of her emotions, realizing she was at the hospital. She tried to compose herself, but the pain was still evident. Though the tears had stopped, her sobs continued.

"How is she doing? What did the doctor say?" I inquired, hoping to provide some comfort.

"She's not doing well. She's still in the ICU. The doctors discovered an issue with one of the valves in her heart, and if they don't operate soon, her chances are slim," Seerat revealed, wiping away her tears, though her voice still quivered.

My eyebrows shot up in alarm. "Surgery?"

This news told me that the situation was worse than I imagined. Yet, there was solace in knowing that the problem could be fixed.

"She'll pull through. Soon, she'll be back on her feet," I reassured her.

"I hope so," Seerat replied, her voice filled with concern. "But I can't help but worry. She's the only family I have."

I nodded in understanding and offered a faint smile. "Where is everyone else?" I asked, noticing the absence of other family members.

"No one else is here. I'm alone," Seerat replied, and my heart ached for her. She had been taking care of her aunt all by herself. Where was her supposed daughter when her mother was in such a critical condition?

"Thank goodness you're here," I said, placing a comforting hand on her shoulder.

"Can I meet your aunt?" I inquired, wanting to offer my support.

* * * * *

Walking down the corridor, I passed the nurses' station and turned a corner until I reached the ICU. A guard sat at the door and instructed me to remove my shoes and put on green coveralls. After following the protocol, I opened the door and entered the spacious room with approximately 15 beds, where the nurse station stood at the center.

Her aunt, dressed in a hospital gown, smiled upon seeing us.

"Hey," she greeted.

"Hey, I'm Meet," I introduced myself with a warm grin. "How are you feeling?" It was a rhetorical question; I already knew exactly how she must be feeling.

She lay on the hospital bed, wearing a flimsy gown, with numerous tubes attached to her body and medications coursing through her veins. Various medical instruments monitored her vital signs, emitting constant beeping sounds. It was disconcerting to witness someone in such a condition.

"I'm feeling better now that they gave me some medicines for my headache and chest pain," she replied.

I fetched a stool from the corner and positioned it beside her bed. "Seerat told me she talked to the doctor, and they said you'll be fine soon." I wanted to instill a glimmer of hope. A bit of hope can work wonders.

"I know she's a gem," her aunt said, glancing at Seerat. Seerat stood beside me, and they exchanged smiles. "I don't know what I would do without her."

"If something happens to me, please take care of her. She likes you," she whispered, her voice strained but clear, her words hanging heavy in the air.

My eyebrows shot up in surprise. Her words caught me off guard, whether it was the effect of the medicines or the shock of the situation.

Glancing at Seerat, I saw her expression shift from blush to shock, her eyes wide open with disbelief. It was as if all her hidden feelings had been bare at that moment.

She quickly interjected before her aunt could divulge any more secrets. "You must be tired; take some rest," she urged, grasping my right hand and urging me to follow her.

But I hesitated. This was an opportunity I couldn't pass up. "Wait a moment. Let me hear what else she has to say," I insisted, ignoring Seerat's glare.

Seerat's cheeks flushed with anger, the pink hue of embarrassment replaced by a fiery red. She was seething, and I knew I was treading dangerously close to crossing a line. But the risk seemed worth it.

Her aunt smiled, fully aware of my intentions. Due to the effects of the medicines, her thought process wasn't entirely clear, or perhaps she was just enjoying teasing Seerat in this state. "At first, she wasn't sure whether to accept your offer to bring the keys from Kritika's house. She hesitated but eventually agreed. She was scared to ride on a bike with you, especially in the dark and inclement weather," her aunt narrated the entire saga.

I was astonished by how much Seerat had confided in her aunt. She had mentioned being close to her, but I had no idea she shared every little detail. I was curious to know if she had revealed our kiss as well.

"She was startled and trembling. Darkness has always terrified my little girl," her aunt gazed at Seerat. I could see the depth of their love. Seerat drew closer, holding her aunt's hand. Her anger had dissipated; she understood her aunt's state under the influence of the drugs and knew she didn't intend to hurt her.

"When she holds you, all her displeasure fades away," her aunt remarked. I had assumed she hugged me because she was feeling cold, but now I realized how little I understood her. It wasn't just me; no man has ever truly comprehended women.

"Even when she suggested you come to her apartment due to the rain, she had doubts. She messaged me about you when she arrived at her apartment," her aunt disclosed. Good Lord, she was sharing every detail with her aunt. That was quite unusual. Now, it's

I Shouldn't Have Done This

not just Seerat who feels embarrassed; I also feel embarrassed. When I look at her, she raises her eyebrows, an expression that says, "I told you so."

Her aunt continued her saga, "After some time, she realized that you are just a naive little boy." Who am I? "Naive little boy" yes, I was a naive boy who kissed her niece. I resisted my urge to tell her.

She continued, "When she kissed you, she knew you were that special guy. Girls have a superpower; they can only tell after the first kiss if they can spend their life with you." That's enough; she told her about our kiss as well. Her aunt knew I was that special guy, but I didn't know.

I was brooding over and submerging myself in alcohol over this. I thought I had made a mistake and that Seerat would never talk to me.

But here she was, narrating everything to her aunt, moment by moment.

That was enough for the day. I didn't want to pull any more strings. I believe it was equally embarrassing for me as it was for Seerat. But I was contented that she wasn't exasperated with me or what happened between us.

"I think I should go now," I said, rising from the stool and returning it to its original position.

"Promise me that if something happens to me, you'll take care of her. She has no one except me," her aunt pleaded, her eyes numb.

"But now she has me," I replied, offering her a feeble smile.

* * * * *

"We strolled past the bustling nurse station and hopped on the elevator to the third floor, making our way to the canteen. Seerat seemed to be avoiding eye contact, creating an air of unease between us. I broke the tension when the elevator emptied, leaving us alone.

"So, am I some kind of special guy?" I asked playfully, trying to lighten the mood.

I Shouldn't Have Done This

She hesitated, "My aunt was under the influence of the medicines, and I don't think she knew what she was saying."

"So, I'm not the special guy then?" I probed, wanting a more straightforward answer.

"No," she replied curtly, not giving it much thought.

"Then why did you tell your aunt I am that guy?" I couldn't let this go, feeling like an investigator on a mission.

"I didn't tell her you are special or anything," she retorted, but I could sense her trying to evade the question.

"Then why did she say so?" I persisted, determined to get an answer.

"We kissed, and I felt..." She paused, noticing the canteen's closed sign. "The canteen is closed."

I had no appetite; my entire being hinged on this moment, my heart racing faster than a Delhi metro train, yet all she seemed to care about was food.

"And your response?" I pressed, attempting to steer the conversation back on track.

But she ignored my inquiry, suggesting we go to another canteen outside the hospital. Frustration simmered within me; she deliberately avoided my question, and I wasn't about to let her off the hook.

Taking the stairs to avoid prying ears, her phone rang, interrupting our conversation. It was her uncle, who had arrived and was waiting for her near the ICU.

"Now you go, he is waiting for me" She kept her phone in her pocket.

"OK." This time, she got lucky, but I won't leave her next time. I walked towards the exit gate.

"By the way, thanks for coming," She said with a cute little smile and left.

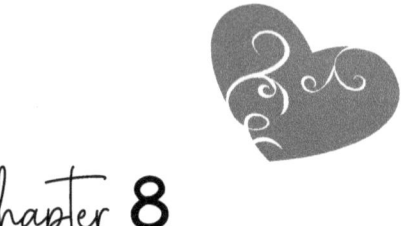

Chapter 8

"*N*early three months had passed since Seerat's aunt left us. The surgery had gone well, and the doctors moved her to the standard ward, optimistic about her recovery. But one fateful night, she experienced sudden chest pain, and before the doctor could arrive, she was gone.

Seerat was inconsolable for weeks after the tragedy. Her uncle and cousin were physically present but emotionally absent. She was closest to her aunt, who had taken care of her since her parents' passing.

I tried my best to offer comfort and support during those difficult times. Time, they say, heals wounds, and slowly, Seerat began to move forward.

As winter engulfed Delhi, so did the pressure of semester-end exams. Most students burned the midnight oil, but my late nights were spent talking to Seerat. Love has a way of making everything else seem trivial.

But as Christmas approached, I knew it was time to take a leap of faith and confess my feelings. The Christmas party seemed perfect, just a few days away. I wanted everything to be perfect.

With a beer in hand, I sat at my study table, trying to come up with ideas. Ankit was texting away, and I asked him for a cigarette, hoping for stress relief. Surprisingly, he suggested I try searching online for proposal ideas.

I Shouldn't Have Done This

Google Baba, as they call it, was my savior in this quest for creativity. Yet, most of the suggestions felt mundane and didn't capture the essence of what I wanted to convey to Seerat.

Frustrated and worn out, I decided to call it a night and try again tomorrow. However, my mind was still racing with ideas, refusing to shut down.

In a moment of inspiration, I threw a pillow at Ankit to share my Eureka moment. I had found it!

Ankit looked bewildered, thinking I found something scandalous online again. But this time, it was about impressing Seerat.

Excitedly, I revealed my idea to him, and my relief was that he approved. Yet, he also warned me about the risks involved, especially if I got caught.

I felt a mixture of courage and uncertainty. After all, this was the love of my life. I couldn't let fear hold me back. But one obstacle remained: how would I enter her apartment without raising suspicion?

Ankit reached into his bag and pulled out a bunch of keys. He tossed them to me, claiming they were magical keys that opened any door. In truth, they were from Kritika, but that was a story for another day.

Empowered by the keys, I was ready to take the leap. My heart raced with anticipation, knowing that this could change everything.

Leaving Ankit in the dark, his sleepy face fading from view, I felt a surge of determination. Christmas Eve would be the day I would finally reveal my feelings to Seerat.

* * * * *

It was finally Christmas Eve, the night I had been planning for. I felt ready for the adventure that lay ahead, even though breaking the rules had been a part of my life. This time, however, the stakes were higher, and danger lurked.

I Shouldn't Have Done This

As the evening progressed, I couldn't even eat supper, and my nerves were too unsettled. Ankit, noticing my anxiety, asked, "All set?"

I gave him a brief nod, glancing at my watch. "I should be going now."

"It's freezing outside. Take my car," he offered, tossing me the keys.

"Thanks, but I'd rather take my bike. It'll be easier to escape if anything goes wrong."

Ankit wished me luck, and I left. The cold wind was harsher than expected, and the dense fog obstructed my view as I rode.

My determination wavered at times during the journey. Was I indeed prepared for this risky endeavor? Yet, turning back now after coming so far wasn't an option. So, I pressed on, driving cautiously due to the poor visibility.

After about 30 minutes, I reached Seerat's society. As I approached the gate, the watchman, dressed in a monkey cap and blue uniform, stopped me. Panic set in; I hadn't thought this through. When Seerat and I had come here before, there was no one to stop us, and perhaps the rain had kept him from his duty this time.

Trying to remain calm, I replied, "I came to meet my aunt."

"Tell me her name, flat number, and phone number," the watchman demanded.

"I don't know her flat number exactly, but she lives in that building," I said, pointing to a building in front of us.

He briefly considered the building before suggesting, "Call her and ask for details."

I pretended to make a call but hung up after a few seconds. "My aunt's not picking up."

"Sorry, Saab, but I can't let you in without proper details," the watchman said with sympathy. "I wish I could help."

Feeling defeated, I took out a five-hundred-rupee bill and offered it to him. "Please consider my situation. I came a long way to meet my aunt, and it was freezing outside. Where would I go at this time?"

He refused the money, saying, "Rules are rules, sir. A few weeks ago, I allowed someone in like this, and my agency threatened to fire me. I can't take the risk."

With no other choice, I left, saddened by the turn of events. As I approached the society's boundary, the darkness and emptiness of the road added to my desolation.

Parking my bike a few yards away, I mustered my courage and climbed over the boundary wall with an adrenaline-fueled rush. Inside the society, halogen lamps illuminated the area, but the cold kept everyone indoors.

I could see Seerat's building just 200 yards away. My heart raced in the deafening silence of midnight. Standing outside her apartment, I felt a wave of uncertainty wash over me. Should I proceed or abandon the plan?

I took Ankit's keys and attempted to unlock the door, but my hands trembled uncontrollably. Fear of being caught and facing severe consequences overwhelmed me.

Struggling to steady my hands, I tried again, and finally, the key slipped into the lock, allowing me to sneak inside just in time.

It was my third time here – the first with Kritika, the second with Seerat, and now, as if I were a thief or a petty criminal.

Stepping into the dark room, I felt relief as the temperature offered respite from the cold. I pressed my shivering hands to my face, trying to regain sensation.

Amidst the darkness, I heard the murmur of two female voices. One was Krittika, but the other remained unknown. It wasn't Seerat, though. Curiosity got the better of me, and I attempted to open her bedroom door, only to find it locked.

I pondered my next move. Knocking on the door risked exposure, potential police involvement, and the spread of rumors in college. The safer choice was to call Seerat and ask her to open the gate – it would ruin my surprise, but it seemed necessary.

As I reached for my phone, I caught sight of the balcony adjoining Seerat's room. An idea took root, and I decided to pursue it. Opening the balcony door, a chilling gust of wind sent shivers down my spine. The night grew even colder and darker.

Glancing around the compound, I assured myself that no one in their right mind would venture out at this hour. But was I in the right mind to do this myself? Doubt gnawed at me, questioning my actions.

Waving off the thought, I skillfully leaped to another balcony, ensuring that my actions remained hidden in the darkness of the night. Not that there was anyone else around to witness my daring escapade.

Once I confirmed the coast was clear, I discreetly peered into her room through the window. The soft glow of her cabin's light revealed her still awake, engrossed in a novel. I never knew she had a fondness for reading, too. Retrieving my cell phone, I dialed her number.

Upon seeing my name on the screen, she affectionately kissed it, and at that moment, the risk seemed entirely worth it. A wild idea to break the window and kiss her crossed my mind, but I managed to restrain my emotions.

Things unfolded even more beautifully than I had imagined in my wildest dreams. "Hi," she tried to sound sleepy, and I must admit, she did a convincing job. If I hadn't been watching her, I would have never guessed she wasn't asleep and had just kissed her me – technically not me but her phone, I think that's close enough!

"Hi, I didn't know you were asleep. Sorry if I disturbed you. I'll call you tomorrow," I played along with her charade.

"No, it's fine," she replied, emerging from her quilt. As always, her beauty mesmerized me. She looked stunning and clad in red polka-dotted pajamas and a matching T-shirt. "Is everything all right?"

"No, I wanted to tell you something; that's why I called you," I used a serious tone to make it sound genuine.

"Hey, what is it? Tell me," a smile on her face a moment ago vanished. She stopped wandering around and took a seat on her study chair.

"I am going to freeze to death out here if you don't open your balcony door right now," I couldn't hold back any longer and burst into laughter.

She looked out the window and shouted, "Oh my God," her voice echoing, possibly waking the entire neighborhood. I was sure half the society was aware of my presence, and they might beat me black and blue.

"Hey, relax! You just blew out my eardrums," I whispered into the cell phone, "Now open the window."

She tossed her phone on the bed and swiftly opened the door. Her expression was a mix of surprise and amazement.

"Can I come in now?" I clapped my hands to bring her back from her stupor.

"Yes, definitely," she closed the door behind me but was still visibly dazed. I questioned my impulsive decision momentarily, but there was no turning back now.

"If you're unhappy to see me here, I can return."

"It's nothing like that. I'm just slightly surprised, shocked, and scared," Seerat emphasized each word.

"So, that means you're not sad?"

"No, of course not."

"So, that means you're happy," I smirked.

She blushed when she realized I had caught her. "I never said that."

"So?" She decided to change the topic.

"So what?" I was enjoying her in this situation so much and didn't want to let her go so easily.

"So what brings you here?" She completed her sentence.

"I am here to celebrate someone's birthday."

"Who told you it's my birthday? I was born in November. I am a Sagittarius," she said proudly.

"Who told you that I am here to celebrate your birthday?"

"Is it your birthday?" she said excitedly, "But you said you were born in August."

"I am here to celebrate Christ's birthday. Merry Christmas," I exclaimed, a smile spreading across my face.

Seerat chuckled, "So, you're here to celebrate Christmas?"

"Not exactly. I'm here to meet you, Senorita," I said, moving closer and holding her hands playfully. She laughed and gently pushed me away.

Suddenly, we heard voices from outside—Krittika and someone else in her room. It was midnight, and they were exchanging merry Christmas wishes.

Turning my attention back to Seerat, I wished her a merry Christmas but resisted the urge to hug her at that moment. "I have a gift for you."

"Really? What is it?" she asked excitedly, seemingly forgetting that we were alone in her room late at night, with her friend standing just outside the door, probably able to hear our conversation.

"Close your eyes," I instructed, half-expecting her not to comply, but she did so without hesitation.

I removed a jar from my bag and instructed her to open her eyes.

"OMG!!" she exclaimed, but this time in a hushed tone. She took the jar from me and hugged me gratefully.

"Oh God, you're amazing! How did you know I love butterflies?" she thanked me repeatedly. It was a butterfly in the jar, and she

I Shouldn't Have Done This

seemed to love it. However, her beauty surpassed even the most beautiful creatures.

I was glad she liked her gift and quickly forgot about the challenges I faced to get that butterfly. "Do you like it?"

"Of course I do! It's the best gift anyone has ever given me."

"I don't think so."

"Why? Don't you trust me? I'm not just saying this because you gave it to me," she said, placing the jar on the table.

"No, I genuinely believe that," I said, reaching for my bag. "Because I have one more gift for you."

"Really? What is it?"

"But first, you have to do something."

"What?"

"Switch off the lights," I requested.

"Why?" she hesitated.

"Just do it for me, please."

Reluctantly, she switched off the lights.

"Now, close your eyes," I insisted.

"I won't close my eyes. It's all dark here, and I can't see anything anyway," she protested.

"Trust me on this."

With her eyes closed, I took another jar out of my bag.

"Can I open my eyes now?"

"Yes, you can," I replied.

When she opened her eyes, she didn't shout like the last time. Instead, she only managed to say, "This is beautiful."

I had filled the jar with fireflies that glowed in the dark, creating a magical ambiance. The faint light from the fireflies illuminated Seerat's face, making her look like a goddess bathed in pure white radiance.

"What do you think?" I asked, observing her closely.

She seemed to struggle for words and choked with emotion. After a moment, she managed to whisper, "It's beautiful," her eyes glistening with tears.

As I moved to switch on the light, she held my hand, signaling me to stop. I respected her wish because she wanted to cherish the moment without disrupting the ambiance.

Drawing closer, I gently held her face in my hands, and she leaned on my shoulder, finding comfort in my presence.

For a while, silence enveloped us, and then she wiped away her tears, standing up. "Thank you so much," she managed to say, offering a warm smile.

The faint traces of tears on the sides of her eyes twinkled in the dim light.

Seerat switched on the lights and pretended as if everything was normal.

"I have one more gift for you."

"How many gifts did you bring? What's in it this time? Dragonflies? Sparrows? Fish?" she playfully guessed.

I retrieved the final gift from my bag, wrapped in red paper. As Seerat unwrapped it, she found a knee-length black dress inside.

"Finally, something normal," she chuckled. "All the gifts you've given me today were thoughtful, and you made my Christmas special."

"Wear it," I simply said.

"You want me to wear it?"

"Yes, that's why I brought it."

"Stupid! I mean, do you want me to wear it right now?"

"Yes! How would I know if it suits you or not? Besides, I wasn't sure about your size either," I teased her, causing her cheeks to turn red. "Now go and change!"

"Go where?"

"Go wherever you change," I said with a playful grin. "What now?"

"But I change here in my room," Seerat said as she sat down and placed the dress on the bed.

"Then change here, I won't mind," I replied.

"I am gonna kill you, Meet!"

"Relax, I was just joking. Go and change in the bathroom," I suggested.

"Kritika and her sister are outside watching TV; what would I say to them?"

"Fine! Then let it be," I said, disappointed as I wanted to see her in that dress.

She switched off the lights. "Face the wall and close your eyes," she said, sensing the sadness in my voice.

"Why?" I knew what she was planning, but I wanted to hear it from her.

"I will change here."

"You mean you will change in front of me?" I teased her.

"Turn around before I change the mood," she mockingly threatened but couldn't resist a smile. "Now turn around," she added.

I complied, feeling hypnotized. My face was towards the wall, and I couldn't see anything, but the thought of Seerat changing her clothes behind me tickled me!

"Have you changed already?" I asked eagerly, unable to wait to see her in that dress.

"Wait a minute," she answered. "Yes, now you can turn around."

As I turned around, my imagination of how she would look in that dress shattered. She was still wearing her red pajamas and top.

"What's this? Why didn't you change?" I was both sad and disappointed.

"Just like that," she laughed, perhaps amused by my expression.

Then she took out a gift from behind her back. I hadn't noticed that she was holding something.

"Merry Christmas!" she wished me, handing the gift to me. "This is for you; open it," she said, switching on the lights.

I Shouldn't Have Done This

I unwrapped the gift, which turned out to be a black suit. It looked amazing, and I thought it might be from some fancy brand. I checked for labels, but there were none.

"This is fantastic! Where did you buy this?" I asked with excitement.

"I made this!"

"You made it for me?"

"No! I made it for my ex-boyfriend, but now we aren't together, so I gave it to you," she joked, laughing at her humor.

To be in love with someone makes you feel good, but when that person loves you back, it makes you feel incredible!

"Try it on! I need to check if it fits you," she said, smirking and pretending to be serious. Now I understand why she initially agreed to change.

"Here? No way."

"Why?" She sipped on a glass of water. "If I can change here, why can't you?"

"But you never changed," I stated the fact.

"But I was ready to change!" she countered.

"Fine, first you change, then I will," I proposed.

"Nope, first you change," she rejected the idea outrightly.

"We will change together," I counter-proposed. "You turn your face to that side," I pointed to the wall where a picture of Seerat in her school uniform hung, "and I will face towards the window." That seemed like a legitimate idea to me.

She thought for a second and raised her brows. I swear I feel like kissing her when she does that. "But don't you dare to cheat; otherwise, I am gonna kill you," she said, switching off the lights and moving to the corner.

"I promise I won't cheat. On the count of three," I took my place. "1, 2, 3," we counted together and turned around.

I took off my jacket and started unbuttoning my shirt. I never imagined that the night would unfold like this. Part of me wanted to turn around and look at her, but I didn't want to break my promise. I glanced towards my left. Although she had switched off the lights, I could see her shadow in the dim light emanating from the fireflies.

She was taking off her top, sending shivers down my nerves. I felt guilty that I broke my promise, but a voice in my head convinced me that I was looking at her shadow and not her.

She put her top on the table and unhooked her bra. I could see her curvy body, lean waist, and taut stomach. I couldn't see the color of her clothes in the shadow, but I imagined it must be as bright as hers.

As she obliterated her clothes, I couldn't hold myself any longer. I turned around and said her name. She turned around and looked at me. I took off my shirt. Every nerve in my body was electrified in that split second before her touch. It was the anticipation of being together in a way that was more than words, in a way that was so wholly tangible. In the twilight and shadow-filled room, Seerat stood close enough for me to breathe in her scent. I wrapped my arms around her, and in one gentle pull, our skin touched. I felt her hand in my hair, lovingly watching it tumble as she released it. Then, her hand moved down my cheekbones to my lips.

I placed my lips onto hers, and she didn't resist this time. Her lips parted, and her tongue brushed against mine, leaving me quivering with excitement.

I lifted her right off her feet, carrying her towards the bed, letting her fall with a soft bounce on the mattress. We locked our eyes together for a moment, just enough for us to feel safe with each other. She blushed and covered her face with both her palms.

She was my drug. A touch of hers and the intoxication was instant, intense to the extent that nobody could imagine. I moved her palms away, but her eyes remained closed. I caressed her skin with my fingers, afraid a heavier touch would break the enchantment. I tucked her hair behind her ear.

I Shouldn't Have Done This

Her scent was driving me crazy, playing with my brain. I don't think it was working anymore; I was utterly instinctive.

I kissed her on the neck and moved down her bust to her waist. Her skin was smooth like the finest silk. Then I was all business, undoing her pajama and pulling it off, kissing from her toes upward, slowly, my hands on her legs, consistently just a little higher than the kisses. She let her back arch in anticipation of where my fingers would soon reach, and as I did so, the first moan escaped her lips.

Chapter 9

I gazed at my reflection in the mirror, still trying to process what had happened last night. As soon as I got home, I reached for a beer to celebrate my triumph. Ankit wasn't around, which I felt was for the best. I needed time to gather my thoughts before facing him.

The question of what I should say to Ankit about last night with Seerat weighed heavily on my mind. Should I be honest about it or simply lie? I knew there was no point in hiding things from my best friend; eventually, he would find out. But I couldn't predict how he would react to the whole situation with Seerat.

Ankit was already aware that something was happening between us, and it would be evident if things went well. The events had unfolded favorably for me, but I never expected it to happen so soon.

I retreated to my room, sinking into my bed. Determined not to overanalyze the situation, I resolved to let things unfold naturally. With that decision, I pushed aside any lingering thoughts of Ankit and allowed Seerat to occupy my mind entirely. Soon, my mind became consumed by thoughts of the events of that morning.

The sun's rays seeped into the dark room, waking me up. It took a moment to realize that I wasn't at home anymore. As I recalled the previous night's events, a smile curled on my lips. Seerat was not beside me; the room was still dim. Even though I had just woken up, I missed her and set out to find her.

As I stood up, I noticed I wasn't wearing anything. Panic surged through me as I searched for my clothes but couldn't find them. My

79

memories of the previous night were blurry, but I vividly remembered her touch—her skin as soft as silk and her scent that enraptured me.

I tried hard to think and remembered tossing my clothes onto the table by the wall. But they were gone. As I bent forward, embarrassed, I heard the door crack open behind me. It was Seerat, and she had caught me in an awkward situation. I quickly grabbed a sheet and wrapped it around my torso, feeling like a fool.

We locked eyes for a moment before she turned her face toward the wall, a mischievous smile on her lips. It was a strange feeling to stand there, exposed in front of her after last night's intimate encounter.

"I... I was looking for..." I struggled to find the right words.

She pointed towards the chair, understanding my predicament without me saying a word. "There," she said.

My clothes were neatly folded on the chair, along with my bag. Trying to escape the awkwardness, she offered to make some coffee. Unable to refuse her, especially knowing she made the best coffee, I agreed and began changing.

She turned toward the wall, and I left the sheet on the table and dressed quickly.

"Meet, I want to confess something," she said suddenly.

My heart pounded in my chest, fearing the worst. Was she about to tell me it was all a mistake and that we should move on? The thought of losing her sent shivers down my spine; even though we weren't officially in a relationship, our connection was beautiful. With my throat almost dry, I managed to ask, "What is it?"

A smirk danced on her lips as she said, "I can see you changing in the mirror." And with that confession, she left the room.

She was wicked, my wicked angel, and I couldn't help but smile despite my embarrassment. After getting dressed, I stepped out of her room. Kritika and the other girl weren't around, leaving the place empty for us. Memories of our last encounter in that room flashed through my mind, and I couldn't help but reminisce about our first kiss, drenched in the rain.

She brought two coffee mugs, and once again, I instinctively chose the one with her picture on it.

"Where is Kritika?" I asked, trying to find a way to break the ice.

"She's out shopping with her sister," came the reply.

Now I recognized the other voice I had heard last night. It belonged to her younger sister, Nikita. Although I had never met her in person, Kritika had mentioned her a few times.

"Didn't you go with them?" I blurted out, realizing it was a rather strange question. I felt like a complete fool, unsure of what to say.

"No, they went shopping for the Christmas party hosted by their neighbors."

"So, you're not attending the party with them?"

"Nope! First of all, I wasn't invited. Second, I don't know her neighbors. And third, I'd rather stay cozy in my bed. It's frigid outside." I couldn't believe she preferred staying home on Christmas night rather than partying outside because of the cold.

This is lame; I can't let this happen.

"Then maybe we should go out tonight, just the two of us," I suggested.

"I don't know if that's a good idea," she hesitated.

"Believe me, it's a great idea," I assured her as I left. "Be ready; I'll meet you at 8."

She accompanied me to the door to say goodbye. "Wear that black dress you never tried on for me." Her cheeks turned red, and her lips curved into a smile. She tried hard not to let it out but couldn't hide her excitement.

A knock on the door interrupted my thoughts. It was Ankit, carrying a shopping bag and wearing a big smile. That was odd; why was he smiling to himself?

It reminded me of an incident earlier in the day when I was smiling to myself, and the watchman of Seerat's society asked me why. He was the same watchman who didn't let me in last night. But

I Shouldn't Have Done This

my smile was because of Seerat. I loved her, and even the thought of her was enough to fill me with happiness.

Was Ankit also in love with someone? He had been acting strangely for the past few days, constantly chatting on his phone and often absent. Now, he was smiling to himself. It should have been a warning sign, but I was too preoccupied with thoughts of Seerat and our project.

However, if something bothered him, he would have told me by now. After all, we had been friends since our school days.

"Why are you smiling? And what's in the bag? And where were you the whole day?" I bombarded him with questions all at once.

"Chill, dude. I went shopping for some new clothes. You won't believe it—I got passes for the Christmas party at The Temptation." The Temptation was the best club, and it was nearly impossible to enter, especially on Christmas night.

"Where did you manage to get those?" I asked, excited by the prospect.

"A magician never reveals his secrets," he replied with a cheesy laugh.

"Well, then the magician will be going to the party alone," I mimicked his laugh.

"My dad gave me these; one of his juniors confiscated them from a couple making out in public." He took out a beer from the fridge. "Do you want this? It's the last one in the fridge."

"No, I'm good," I replied, torn between wanting to go to the party and keeping my promise to spend the evening with Seerat. "Anyway, I can't make it. I promised Seerat I'd be spending the evening with her.

"She can come too if she wants!" Ankit said, taking a sip of his beer. "Don't forget to stock up."

"Wait, she can come too? How many passes do you have?" I asked, amused by the possibility, given how difficult it was to obtain even one pass.

I Shouldn't Have Done This

"I didn't count. Maybe five or six."

"Oh, Lord! You're a lifesaver!" I exclaimed, giving him a grateful hug. "This night is going to be extra special for me."

"Could you ask Seerat if she can convince Kritika to come with us? You'll be occupied with Seerat, and I wouldn't want to be alone there. It'd be nice to have someone to talk to," Ankit requested.

"Sure, but are you just looking for someone to talk to?" I teased playfully. I dialed Seerat's number and explained everything to her. She spoke with Kritika, who was willing to come, but she couldn't leave her sister alone at home on Christmas night.

"That shouldn't be a problem; we'll figure something out," I assured before ending the call.

* * * * *

I casually admired her outfit; she looked stunning in the black dress I had given her. The dress fit her perfectly, accentuating her figure, especially her beautiful bust. Just the thought of touching her again made me smile.

Her fiery hair hung loose down her back, and her lip gloss gave her lips a pink, shiny appearance.

"You look beautiful tonight," I complimented her, surprising myself as I had never said those words to another girl. It felt right in this moment, though.

"Thank you," she replied softly, avoiding my gaze. "You... would you like something to eat?" she smoothly changed the subject, showcasing her wit.

"No, I'm fine," I replied, sitting on the couch. "Where's Kritika? Isn't she ready yet?"

"About Kritika, I'm sorry, but she isn't coming," Seerat said, with pity in her eyes as she glanced at Ankit, who looked at me angrily while I tried to comprehend what was happening.

We discussed everything earlier, and Seerat assured me everything was set. Nikita was supposed to go to her parents' house, and Kritika

I Shouldn't Have Done This

was joining us. I informed Ankit, and he took an hour to prepare, planning every detail of the night. Now, Seerat was saying that Kritika wasn't coming.

I didn't know what had gone wrong or when.

"Kritika had planned to leave Nikita at her parents' house, but unfortunately, someone from their distant relatives passed away, so she has to stay here with Kritika. She can't leave her alone on Christmas night," Seerat explained, looking puzzled.

Ankit quickly interjected, "Where are they now?"

"They just went to a nearby shop to get some cold drinks and chips for the night. They'll be here any moment," Seerat replied.

"What the...?" Ankit's frustration was evident. He had entry-pass for the best club and had meticulously planned the entire evening. Now, she would spend it eating chips and having cold drinks on her couch in pajamas.

"Do you guys need any coffee?" Seerat asked, tucking a strand of hair behind her ear.

"Yup," Ankit replied.

"No," I said almost simultaneously. Though technically, he said it before me, it was just a few microseconds, which didn't matter.

Ankit was clearly frustrated. "Dude, look at her; she's all dressed up. She isn't going to the kitchen to make coffee for you in that dress."

"No, it's fine, really. I didn't ask out of courtesy," she insisted as she rose from the couch to prepare coffee for both of us.

"No, it's fine, we'll grab something on the way," I replied, rising to leave as well. I glanced at Ankit, expecting him to take the hint—a cue he consistently failed to pick up.

"I'm not leaving until I talk to her," Ankit declared, taking out his phone to call her just as she arrived with a bag of chips. She seemed to have bought enough for the entire society, doubling as a distributor for the chip manufacturer.

I Shouldn't Have Done This

Behind her, another girl was carrying cold drinks in both hands, probably Nikita. I had imagined her as a young girl, around 8 or 10, but she was a teenager, possibly 17 or 18. She wore a borrowed t-shirt barely fitting her, and her pajamas seemed too big for her small frames.

"Seerat told us you aren't coming with us," Ankit confronted her, not bothering with pleasantries.

"Yes, she was right," she replied, placing the bags on the table. "I was supposed to drop her off at our parent's house, but then a distant relative passed away, and now she's staying with me."

"But you said you were joining us," he retorted, his tone laced with accusation. I exchanged a puzzled glance with him, wondering when she had mentioned this. "I mean, you mentioned it to Seerat," he clarified, though his explanation felt unnecessary given the tension in the air. It was an odd addition, one that seemed to deflate the drama of the moment.

"I don't have any other option. I can't leave Nikita alone, and I can't go clubbing all by myself on Christmas day," she explained, her voice trembling as she took a gulp of water. Was she crying?

"Why was everybody behaving so strangely that night? Or was it just me who was missing something? The truth was, at that time, I didn't know what was really going on.

Ankit let out a long sigh and slumped onto the couch, his hands buried in his hair. His reaction seemed extreme, hinting that there was more to his desperation. I could sense it; there was something beyond wanting Kritika to come out with us. Was he in love with her? Or did they both have feelings for each other?

But if they did have mutual feelings, why would she refuse to join us? Perhaps she wanted to come but didn't want to leave Nikita alone on Christmas night.

"Nikita can come with us," I suggested, but everyone except Ankit looked at me as if I had committed a crime. The spark was back in his eyes.

85

I Shouldn't Have Done This

He moved closer to Kritika, saying, "That is a nice idea. She can come with us."

"No, she can't. She's just seventeen," Kritika responded, sounding confused.

"That shouldn't be a problem," Ankit replied with a mischievous grin, glancing back at me. I knew exactly what he had in mind.

"As per the rules, you can't enter a club until you are eighteen," Kritika pointed out.

"Forget the rules; rules are meant to be broken. Now go get ready," I chimed in, taking a seat while the siblings went inside to prepare for what promised the best night of their lives.

Chapter 10

"We don't have the whole night. Get ready fast!" Ankit shouted, glancing at his watch impatiently. They seemed to be taking forever to prepare for the Christmas party, which wasn't such a big deal, according to me. We've attended parties before, and Ankit had never acted this way.

"Man, cut them some slack. Let them take their time," I said, giving Ankit a disapproving look, trying to remind him to be patient.

Seerat finally emerged from the room. "Ah, sorry they took so long. I know, but they are ready now. They'll be here in two minutes, and then we'll all be set to go." I wanted to emphasize to Ankit that making the girls feel guilty for taking their time wasn't fair.

"There's no need to apologize. It's just..." I tried to explain the situation to Seerat when the siblings finally appeared.

Kritika, as always, looked stunning in her black dress with no sleeves and a hint of cleavage. Her hair hung loosely, and she seemed a bit shy, avoiding direct eye contact.

"You're looking beautiful," Ankit complimented her, trying to adjust himself in his seat as if he was a bit uncomfortable.

"Thanks," she replied with a wry smile, but she didn't linger on the compliment. "I... I'll go get the keys." I wasn't sure, but it seemed like she also noticed Ankit's unease.

I had seen her in Western dresses, and she always wore them elegantly. But today, there was something different. The outfit was slightly more revealing, but instead of judging, I appreciated her confidence.

I Shouldn't Have Done This

She always looked charming; she was, in fact, the most attractive girl in our college. But today, she seemed incredibly captivating. Her allure was undeniable, and it was easy to see why Ankit was at a loss for words.

Seerat giggled, standing at the far end of the drawing room, observing the whole situation. "You also look fabulous, kiddo. Wait a minute; these earrings would look good with this dress." She handed her a pair from her bag.

Kiddo? In what universe do you call her kiddo? She was a perfect beauty. She wore a tight dress that ended well above her knees. Her hair was shorter than Kritika's, a little curly around the head. Seerat was standing right beside me, and she was no less than Kritika in any aspect.

But yes, she was still a kid.

"We better go now," Seerat said, and everyone followed her lead out the door.

* * * * *

The nightclub we entered surpassed all my expectations. It was a double-story building with a huge, muscular man adorned with ear piercings guarding the entrance. A velvet rope cordoned off the entrance, and a long line of people waited outside to get in.

Cutting the line, we showed our passes to the guard. To my surprise, Ankit had VIP passes. He confidently removed the velvet rope and led us inside.

"Can you show me your IDs, please?" asked a guy in the same attire, sporting a brilliant smile. Everyone looked at me, making it clear that they didn't have their IDs on hand. Without wasting any time, I asked them to hand over their IDs to me. Kritika handed hers to me with a blank expression, and I nodded in assurance. I wanted them to have faith in me.

Nikita gave me her ID, and I slipped it into my back pocket. I handed over the IDs to the guard, except Nikita's.

I Shouldn't Have Done This

"These are only four IDs, sir," he observed, checking the IDs and giving them back to me.

I discreetly slipped 2000 rupees into his hand while taking back the IDs. "Here is the fifth ID."

He glanced around and tucked the money into his back pocket. "You're good to go, sir."

"Smart guy," I said, tapping his shoulder as he opened the gate leading to the club's main area for us.

The inside of the building was spacious, with a massive dance floor in the middle and a mirrored bar spanning three of the walls. The ceiling extended two stories above, with several balconies lining the walls reached by private staircases.

The guy at the door informed me that our table was on the VIP balcony in room number five. We asked a bartender for directions. It seemed like the people from whom Ankit had confiscated these passes were big shots.

After a quick stop at the bar, where Seerat and Kritika ordered cocktails—a Long Island Iced Tea and a Screwdriver—I ordered Rum for Ankit and me.

"What would you like to have?" I asked Nikita. She looked amazed, her eyes wide open as she gazed at the bar.

"No drinks for her," Kritika intervened before Nikita could answer. "Just order some cola or juice for her."

Nikita's amazement turned into frustration, and her smile disappeared. "I'm fine, I don't need anything."

Sensing her frustration, I didn't want to spoil the night, so I decided to handle the situation.

"It's not fair, Kritika. Let the kid enjoy the party. There's no harm in one beer." Before she could say anything, I ordered one beer for Nikita.

"Okay, but just one beer," Kritika said with a stern look on her face.

Nikita looked at me and thanked me, and the smile returned to her face. We took our drinks and went to our table. Though the club was thumping with loud music, it was relatively quiet inside this room.

We all settled down and enjoyed our drinks. The music was loud enough to enjoy yet soft enough to hold a conversation.

"That's my favorite song! Come on, let's dance!" Nikita almost screamed when she heard an English song playing. She stood up, beer mug in hand, and urged us to join her before the song ended.

"I better go with her," Kritika said, following Nikita's lead, and Seerat and Ankit joined in as well.

"Aren't you coming?" Seerat asked when she noticed I was still sitting.

"Maybe after two more Morgans," I replied, lifting my drink and taking a sip.

Eventually, Seerat joined the dance floor, pushing her way through the crowd. I stood at the balcony's edge for the next few minutes, sipping on a few more Morgans. I kept the door closed to shield myself from the grating music. Though I declined the invitation to dance, I couldn't take my eyes off Seerat. Her moves were sexy and flawless, captivating everyone around her.

As I watched, I noticed a guy approaching Seerat. They shook hands, and then he hugged her. Jealousy reared its ugly head inside me. She was my girl, and no one else should be dancing with her when I was present.

I reached out for her and tapped her shoulder. She introduced me to the guy as "Meet, my..." but hesitated before completing the sentence with "friend."

Those words hit me like a storm. I am just another friend to her when she meant the world to me. I felt sad and disappointed. I left the dance floor and headed to the bar, ordering another round of Rum.

I Shouldn't Have Done This

I felt like telling her how I felt, but I didn't know how to express it. It was the first time in my life I felt so clueless. I had fallen hopelessly in love with her, and I didn't even know if she felt the same way. I hadn't even asked her to be my girlfriend, and she hadn't considered me her boyfriend.

Seerat came near me, rubbing her hands on my shoulder. "Hey, honey, what's been bothering you? Are you sure you're all right?"

"I don't know," I said in a gravelly voice, my heart breaking inside me. I was hurt and conflicted, and I couldn't find the right words to express myself.

"It doesn't look like everything is fine," Seerat said, ordering something for herself from the bar. "Why did you come here like this?"

"I don't know, and you know what, maybe I don't even want to know," I repeated, feeling lost in my emotions. "Yes, everything is fine," I lied, not wanting to burden Seerat with my feelings.

"But it certainly doesn't look like it," she replied, looking at me intently. "Why don't you tell me what's really bothering you?"

I sighed, feeling a mix of frustration and relief. "I don't know," I said, my voice wavering. "I just don't know."

The nightclub surroundings, with its scattering lights and loud thumping music, failed to amuse me anymore. The suffocating atmosphere made me yearn for fresh air, but I didn't want to spoil the night for the others. I suppressed the idea of leaving and decided to head to the smoking area near the bar for some respite. Ignoring Seerat, I walked away.

Stepping out onto the open porch, I finally found a place to breathe. I took out a cigarette from my pocket and lit it, finding solace in the quietude. The area was sparsely populated, with only a couple standing in the far corner near the fire exit. The girl, dressed in a tight white t-shirt and blue denim, leaned against the wall with her left leg for support. The guy leaned over her with a cigarette in his right hand and his left hand on the wall. They were immersed

I Shouldn't Have Done This

in conversation, sharing laughter and tender kisses without any hesitation, showcasing their love for all to see.

Observing the couple, I couldn't help but feel a pang of jealousy. They seemed genuinely in love, unafraid to express it in public. My mind drifted to Seerat, and I couldn't deny the frustration I felt about not being on the same level of affection with her. I decided to move to the other corner to give the couple some privacy.

As I turned, I saw a dimly lit lane near the smoking area, seemingly used as a service exit. My eyes fell upon another couple engaged in a much more intimate display of affection. It made me feel uncomfortable, and I quickly turned away. The guy noticed me, and embarrassment washed over me. I recognized him; it was Kartik, and he was with Nikita. She seemed to be in an intoxicated state and was not fully aware of her surroundings. Anger surged through me.

Without thinking, I walked toward Kartik and swung my right fist, connecting it solidly with his jaw. In a flash, I leaped onto Kartik, straddling him at his stomach and wrapping my hands around his throat. I bore all my weight down, tightening my grasp as Kartik's eyes widened in fear. He desperately dug his fingers into my arms, trying to relieve the pressure, but I wasn't in the mood to spare that bastard. I couldn't pinpoint the exact reason for my anger. Was it because of his behavior with Seerat or because he took advantage of Nikita? All I knew was that I had to teach him a lesson.

Amidst the chaos, I heard a girl crying out for help, but only a few brave souls dared to step forward. Someone called for the bouncers, and people began to gather around us. Realizing I didn't have much time to make my point, I decided to tighten my grip.

As I continued to stare at Kartik, his face turning red, Seerat's voice reached my ears. She begged me to stop, her eyes filled with tears. Still, I remained unyielding, ready to make him pay for his actions.

However, Seerat came in front of me, her tearful eyes pleading with me to release Kartik. My anger was overwhelming, but her presence managed to break through the rage. I released his neck, and Kartik coughed and sputtered, massaging his throat.

I leaned in closer and snarled, "If you touch her again, I will kill you. I swear to God, I won't think twice."

Two bouncers in black t-shirts approached us, and I recognized one of them as the guy who had let us inside earlier. They held my hands, trying to calm the situation. I pointed towards Kartik, who was still struggling to stand up, and said, "There's no need to hold me. I'm leaving. If you want to throw someone out, throw this guy. He was trying to take advantage of this girl."

Nikita stood with Kritika and Seerat, still not fully in her senses. She mumbled, "Don't tell this to Father, please."

"Let's leave," I said, shrugging my shoulders. The bouncers released me, understanding the gravity of the situation.

"Not so fast," one of the bouncers said, "This might lead to a police case; you have to give us some details before you leave."

"You guys go; I will come once this is all sorted out," I told Ankit, gesturing for everyone to leave. The night was ruined, and I didn't want them waiting here any longer. Especially Nikita, who could barely stand.

Ankit nodded, understanding my concern. He handed me the car keys and said, "We'll take a cab; I don't think I can drive."

"I will stay with him," Seerat said, standing by my side as the others left.

As the rest of the group departed, I stayed behind with Seerat and the bouncers, ready to face the consequences of my actions. The gravity of the situation began to sink in, and I hoped I hadn't crossed a line I couldn't come back from.

As we left the club, the night was far from what we had hoped for. Emotions were running high, and the sense of confusion and uncertainty gnawed at me. Seerat's presence by my side offered some comfort, but the questions about our relationship remained unanswered.

Chapter 11

"I will drop you back at your place," I said to Seerat, giving her an apologetic smile as I took a turn that led us onto the highway. She hesitantly returned the smile.

At the club, we didn't spend much time. We were sitting in the main office when a police officer arrived. I narrated the entire incident to him, and instead of filing an FIR against me, he warned Kartik and advised us to resolve the matter amicably.

Despite my explanation, Seerat was still upset with me. Perhaps she believed I acted out because she was dancing with the curly-haired guy.

Though it was the last week of the year and the peak of winter in Delhi, it wasn't too cold outside. The roads were clear, and there wasn't much fog, unlike most days with limited visibility. The traffic was also lighter than usual, with only a few trucks leaving Delhi in a disciplined queue, resembling children returning to class after the morning assembly. This gave us a wide five-lane road to drive on.

I glanced at Seerat; she was looking outside the window, lost in her thoughts. Her silence drove me crazy, and I couldn't bear it. "Hey, listen, I am sorry for everything that happened back at the club," I said, pressing the accelerator harder.

"Sorry for what?" She turned her face towards me. "Instead, I should thank you for saving Nikita from that bastard. If you weren't there, he might have raped her."

Her response perplexed me. "So you are not angry at me?" I questioned. It seemed that understanding a woman's emotions was a challenging task.

"No, absolutely not. In fact, if you weren't there and something had happened to Nikita, I wouldn't have been able to forgive myself. How would I have faced Kritika?" she revealed her true feelings.

"It's not your fault. That guy was a total jerk, and you can't blame yourself for what he did," I tried to console her, but her tears kept flowing.

"It was my fault; I had introduced him to Nikita," she confessed, revealing something I didn't know. She continued through her sobs, "When I was dancing with Kartik, and after some time, you came. I thought you weren't happy to see me with him, so I introduced him to Nikita and came looking for you. I didn't know he'd have such heinous intentions."

"Don't cry; there was no way you could have known. You meant well for everyone; don't blame yourself for his mistakes," I reassured her, trying to offer some comfort.

"It was a perfect day; everything was so perfect, and it ended this way," she said, her voice filled with gloom. Now, I understood that her emotions weren't directed at me, and I was determined to lift her spirits.

"Who says the day has ended?" I looked at her with a smile and took a turn, signaling that the night was not over yet.

* * * * *

"I haven't been here before," she said, rubbing her palms together to keep herself warm. We were walking beside a lake, trying to reach the end. It was around 2 a.m., and there was no one around. The grass was wet with dew.

"Here, take my jacket," I offered, helping her put it on. She said nothing, just smiled – a smile I would die for. There was something special in her eyes, something I hadn't seen before.

I Shouldn't Have Done This

"Would you like to sit?" I asked when we reached the end of the lake. Once again, she didn't say anything but nodded in agreement. Why was she so quiet?

We sat on the boundary wall under a tree near the lakeside and looked at the moon. It wasn't a full moon or crescent, but it looked marvelous.

"So you said the day was perfect; what did you mean by that?" I probed, hoping for some compliments. I wanted to know her thoughts about our time together last night and the gifts I gave her.

"Yes, it was," she replied, shifting her gaze from the moon to me. "The club, music, dancing, you, me, Ankit, Kritika, and Nikita – everyone was so happy and enjoying the night." She paused for a moment, giving nothing away. "I don't even remember the last time I was so happy and excited about Christmas. Today, everything felt special – something I haven't felt in a long time," she sighed.

Tears rolled down her cheeks, and she continued, "I was just a little kid when my mother left me, but I still remember how we used to celebrate every festival." The memories of her mother brought a smile to her face. "Not just festivals, we celebrated everything – my first day at school, when my father bought a new car, when my mom got me a puppy. She used to make cute little dresses for me, dress me up in them, and paint me."

I interjected, "What do you mean by 'paint you'?"

"She liked to paint; she made like a thousand paintings of me and hung them all around the house. I still remember watching her paint, wearing her long blue shirt and holding a brush in her hand, focused on her canvas. She moved her painting brush like a magician with his wand. And her paintings were no less than magic. She used to tell me to sit still. I still remember how she smelled. I can still smell her and hear her voice. But she doesn't talk back to me anymore." Her eyes became teary, and so was mine, but I swiftly wiped away the tears.

I Shouldn't Have Done This

My heart went to her – a poor little girl who had seen so much at a young age. I noticed her trying to hold back her tears, but they still fell, and she wiped them when she thought I wasn't looking.

"I wanted to be a painter like her. She meant the world to me, and then she died, leaving me and my father alone. My father was a true gentleman – the kind of man I hadn't seen in my entire life. He did everything he could to make me smile. When I was eleven, we used to go on road trips, just him and me, and sometimes my aunt and her daughter would join us. But mostly, it was just the two of us. I didn't like going with my cousin; she always ruined everything," she smiled as she reminisced.

She wiped away another tear as I turned my head to give her some privacy. "During those trips, sometimes he had to drive all night, and sometimes the roads were so deserted that there was no one else. It would be completely dark outside, and I was scared of the dark, as any little girl would be," she paused, taking a deep breath. "But deep down, I felt safe, knowing that the guy behind the wheel was my dad. He was my superhero, who could drive all night without feeling tired and see far away, even in the darkness. Just when I started feeling that everything would be fine, he passed away, too. My dad was my hero, my teacher, and my best friend. He always came through for me, and then he died, leaving me all alone. No one to look after me. Tell me, Meet, how is this fair? My parents were the best human beings I can imagine, and they both died way too young. How is this fair? I was stranded and had to live with my aunt. Yes, she was good to me, but can't take my parents' place. Tell me, how is this fair to me, to my mother or even to my father? God has always been unfair to me; he is selfish and can't see me happy."

I didn't know what to say to her. I held her hands, and before she could wipe her tears, I gently brushed them away from her cheek. My thumb caressed her face, and she closed her eyes, leaning in. It was a perfect moment; everything felt calm and silent, and the only sounds were the rushing wind and the rustling leaves. I closed my

I Shouldn't Have Done This

eyes and leaned in for a kiss. I was elated to be with a girl many can only dream of being with. Just before our lips met, she pulled back.

"I think we should go; it's quite cold out here." She gathered her belongings and stood up. "By the way, thanks."

I was disappointed; I had wanted that moment to end differently, but I put on a smile and asked, "Thanks? Thanks for what?"

"Thanks for saving Nikita from that bastard, thanks for making Christmas so special for me, thanks for all those lovely gifts, and thanks for not letting Christmas end on a bad note. I owe you; I owe you big time. Tell me, what can I do for you?"

"There's one thing I want. Can you give it to me?"

"Yes, I guess. What do you want?" she sounded slightly confused but still willing to entertain my request.

"I want what every guy in this world wants at this hour of the night."

She arched her brows, waiting for me to finish my sentence, and when I didn't, she asked, "What do you mean?"

"I need something to eat. I'm damn hungry."

"So am I..." We both chuckled.

* * * * *

"Where are we going?" She asked as I turned onto the Ring road from the main highway.

"It's not a fancy place, but they serve great food," I assured her. "Don't worry; it's not too far from here. Only 20 km down the road, and we'll be there."

City roads were no different from the highways at night. It was mostly empty, and we hardly spotted any vehicles, especially in the winter. It didn't take much time to reach our destination. The flyovers and main roads, typically bustling with people during the day, were quiet and deserted at this hour.

"It hardly took any time to reach the destination. We crossed one flyover after another and arrived at Naraina. Instead of taking the flyover, we opted for the main road. As we approached a crossroad, the signal turned red. Glancing around, I noticed no other vehicle in sight, so I impulsively decided to jump the signal," I explained.

"Hey, you jumped the signal," Seerat exclaimed, playfully fisting my left arm.

"Nobody was there. For whom was I supposed to wait?" I responded, trying to maintain a mischievous tone.

She playfully scolded me, "There are rules, and you should follow them."

"Rules are meant to be broken," I snorted, adding a hint of defiance.

After a minute, I decided to take a U-turn and brought the car to a stop. The area, usually bustling with activity during the day, now wore a deserted and slightly eerie appearance due to the late hour.

"We have arrived," I declared, opening the car door to step outside.

"We have? There isn't a single shop around here," Seerat remarked, perplexing.

"Is it?" I walked to a nearby shop and knocked on the shutter. A young man, probably in his twenties, lifted the shutter and stepped out.

"What would you like to have, sir?" he asked politely.

Seerat appeared both amazed and slightly wary, perhaps thinking that I might be getting involved in something illegal.

I gestured to the guy, signaling him to approach the car. He walked over, and after a hesitant moment, Seerat rolled down the window.

"What would you like to have?" the guy inquired, displaying the menu.

As he read out the variety of paranthas available, Seerat's eyes widened, and we couldn't help but laugh, finding the situation amusing.

I Shouldn't Have Done This

"I don't know. Go ahead and order," Seerat said, encouraging me to decide for her.

I ordered my favorite mutton parantha, and in just five minutes, the guy returned with two plates of delicious paranthas. The aroma of the butter melting over the hot paranthas was irresistible, and I couldn't wait to dig in.

"It's delicious," Seerat said, her mouth still full as she tried not to burn herself on the hot paranthas. But the temptation was too great, and she couldn't resist taking another bite.

"I wonder how you've never come here before," I said, genuinely surprised.

"Yes, even I wonder, considering I've spent countless nights during my teenage years wandering the streets of Delhi and exploring all sorts of places. I must have ended up here at 3 in the morning on multiple occasions for these delectable mutton paranthas," Seerat replied with a smirk.

"You are a mean tease," I playfully chided her, revving the engines and accelerating the car.

"Yes, indeed I am," she humorously bowed down, pretending to accept the "honor." "But I must say, you're also quite the badass."

As I glanced at her, a perplexed expression appeared on my face. "I am a little offended by that," I admitted.

"Is it?" She switched on the stereo, and a radio host's nonsensical chatter filled the airwaves. Despite the noise, I found myself captivated by her voice. "Well, it was a compliment. You are bad with compliments. You should learn to recognize them and, most importantly, to honor them. You have a terrible problem, and do you know the worst part? You don't even know it," she teased, tilting her head with feigned sympathy.

Her chatter and radiant happiness filled the car as we made our way back home. It seemed like no time had passed when we arrived. I felt a pang of disappointment, knowing that this beautiful night had ended and we had to part ways.

Stopping the car in front of her building, I got out to open the door for her. "So here we are," I said, running my hand through my hair.

"Yes, we are," she replied with a half-hearted smile, avoiding direct eye contact. "I guess it's time to go. Thanks a lot; it was a wonderful evening." She bid her farewell and left without any physical affection, leaving me feeling the emptiness of an unfulfilled dream.

In my mind, I had envisioned that by the end of the day, we would be together, sharing intimate moments as a couple. However, that dream seemed to crumble before my eyes.

Determined not to let this opportunity slip away, I couldn't bear to drive home with such regret. Even though a few things didn't go as planned, the night unfolded beautifully.

"I can't go back like this," I murmured, unsure if the words were meant for myself or the voice in my head. I quickly decided to go back and share my true feelings with her.

As I approached her doorstep, I pondered what to say. Maybe I could ask for a glass of water or a cup of coffee, cherishing the moments when she would make it for me. Or better yet, I could mention that I needed my jacket back, as my driving license was in its pocket, and I couldn't drive home without it. Those words echoed in my mind, giving me the courage to knock on her door again.

"I went up the stairs and stood in front of her door. I decided to go with the 'I need my jacket back; my license is in the pocket' thing. But what if she returned my jacket and didn't even ask me to enter?

My heart was beating so fast, like a drum at a carnival. I could hear its rhythmic thumping. I thought I might have a stroke; I felt powerless, and my legs turned weak, but I managed to knock on the door.

I Shouldn't Have Done This

All the confusion in my head cleared itself when she opened the door. I placed my lips onto hers and held her in my arms, hugging and caressing her body.

She had changed her dress into night clothes, yet she looked amazing as always. I wished that moment would never end. We realized it wasn't an appropriate place, but we couldn't control our emotions and let go of each other from the embrace.

I closed the door behind me and headed to her room, still holding and kissing her, careful not to bang on anything or make any noise.

When we entered her room, we didn't care anymore. We didn't bother closing the door or switching off the lights, as there was no time for this.

We got straight into bed and undressed each other, exploring each other's bodies, finding the door to salvation, fondling like there was never enough of her for me. Funny enough, I wouldn't be here now if I had made a different decision. If I had driven back to my home, my fate would've been different because, in any other universe, I would never be truly complete if I existed without you.

I grabbed her waist, pulling her up close against my chest. My hands gently glided through her hair as I looked at her in a way I had never done before. Her eyes were like candles in the night; their light shone like a spark of passion and desire. A small but teasing smile crept upon her face, and goosebumps lined her skin, the kind one gets when nothing else matters except right now.

We kissed each other as if it were the end as if we would never meet again. And indeed, it was.

After we finished, I told her how I felt about her, how she had made me complete, and how I wanted to spend the rest of my life with her by my side.

"No," was the word that she said.

Before I could ask her anything, she continued, "Meet, you are a great guy, but there is something that I want to tell you. I can't be with you anymore, and this may seem strange, but you can't ask me why."

The moment her words stopped was the moment my heart broke. And the biggest irony was I didn't even have the right to ask her why. I felt that I had been executed without a trial. Because I swear to god, if I knew what made her say that, I would do anything to make it right. To make things work between us.

I got off the bed and put on my clothes. I looked into her eyes; they were distant and cold. Those were the same eyes in which, a few moments earlier, I saw love for myself.

"You are a mean girl indeed, and that is not a compliment," those words came out of my mouth unruly.

I walked to the door; my mind was not working; I never thought the night would end like this. She came with me to the door, and when I was out, I turned back for the last time and looked into her eyes.

My eyes begged for love, for her to take me back or at least tell me what I did wrong that she adjudged such a cruel punishment for that.

She understood what I wanted but didn't say a word. She just shook her head and closed the door on me once and forever.

It was strange how we studied that time is relative, how sometimes hours can feel like minutes, and sometimes a single second can last for a lifetime. For me, that one second would never end when she shook her head and closed the door for me. Everything else just ceased to exist for me. The second that haunted me every night for the rest of my life.

Chapter 12

I thought this might be the beginning of a new story, but it was the end of the most beautiful chapter of my life. A chapter where everything was perfect and consummate. But the day didn't end similarly for everyone. For me, it was mournful, but for Ankit, it was propitious.

When I unlocked the apartment door, Ankit and Kritika were sitting in the drawing room, and upon seeing me, they seemed a bit scandalized. Kritika stood up and said, "I will catch up with you guys later," giving Ankit a meaningful smile. I wasn't sure what was happening between them, but something had been brewing that I had overlooked before. Even Ankit had a broad smile from ear to ear. The signs were there, but I had been indifferent to them.

As Kritika left, Ankit hugged me, "Bro, I am in a relationship with this girl. I can't believe it. Do you know what the best part is? She proposed to me."

If it had been any other day, I would have celebrated this occasion in the best possible way, but that day, my heart was filled with sorrow. I didn't want to ruin it for Ankit, so I wore a smile to make him happy. Despite my immense pain, I was genuinely pleased for Ankit.

"How did it happen?" I sat beside him and patted his shoulder. "How is Nikita? Is she fine?"

"Yes, she is fine now, but Nikita was pretty scared when we exited the club. She wasn't saying anything. It seemed like she was in a deep shock. Even Kritika was frightened and clueless. Honestly, I was scared, too, not because of your fight with the little curly-haired rat but because of her condition. She was shivering, her hands were cold, and she wasn't even crying – just looking blankly. Her eyes were cold and distant.

Even on our way back home, she remained still as a statue. Kritika tried her best to console her, rubbing her hands and assuring her that everything was fine and she was safe. But Nikita didn't react as if she was in some other world.

When we reached her apartment, Kritika asked me to stay with her as she was scared.

"Wait, don't tell me what happened today; tell me from the beginning."

"Do you remember when Kritika first came to teach us computers, and you got your hands burnt?"

"Yes, of course I do." That pulled some of the most painful strings in my heart. If my hand hadn't burnt that day, Kritika wouldn't have asked Seerat to help me write my exams. I wouldn't have fallen in love with her and wouldn't have had to bear all this pain.

"Yes, after that, she didn't come to teach us again. You got Seerat to write your exams, and all this left me miserable, and I was sure I would fail in exams."

"I am sorry; I didn't realize you would fail because of me. Why didn't you call Kritika to teach you?"

"I didn't know her then; she was your friend." He defended.

"You could have asked me to call her."

"Your hand was burnt badly, and I could feel the pain. I didn't want to disturb you with such things. Anyway, that is trivial now. Don't disturb me; let me come to the point." He was enthusiastic about telling his story, so why wouldn't he be? After all, he got what he wanted.

"Okay, I won't disturb you now."

Ankit narrated everything.

"So, I went an hour earlier to college, hoping to catch someone from class and get some topics cleared so that I could at least pass my exams. I was standing with some guys when she came to me."

"How is Meet now? Yes, she came to ask about you. After some chit-chat, she asked me about my preparations. That is when I confessed about my horrific situation."

"I didn't know you were that bad with computers," Kritika laughed at me.

"Yeah, I am horrible with computers," I gave her a rattled smile. She asked me to come with her and taught me some crucial topics. That was the first time I spent some alone time with her. However, due to the immense fear of flunking, I concentrated only on the books and not on the little red mosquito bite on her quintessentially youthful pink cheeks. If it weren't for her, I would have flunked.

In the evening, I sent her a thank-you message. After an hour, she replied with a smile, and I thought that was the end. But indeed, it wasn't. God had other plans for me. After a few days, I got a call from her. I was confused at first. I never expected that Kritika would ever call me. I picked up the call. She sounded tense, and I got scared, "Hi, it's me, Kritika. How are you?"

"I am good, how are you? You sound tense; is everything alright?"

"Nope, I mean yes. I just want to ask you for a favor." I sensed she wasn't sure about asking me for this favor.

"And what is it?"

"Can you help me with the production technology exam? I don't know anyone from Mechanical who could help me except you and Meet. Meet's hand is burnt, and I don't want to disturb him." She justified her situation. I couldn't hold myself and burst into laughter. Karma is a bitch. Only a few days earlier, I asked for help, and she laughed at my condition. Yeah, but she helped, and now it was my turn to return the favor.

I asked her to come home, but she denied it, so we decided to meet in college. No exam was scheduled that day, so few people were around. Surprisingly, our college looked completely different, a lot scarier, when nobody was around.

After finishing our studies, we both felt hungry and decided to eat something. We looked around but couldn't find anything good to eat.

"Why don't we go to my house and eat something there? You have done so much for me; I could at least do this for you." She looked for something in her bag and took out a thing wrapped in a yellow wrapper. It was a chocolate; she opened it and took a bite. She got a little caramel on her scarlet lips. She had the most sensuous lips I had ever seen.

I was hypnotized and forgot that humans have to blink to look normal. She noticed me staring at her. With a strange look, she arched her brows and offered me chocolate, "Do you want some?"

That was enough embarrassment to pull me out of the trance. "No, I was thinking of something."

"What?" She took another bite of her chocolate. This time, I was careful enough not to get caught again.

"I haven't been to your house before." That doesn't sound like a big issue. There is always a first time. She gave me a strange look again.

I think I said, "I mean, I haven't been to any girl's house before." I confessed.

"What?" She looked at me and burst into laughter. "What do you mean you haven't been to a girl's house before? Don't you have a girlfriend?"

"No," I felt mortified. I bowed my head and started looking at the turf on the ground.

"You know what? You are adorable." She gave me a lovely smile and gently caught my cheeks, and it turned red. Not because she saw it but because I was blushing.

So it was my first time in a girl's room. It wasn't like a boy's den, clumsy and smelly. It was nicely decorated and smelled so good.

I Shouldn't Have Done This

"What would you like to eat?" She sat on a sofa beside me.

"Anything you would make." I was so tense. I felt like a student sitting in front of an examiner. Kritika sensed the unease and decided to take the matter into her own hands.

"I have heard that your father is a police officer. Is he strict? Is it because of him that you are such a sissy?" She said with a stern face. She pressed her lips hard, trying not to laugh.

I knew she got it, so I didn't say anything in my defense. As they say, be part of it if you can't resist. So I joined her.

I felt good just by talking to her. It was indeed fun. We talked about so many things; we talked about everything. In a short while, we were discussing our secrets with each other. I felt that we had known each other for a long time.

"I should go now," I said as I stood, preparing to leave.

"You are such a darling; I owe you one." She came over and hugged me. At that moment, I felt like I had everything. Life seemed perfect, and I had no complaints. "Tell me, what can I do for you?" she asked.

"There is something you can do for me, but let's wait until the results are out," I replied.

She looked astonished; she had never expected I would ask her for a favor. "What is it? Tell me now," she insisted.

"No, not now. Only after the results come," I said, waiting for the right moment.

* * * * *

Exams had finally concluded, and the moment of truth had arrived with the release of the results. Although my grades weren't exceptional, I felt relieved that I hadn't failed in any subject. However, my thoughts were consumed with concern for Kritika. Anxiously awaiting her call, I decided to drop her a message and be patient.

As time ticked by without a response, worry gnawed at me. It seemed like she might have faced failure in her exams. Wanting to

I Shouldn't Have Done This

be there for her, I held off calling, sensing it might not be the right time.

Resolving to meet her in person the next day, I spent the night contemplating how to comfort her. The following morning, I tried reaching her over the phone, but to no avail. Filled with determination, I headed to the computer department, knowing where she spent most of her time. However, when I arrived, I was met with an unexpected surprise; the result was displayed on the notice board. I checked it, and to my surprise, Kritika had emerged as the topper of the computer department.

I had never realized that she was so intelligent. In my mind, she had always seemed out of my league. The feeling of disappointment dissolved, replaced by a newfound ray of hope. As I turned around, I heard someone calling my name – Kritika herself, approaching me with her friends.

"Such a nice surprise; I never saw you here before," she said, coming over to hug me. All my worries seemed to vanish at that moment.

"I came here to meet you. By the way, congratulations," I replied, genuinely happy about her achievement.

"Thank you! Let's go to the canteen and talk," she suggested.

She expressed her gratitude over coffee and a cold drink, asking how to repay the favor.

"There is something you could do for me, but I'll wait till the right time," I replied, not wanting to burden her with my request.

"Don't be shy; you can share anything with me," she said, pinching my cheeks playfully.

Encouraged by her warmth, I confessed, "I could use fashion advice. Unlike yours, my style is outdated, always looking classy and stunning."

She laughed initially but readily agreed to help, and I felt grateful for her generosity. That day, I learned that sometimes all it takes is to ask for help, and people can surprise you with their kindness.

109

I Shouldn't Have Done This

"Day after tomorrow, pick me up from my apartment at 10 in the morning," she said with a smile.

With a newfound excitement, I looked forward to receiving her fashion advice and cherishing her friendship even more.

* * * * *

When the day arrived, I picked her up precisely on time, feeling excited for what was essentially a friendly outing. Yet, it was the closest experience to a date I had ever had.

"So, where are we going?" I asked, eager to begin the day's adventure.

"Just follow the directions, man, and keep driving," she replied, looking stunning as always.

After about an hour of driving, we arrived at a big mall. It was my first time there, and I couldn't help but ask, "Do you buy your clothes here?"

"Always," she replied proudly. "Where do you usually buy yours?"

"From Chhotu Garments," I said, to which we both laughed.

During our shopping spree, I tried on many clothes I had never considered wearing. Whenever I emerged from the trial room, she would shake her head and make funny faces in disapproval. By the end of it, I was both hungry and frustrated. Shopping with a fashion-savvy girl is no easy task.

"Let's go eat something now," I suggested, needing a break from trying on more clothes.

"Fine, we'll go eat, but at least let me try this dress," she said, holding up a grey dress and heading back to the trial room without waiting for my response.

Standing outside the trial room with her sling bag in hand, I couldn't help but recall how my father used to wait outside trial rooms for my mother. He was an Assistant Commissioner of Police in Delhi, yet he never minded doing it for her. I tried to act casual,

110

I Shouldn't Have Done This

but the girls standing nearby giggled, making me self-conscious. I moved away to avoid their prying eyes.

Suddenly, my phone rang, and it was Kritika. "Where are you?" she asked.

"I am near the trial room; where are you? I can't see you."

"How can you see me? I am still inside the trial room. Please come here; I'm stuck."

"Are you all right?"

"Don't ask anything, just come inside and keep your eyes closed."

Curious and concerned, I followed her instructions and entered the trial room with my eyes closed, promising not to open them.

"Don't open your eyes," she reminded me again, more as a threat than a reminder. "I got stuck in this dress, and now I can't escape it. So, help me take it off without tearing it."

Suppressing a laugh, I said, "You're getting fat."

"Stop laughing and help me."

"How can I help you without opening my eyes? I'm going to open them."

"No, don't open them. I'll guide you. Help me take my arm out of this dress." She gave me instructions, and I reached out to find her arm with my eyes still closed. It was like playing a blind man's bluff. My hand touched her bare skin, which felt incredibly soft and smooth. I tried to keep my composure, fighting the urge to open my eyes and admire her flawless body or, worse, kiss her.

"Don't move your hand; I feel ticklish," she said, returning me to the task. "Just bring your hand up here and help me take my arm out of this dress."

It wasn't as simple as it sounded. I had to guess where her arm was, trying to ignore the discomfort in certain parts of my body and fought the temptation to open my eyes.

I moved my hand a little up and touched something soft and unexpected. I immediately pulled back my hand. My discomfort peaked as I realized what I had inadvertently touched.

I Shouldn't Have Done This

Feeling guilty and scared that I had crossed a line, I stood there, blushing and unable to find the right words.

All Kritika could do was laugh and tease me, "Look at yourself! You look so scared. Are you going to pee your pants?"

Embarrassed, I couldn't respond, but I was relieved she seemed to find humor in the situation.

As the incident unfolded, it brought us closer, forging a deep friendship. Our days were filled with endless chats and shared secrets. We greatly admired you and Seerat, believing you were a perfect couple. She often talked about your adorableness, so she entrusted me with her apartment keys to pass them on to you.

Your courage to stand up for her sister against Kartik reinforced her conviction that Seerat couldn't find a better guy than you.

When we finally arrived at her home, Nikita remained visibly shaken and scared. Kritika tried her best to comfort her, but Nikita seemed unreachable.

Feeling a rush of protectiveness, I approached her bed and held her hands tightly. "I promise you, if anyone ever dares to touch you again, I will ensure that person never draws another breath, regardless of the consequences."

Her tear-filled eyes met mine, and she started crying uncontrollably. I embraced her, offering a sense of security she desperately needed. Slowly, the sobs subsided, and she fell asleep in my arms.

"It's time for me to leave. Take care of her, and if you need anything, don't hesitate to call," I said as I prepared to go.

"How will you get home?" she asked, concerned.

"I'll manage. I'll book a cab. Please, take care of yourself."

"I'll drop you off. It won't take much time."

"No, you should stay here with her."

"She's sleeping soundly. I'll be back before she wakes up."

Gratefully, she insisted on dropping me off. "I never expected tonight to turn out this way. Thank you for being there when I

I Shouldn't Have Done This

needed you the most," she said, sitting beside me and holding my hand while resting her head on my shoulder.

"I'm here for you, always," I assured her.

Then she hesitated and finally confessed, "There's something I need to tell you, but please promise me you won't judge me."

I nodded, giving her my word.

She took a deep breath and said, "I have been through a terrible ordeal. Not once, not twice, but several times, I was raped."

Horrified by her revelation, I held her hand tighter, offering my silent support.

"I was in the fifth standard, and that guy was my tutor. Initially, everything was fine, but once, when I couldn't do my homework, he asked me to take off my top, and when I said no he threatened to beat me. I told my mom, but she didn't believe me. Even she said if you won't do your homework, he is gonna beat you. Slowly, he became more barbaric and inhuman. He asked me to take my clothes off and beat me. It was so painful." A tear rolled down her cheek.

Rage consumed me, urging me to exact vengeance upon him then and there. "I couldn't comprehend his actions, but the agony was unbearable. Each day, he inflicted beatings upon me. I fabricated excuses to escape, yet my mother, misled by his facade, punished me and left me alone with that demon. Sleep evaded me, my nights tormented, my existence morphing into a living nightmare until my father witnessed his unspeakable acts. He nearly ended him. Even now, the specter of that fiend haunts my dreams, leaving me trembling and gasping for air. "Filled with anger and compassion, I promised, "I will be by your side, supporting you through everything."

She gazed into my eyes, clasping both of my hands in hers. "If you truly love me, promise me you'll always stand by my side, just like you did today."

113

I nodded in solemn agreement, and she leaned in, pressing her lips softly against mine.

"Where is that monster now?" Though I knew it wasn't the right moment, I couldn't suppress the question. The words spilled out, propelled by a surge of emotion.

"I don't know. Perhaps he's dead. But I don't want to dwell on him anymore. Promise me, instead, that you'll love me unconditionally."

It was then that you entered Meet. For the first time, both of us are in a relationship.

"No, we both ain't in a relationship."

Chapter 13

"It has been two years; you can't remain mired in this place forever," Ankit asserted. Technically, we never broke up, as we were never in an official relationship. I had proposed to her, but she promptly declined. Since then, Ankit has been an unwavering support, a rock by my side.

"Look, I'm almost there. It's nearly completed," I proudly gestured to the cutting-edge prototype of the project I have dedicated myself to for the past year and a half. "Life has never been more fulfilling."

"Fulfilling?" He shot me a reproachful look. "Look at you. You were intoxicated." He settled into a chair beside me.

I straightened up in my seat. Yes, that was the place where I used to spend most of my time after the rejection. After Seerat had turned me down, only one thing had comforted me—alcohol. A little alcohol a day kept the pain away. But now, it wasn't just about numbing the pain; it helped me focus and concentrate.

"So what? You are behaving like you don't drink? What's the big deal?" I took another sip from my glass.

"The big deal is it was 10 in the morning." I checked my watch; it was indeed 10. I promptly rose, intending to take a brisk shower. "Where are you going? You haven't slept for like three days."

"Last night, I slept for two hours. I had a meeting with Tushar Sir at 11 and was already late."

"I can't understand why you're still in contact with that delinquent."

115

I Shouldn't Have Done This

Let me tell you about Tushar. After that fateful day, I channeled most of my time into introspection, trying to fathom what went wrong. Ankit implored me to direct my energy into academics.

I immersed myself in my studies, avoiding socializing as the mere thought repulsed me. During the summer break, while Ankit spent time with Kritika, I had little to occupy my days. That's when I decided to undertake an internship.

I applied to various companies and received a call from a startup founded by a man who had returned from the States after 12 years. Excited, I prepared ardently for the interview.

That was my initial encounter with Tushar. He was the most generous person I ever met. Just kidding, he was the epitome of inconsideration and insensitivity. I'm sure many can relate; almost everyone encounters someone like him at some point in their lives.

During the first ten minutes of the interview, he made me realize that I am just loath of useless meat, a burden on the face of the earth, and it doesn't matter how much I try; I will never succeed in my life.

Nonetheless, I persevered and secured the position. Our small team worked diligently on a project for one and a half years. Upon obtaining a patent, my name adorned the list of contributors. We were poised for mass production when the company Tushar once worked for in the States filed a lawsuit against him, forcing him to suspend production and dissolve our startup.

Undeterred, I embarked on my project and sought Tushar's assistance to bring it to fruition. The next day, he was departing for the States, and I needed to meet him before his departure.

"Don't bother preparing dinner for me," I told Ankit before leaving the apartment.

"Return on time; you have plans with Mahika."

I had completely forgotten about her. Mahika was Kritika's school friend. For the last year, Kritika and Ankit forced me to go out and meet new girls. But the idea of dating and getting into a

116

relationship ridiculed me. Or it might be the fear of falling in love and getting hurt again. Whatever it might be, I avoided the idea of meeting someone.

Until last week, I had been caught in a rut. Stuck in my project, drowning my sorrows in alcohol, and lacking many close friends, I found solace in the company of Kritika and Ankit. However, seeing them together often reminded me of the void left by Seerat's absence.

"I can't bear to see you like this anymore," Kritika's words pierced through my haze as she exchanged a meaningful glance with Ankit.

"I'm equally tired of witnessing your self-destruction," Ankit said, pulling a chair beside me. "I've been by your side through every hardship—from the moment that arrogant woman walked out on you to the nights you silently shed tears. But enough is enough. It's time for you to reclaim the happiness you deserve. You can't continue sacrificing yourself for someone who doesn't appreciate you."

Already feeling the weight of depression pressing down on me, I found myself reluctantly agreeing to meet someone new—Mahika. Kritika had shared that Mahika, her childhood friend, had recently graduated from a fashion school and was now working for a prestigious design firm catering to women's fashion.

* * * * *

Kritika, an angel in my life, had already shared everything about me and Seerat with Mahika. So, she was the one at the helm that day. Kritika had told me she would pick me up at eightish.

At precisely eight, Mahika's voice came through the phone, "Hi, I am waiting at the gate of your society." Was she waiting beforehand, eagerly counting the minutes until it struck eight?

"Oh, hi, please come up," I responded.

"No, I'm fine. Please hurry; we're running late."

I couldn't see her when I reached the society gate, so I decided to call. However, nobody answered my call. Instead, a black sedan

I Shouldn't Have Done This

halted near me, and a girl came out. It was Mahika. I had seen her photos on social media, but she looked even more gorgeous.

I extended my hand for a handshake, but she surprised me and hugged me.

"Hi, I'm Meet," I fumbled. It probably wasn't the best first line, but in my defense, her touch drove me crazy. It had been a while since a woman had touched me like that.

She laughed, and I joined her, realizing my sheer idiocy.

As we settled in the car, Mahika looked stunning. Her dark hair was smoothed out, and her flawless latte skin complemented the velvety pink lipstick she wore. She dressed elegantly in a sleeveless black top, paired with stunning earrings and faux leather pants. I wondered if she always looked so fabulous or if she dressed up just to meet me. Meanwhile, I felt a bit underdressed in my simple jeans.

"Where are we going?" I asked.

"Just wait and watch," she replied with a mysterious smile, adjusting her seat and fastening her seatbelt.

"Can I tell you something?" I ventured.

"Mm-hmm..."

"You look gorgeous," I said sincerely, not trying to flirt but genuinely appreciating her appearance.

"Are you trying to impress me?" she teased, turning her face towards me and sniggering.

"Are you getting impressed?"

"Nope..." Mahika rolled her eyes at me.

"Besides being sexy, what do you do for a living?" I inquired.

She mockingly feigned resentment. "Didn't Kritika tell you?"

"Yes, she did mention that you're a fashion designer. But I want to hear from you. What do you do? How does it feel? You know, insider stuff."

"I'll show you, one day" she said cryptically, taking a turn that led us to a restaurant.

I Shouldn't Have Done This

"Is this The Sensation?" I recognized the exclusive restaurant, known for its difficulty in getting reservations.

"You don't like this place?" She parked her car and touched up her lipstick.

"No, nothing like that. How are we supposed to get in without reservations?" I asked with a genuine concern.

With a sly smile, she replied, "No worries, I know a guy."

"A guy?" I raised an eyebrow, curious about her connection. "Wait, who's this guy?" I nodded, trying to keep my composure. "And how do you know him?" I reassured myself that it was nothing to worry about, but the words spilled out before I could stop them.

"He used to be my boyfriend. Well, now we're just friends." The color drained from my face as I struggled to find the right words. Everyone has a past, I reminded myself. I even briefly connected with Seerat once, though we don't hang out anymore. But is it expected to hang out with an ex? "Why do you always take things so seriously?" I cursed myself for overthinking

"Relax, I was just joking. He's not my ex. He's my friend's cousin. Now that your investigation is over, can we go?"

"Sure, but if he were your ex, it would be kind of strange, don't you think?"

"Why?" she asked.

"I mean, having your past and future all under one roof with you."

She rolled her eyes. "Aren't you being a bit dramatic?"

"No, I'm just a believer. And I believe in myself."

"Kritika mentioned you haven't dated anyone in years. Doesn't seem like you're out of practice," she pointed out.

Anything remotely related to Seerat triggers a flood of memories in me. I remember the first time I saw her, the day we held hands, our first kiss, our first intimate moment together, and the painful day she rejected my love without explanation. These memories

119

haunt me every day, a movie about a love that was never meant to be.

Inside the restaurant, the ambiance is ethereal. The music is loud and lively, blending with the patrons' voices. The crowd radiates sophistication, filled with executives and entrepreneurs from leading global companies who probably earn millions a month. Mahika glides through the warm bodies to order an Irish beer.

"What would you like to have?" We sit at the bar, watching the guy singing a love song for his girl. It's not a karaoke night, but he has a special request.

I look into her eyes and say, "One top-shelf single malt straight up," then turn to the bartender.

"Are you trying to impress me?" she teases.

"Are you getting impressed?" I ask.

"Maybe, or maybe not." She plays hard to get. "You seem like a connoisseur of drinks." She challenges me with a playful smile.

"Yes, try me." I lean closer to her and whisper in her ear.

"In your dreams." She takes a sip of her Irish beer and rolls her eyes.

"My dreams, my rules then," I said with a wink.

"You wish."

"I wish for you." We take our drinks and move to a side table for a more intimate conversation. "Tell me something about yourself."

"What do you want to know?" She enquired

"Anything – your childhood, dreams, work, past relationships, family."

"My childhood was complicated. I went to a school that promoted strict religious values, where makeup was forbidden, and dating was taboo. All these things didn't bother me; I was a tomboy back then – gawky, lanky, and not interested in boys."

"You're kidding; you look like a love goddess straight out of heaven."

I Shouldn't Have Done This

"Yes, I know. I was a late bloomer, but at least I bloomed." She finishes her drink and orders another one. "As for my mom, we never spent much time together. She's an activist, always campaigning for social or political change."

"Do you want to have something else?" She hands me my drink.

"No, I'm good. Please continue." I didn't want any interruptions in between.

"Right now, I'm not dating anyone, and if I were, I wouldn't be here with you."

"What about your past relationships?" I genuinely wanted to know her, so I asked.

"I dated a few guys, but nothing serious. There was a guy named Saurabh whom I kinda loved."

"So what happened?" interested me couldn't stop.

"He turned out to be a jerk. After that, I decided to be more careful with my heart, and my 'sacred garden' is now off-limits for trespassers."

"How can someone get a pass?"

"Now the rules are stricter. First, they must apply and then undergo an initial screening followed by an observation period. In the end, they have to pass an exam and do the registration, and voila, they are welcome to my 'sacred garden.'

"What else? You already know Kritika. We live just two houses away from each other. We learned to crawl together, speak together, and go to school together. We grew up together. She's there in my oldest and fondest memories. I don't have a birthday pic in which she isn't present. We're BFFs."

"I thought Kritika was Seerat's best friend."

"Kritika hates that bitch," was a revelation to me. A pang of agony pricked me when she used such harsh language. It seemed I still couldn't bear to hear negative things about her, but I didn't interrupt Mahika.

"Why does Kritika dislike Seerat if they live in the same flat?"

I Shouldn't Have Done This

"Just because they live in the same flat doesn't mean they're best friends. They didn't know each other until Kritika moved there. Seerat used to live there beforehand. Kritika just wanted to save money, so she had to live with her."

"Yes, but why does she dislike her?"

"That I can't tell you."

"You can trust me, I won't betray you." I signaled the waiter to repeat our orders.

She thought for a second and made a few faces. "Fine, but you have to take this to your grave."

"I promise." I locked my lips and tossed the imaginary key away.

"Kritika dislikes Seerat because..." She deeply breathed, "Kritika believes that Seerat snatched you from her." She almost said this in one breath. This revelation struck me like a thunderbolt.

"Do you remember your Freshers' meet? When you dropped her?" I nodded.

"The moment you left the apartment, she called me. She had a huge crush on you. She told me everything about you and seemed so happy when she talked about you. Her fondness grew daily as time passed until she introduced you to Seerat. You and Seerat hit it off, and she got sidetracked."

All this was shocking for me. After all these years, I never realized that Kritika had feelings for me. Kritika is indeed a wonderful person; every guy would be happy to have her in their life. She has always been kind to me. If it weren't for Kritika, I wouldn't have come here to meet Mahika. She has always been a good friend.

"But that wasn't the reason behind her hatred. Yes, you loved Seerat, and Kritika didn't like it, but she believed that you couldn't force someone to love you, and it wasn't Seerat's fault. What do you think?"

I was listening to all of this with a stern face. Mahika looked at me. "Are you even listening to what I'm saying?"

"Yes, definitely," I nodded in agreement. "Definitely."

She ordered another drink for herself. "Would you like more?"

"Sure." We asked the waiter to repeat our orders.

"The reason Kritika dislikes Seerat is that she left you. She believes that it's impossible to find a person like you. Everything you've done for Seerat was touching and propitious. That's why I said yes when she asked me to go out with you."

I ordered one more whiskey for myself; I needed alcohol to assimilate all of this.

She held my hand. "I think you should stop now. You've already had enough."

Her hands were sleek and lustrous, just like the rest of her. I moved my hand to intertwine my fingers with hers. Her hand fit perfectly in mine, and her slender and graceful fingers filled the space left in mine.

I believe that Kritika is right. I loved Seerat with avidity, and what did I get in return? I should not miss this chance with Mahika that Kritika has given me.

Mahika is a wise, independent, and successful girl who knows what she wants. She's even prettier than Seerat – any guy would be lucky to have her.

"I think we should go now."

"Fine, let's have one more drink, and then we'll leave." I knew that I had a little too much drink

The next morning, I groggily blinked my eyes open to find myself in unfamiliar surroundings. A pounding headache only added to my disorientation. Why was the hangover hitting me so hard? As I struggled to piece together the events of the previous night, it felt like my memory had been wiped clean, leaving me with nothing but a blank slate.

Mahika kindly filled me in on what had transpired: apparently, on our way home, I had dozed off, prompting her to bring me back to her place.

I Shouldn't Have Done This

"Why did you do all this for me?" I looked into her eyes "I was a mess yesterday; you didn't even know me, and we were not even friends."

"Yes, we never met before, we were not friends, and you were something more than a mess, but yesterday, you said something, and those were the most beautiful lines I have heard. Under the influence of alcohol, you believed that I am Seerat..." Her voice faded, and the memories from last night flashed in my mind like a movie.

Everything she was doing reminded me of Seerat. After some time, my mind tricked me into believing that she was no one but Seerat. Who came here to meet me after all this time I spent without her, and I can't lose her again. I held her hands and said "I might not be the guy you dreamt of while growing up, or I might not be the most competent person you've ever met, but my love for you is paramount. If I knew how to live without you, my life would be much easier. Every day feels like a battle, and I'm fighting against the agony of living without you, but it's a war I can never seem to win. I've tried drowning myself in work, hoping to numb the pain, but no amount of success or achievements can fill the void you left in my heart.

I renunciate my sleeps as the dream of you leaving me still haunts me, tormenting me every night. The mere thought of you slipping away from my grasp shatters my soul, and I wake up in cold sweats, my heart racing, fearing the reality of a life without you.

If I could pray to the almighty the way I pray for you, I believe I would be in heaven. But even the heavens feel hollow without you by my side. Every place, every moment, and every breath I take lacks meaning without you in it. I can't envision a life without you. You are my sun, my moon, and my stars—all I need to light up my world.

I wish I could quit it all—this never-ending ache, this emptiness that gnaws at my very being. But dying without you wasn't part of

I Shouldn't Have Done This

the plan. Instead, a flicker of hope remains—the hope that you will return to me when you see me agonize. When you are here with me, I can't bear the thought of letting you go again. I'd rather cling to you with all my strength, cherishing every second, every minute, every hour I have with you.

My heart is an open book; every page is filled with my love for you. I may not be perfect, but my love for you is. It knows no bounds, no limits. So, please, come back to me, and together, we can rewrite our love story. Let's create a new chapter—a chapter where we can heal and find solace in each other's arms.

I promise to hold you close, to treasure you, and to cherish the love we share. Life without you is a life half-lived, and I'm not willing to settle for anything less than our forever together. I'll keep hoping, keep loving, and keep waiting, for you are the missing piece that completes the puzzle of my heart."

"I would be lucky to have someone in my life like you. I cried when you said all this. I was thinking about that girl who left you. She must have a very barbaric heart to say no to you." A tear rolled down her cheek. "You are still in love with her. Just go and get her. I know your life is incomplete without her. No matter what you accomplish, it would be incomplete without her."

"Go get her" were the words I've longed to hear for the last three years.

Chapter 14

Spring had arrived in Delhi, adorning the city with blooming flowers and bidding farewell to the good old classic winters. Amidst this season of change, Mahika had always been a great source of support. Though we never went on another date, our friendship grew stronger. Perhaps fate had other plans, as Ankit seemed preoccupied with Kritika. After learning about Kritika's feelings for me through Mahika, I felt spending too much time around her wouldn't be appropriate. So, I poured all my energy into my work, aiming to patent my project and achieve my long-cherished dreams.

Despite my determination, I did make time to go out with Mahika occasionally, primarily to support her during her shows. Last month, when she was promoted, we celebrated at the same bar where our paths first crossed. This time, I made sure not to embarrass myself, and to my surprise, we took the stage together, leaving the audience thoroughly entertained. It's interesting how people often claim that a boy and a girl can't be friends, but a boy-girl duo can create magic. Such friendships are rare because many people let their overflowing hormones get in the way. But once you're immune to that attraction, it's the best thing to happen to anyone.

As our college days approached their conclusion, companies flocked in for placements every day. This period marked a crucial time in our lives, and I was acutely aware of its significance. However, I was entangled in preparations for the college fest, neglecting my project. It's as if a little nincompoop inside my head kept pushing me

I Shouldn't Have Done This

to prioritize the fest, and unfortunately, that nincompoop seemed to reside with me most of the time.

Ankit convinced me to join him as a coordinator for the technical events. While the core team had initially assigned him the responsibility, he felt inadequate for the role and proposed my name alongside his. Then, he cleverly resorted to emotional blackmail to secure my assistance.

Standing alone on the top floor of the building that molded us into engineers, I looked down at the jubilant students immersed in the festive spirit. When I first arrived at this college, I craved these vibrant vibes, but over these four years, I had transformed, and so had my priorities.

Delhi's winter held a special place in my heart. The cold winds, foggy skies, winter dew, and long queues everything about Delhi during this season was astounding. It was a time when the perfect date required no effort at all just strolling hand in hand, enjoying ice creams, and sharing heartfelt conversations. I had always yearned for this but never had the opportunity to experience it.

Losing in thought, I heard a familiar voice behind me as I stood alone. It was Kritika, her black sling bag hanging near her waist as she checked her phone screen before putting it away.

"Just came to grab my jacket; I forgot it in class today," I lied, trying to appear nonchalant. "What about you? What brings you here?"

"I was looking for Ankit. Seems like his phone is dead again," she said, joining me. "We haven't talked much lately. How's life treating you?"

"I've been quite busy with my project, trying to catch up on everything," I replied, attempting to meet her gaze, but it felt like she was peering into my soul.

"How's everything going, really?" she asked with genuine concern.

I Shouldn't Have Done This

"Good, actually, great. I'm almost finished with my project, and my grades are also good. So, I'm hopeful for a good job," I responded, but I could sense that Kritika saw through my facade.

"No, I mean... I was asking about Seerat. Are you still not over her?"

I hesitated for a moment before admitting, "No. I mean, I'm fine. It's in the past now, and I try to forget about her."

"Lying to me is one thing, but please don't lie to yourself," her voice trembled, and she turned her face away to conceal her tears. "Till this day, I can't help but feel guilty that I introduced her to you. If it weren't for me, maybe you would have been happier. I feel like I ruined everything for you. If you can't move on, I won't be able to forgive myself."

"If I could let go, I would," I reassured her, my heart heavy with the weight of my emotions. She turned her face back to me, her eyes filled with understanding.

"It's the most frustrating feeling, loving someone who can't love you back. Why can't we fix our lives the way we mend things? People say I'm an engineer, capable of creating things, but it seems I can't engineer my own life," she poured out her feelings, and I felt an instant connection with her pain. "Every night when I close my eyes to sleep, I see her closing the door on me. When I'm alone, she says, 'We can't be together, and I can't tell you why.' It's as if I'm lying on a cold steel surface with a hundred bricks on my chest suffocating me. Sometimes, the pain becomes unbearable, and I wish those bricks would shatter my ribs and pierce my heart just to end it all. I feel empty inside, and the constant headaches from obsessing over her drive me insane. I want to call her and ask what I did wrong or if I deserved this. Pretending to be normal is exhausting. People ask how I am, and I say I'm fine, but I'm not. I want to cry; I can't hold it in anymore. Yes, I made a mistake, I might have loved the wrong person, but I loved her, and I can't undo that. I still love her. Even now, if I knew where she was, I would go and ask her why she did this to me."

"Then go and find her." I was taken aback by Kritika's unexpected encouragement. "Remember your first year when you were studying computers?" she asked.

I nodded, unsure of where this conversation was heading. It was becoming a bit frustrating.

"When you write code for a program, is it always correct the first time?" she continued.

"No," I replied, trying to grasp her point, "What's your point?"

"So what do you do?" she asked.

"I used to debug it," I answered, still unsure of where she was going with this.

"Exactly my point. Life can't be perfect; you have to debug it. Look back, acknowledge your mistakes, and try to rectify them. And if you face difficulties, don't hesitate to seek help. You're not a superhero; don't be so hard on yourself," she said, reassuringly smiling. "And remember, sometimes we have to rewrite the entire code."

"I'm afraid. I don't know what to say when I meet Seerat," I admitted.

"Fear is like a monster; it crawls under your skin, gets into your brain, and makes you doubt yourself. Tomorrow, if you were driving on the highway and your car crashed into a truck, and you were about to die in a few seconds, I wouldn't want you to think, 'What would my life be if I had asked her at that moment?'" Her words resonated deeply. "So go find her and talk to her."

"But what if she says no again?" I worried.

"It doesn't matter what she says to you; all you need is closure. Once you have it, you can move on," Kritika reassured me.

"It's not easy. I don't even know where Seerat is. I haven't had any news of her since she left your apartment. I tried to find her on the Internet but found nothing. It's like she was either a ghost or a

Soviet espionage agent who came into my life for some purpose," I joked, momentarily bringing a smile to both of our faces.

"You'll find her. The world is a small place," she encouraged.

"And yet I never ran into Bill Gates or Elon Musk." I again joked to make the atmosphere light. "Besides, I wanted to meet her now, not when she's married to someone else and has two kids," I replied, feeling frustration and longing.

Kritika smiled, wiped away a tear, and patted my shoulder. "Look at yourself; you and Ankit look perfect together. I always envy your relationship. I wish I could have something like you guys have." I complimented

"Don't mention his name in front of me. It's not as perfect as it looks," She warned, her emotions flaring up.

"Just a few moments ago, you were looking for him," I pointed out, slightly puzzled.

"I was lying. I was hiding from Ankit. I thought he would never come here to look for me," she said, breaking into tears.

"He didn't tell you?" she asked.

"No, he didn't" I was clueless; I didn't know what to do next. Should I call Ankit? That is not gonna work; it will only make it worse. I asked myself to take a deep breath to calm down.

"Tell me what happened; you'll feel better," I said, gently holding Kritika's trembling hand to comfort her.

"Do you remember his birthday last month?" she began. I nodded, urging her to continue.

"I asked him what he wanted for his birthday," she paused, searching for something in her bag. Not wanting any interruptions, I asked, "What did he say? What did he want?"

Kritika stared at me, her eyes filled with fury. "He wanted what every guy wants."

"A PS4?" I naively replied.

I Shouldn't Have Done This

"No," she stretched out the revelation. "Sex. He wanted to have sex. At first, I didn't want to, but ultimately, I gave in, thinking that we'd been together for three years."

I didn't realize that Ankit hadn't been sexually active for the past three years. Now, his obsession with porn seemed to make more sense.

"So, what's the problem?" I questioned. Ankit wanted sex, and Kritika was ready for it. I couldn't see what there was to cry about unless Ankit had some serious masculinity issues.

"He had done all the preparations, and we were ready, but then he said..." Kritika started sobbing again, and I became convinced that Ankit was indeed facing some sort of erectile dysfunction. What else could it be?

Kritika sniffled and continued, "He wanted to go raw. Initially, I was hesitant, but I didn't want to ruin the night. Thinking that I was in the non-fertile period of the month, I said yes. Now I'm a week late for my periods."

I never thought I'd encounter such a situation in my life a girl who used to like me, now dating my best friend, telling me about their intimate details and potential pregnancy. It was an unexpected twist of fate, and I wondered what my role would be an uncle, perhaps?

"You did tell him all of this, didn't you?" I asked.

"Yes, I told him everything, but he was such a douche about it. He shouted at me, blaming me for saying it was the non-fertile time of the month. He said it was all my fault and stormed out of the room," Kritika lamented, struggling to regain her composure. "Now, I don't know what to do or whom to talk to about this. I'm sorry; I shouldn't have burdened you with all this when you already have difficulties."

In my life, I've seen and experienced a lot, but one thing I couldn't bear was seeing a girl crying. I pulled Kritika closer and hugged her reassuringly, "Everything's going to be alright."

I Shouldn't Have Done This

"Let me call him and talk to him," I suggested, taking out my phone and dialing Ankit's number.

"Finally, there you are! I've been looking for you for hours. Why was your phone switched off?" Ankit asked Kritika as he approached us.

I went near him and whispered, "She has told me everything. Why have you been such a jerk?"

Ankit's expression softened, and he admitted, "I know I acted like a jerk. I was scared and didn't know what to say; I freaked out. But I want you to know that I love you, and no matter what happens, I'll always be here for you. If you're pregnant and want to have this baby, I'll take care of both of you." He hugged Kritika, wiping away the tear from her cheek.

It was heartwarming to see them together loving, caring, and teasing each other. When they were together, they didn't need anyone else. I decided to leave them to bridge their differences, hoping that one day I would meet Seerat again, and this time, I wouldn't take no for an answer.

* * * * *

"If only life went as planned, I'd be on Mars. But it never does, and we must learn to maneuver around it. Ankit and I were fortunate to join a significant market giant focusing on innovative environmental solutions. I was assigned to the research and development department, and Ankit found his place in production. The initial excitement waned as the work turned monotonous, repeatedly running repetitive tests for the same model.

After enduring five months of this, I couldn't take it any longer, so I decided to quit and start working on my projects. Two months later, when Ankit came home, he was furious and frustrated. "I don't know what that jerk thinks of himself," he said, grabbing a cold beer from the fridge and downing it in one go.

132

I Shouldn't Have Done This

"Calm down, relax, and tell me what happened." It wasn't new to me; he had been arguing with his boss for the past month.

"He thinks I'm an uneducated fellow who got into this college because of my father," he vented, sinking into the sofa. "I'm not gonna work for that jerk. So, what are you working on?"

His sudden interest in my work thrilled me, "I'm working on a drone…"

"And I'm working on wheels; what a breakthrough," he interrupted me, crossing the line with his frustration.

"Ankit, relax and listen to me. I've been working to increase the payload a drone can carry. My idea is to use it for defense purposes. Imagine if we could mount a gun on it and operate it remotely. It could be a lifesaver for soldiers fighting in the woods against Maoists. If I can achieve this, it has the potential to save many lives. I'm also working on improving its maneuvering capabilities; it should be able to navigate through narrow routes in the woods."

"That's interesting, and we can work on it together," a smile replaced the anger on his face. "But I believe this technology already exists."

"Yes, you're right. The US and China already have it, but India mostly imports it from foreign countries. If we can develop it here in India, it will be economical and beneficial for us. We don't have to depend on others, and you know that the US is famous for putting sanctions, and who knows that one day they put sanctions on this also. Once we own the technology, we can modify it for other purposes."

"What's the status? How much progress have you made?" he inquired.

"I've made significant progress. I've worked on the size, maneuverability, and payload, and the results are impressive. However, I must test it with a gun to address challenges like recoil. I'm not sure how the drone will behave when an actual gun recoils during firing."

I Shouldn't Have Done This

Ankit nodded, brooding for a moment. His intense expression indicated he was about to come up with something. "So, what do we need to do now?"

That wasn't the reply I was hoping for. "I was thinking of showing it to DRDO or some organization that can help us, but it's not that simple. First, I'm trying to get an appointment but struggling to secure one. And even if we get an appointment, we need everything to be perfect."

"Why don't we show it directly to military personnel? My dad's friend is a Colonel in the Indian Army. They went to school together, and he might be able to guide us."

That's what I admire about Ankit; he has exceptional networking skills. Whenever there's a problem, he always knows someone who can help.

"What are you waiting for? Just call your dad and tell him everything," I encouraged him.

Chapter 15

"What are you doing?" I asked Ankit when he took out two suitcases. "We are going there just for two days."

"Yes, but man, you are talking about Kashmir. It's the most beautiful place on earth."

I had always wanted to go to Kashmir; it was one of my wishes since childhood. When I was twelve, my dad called me one day and said, "Go pack your bags, son; we are going to Kashmir for vacation." He told me he had already booked tickets, and we would stay there for a week. I was thrilled and immediately told all my friends about it. Everyone was so jealous because just two weeks ago, our teacher had taught us about Kashmir and described how beautiful it was. We were all set to leave, and we had to cancel our trip when the day arrived.

I was upset and angry with my dad; I thought I would never forgive him for ruining my dream vacation. My friends made fun of me the next day at school, and it was a nightmare. I didn't talk to anyone for the rest of the day. After a few years, when I grew up, my mother told me the truth. There was a militancy attack in Kashmir the day before we were supposed to go there, and my dad didn't want to say to me. He came up with an excuse about having to work at the office to protect me from the harsh reality.

Since then, I have always longed to see Kashmir, but I never got the chance until last week when Ankit's father scheduled our meeting with Major Brar in Kashmir. I couldn't jeopardize this meeting; it was crucial for our project.

135

I Shouldn't Have Done This

"We are not going there for a vacation," I said firmly, trying to make it clear to Ankit.

"I know we are going there to discuss our project with Major Brar, but we won't talk to him all day. In the evening, we can go sightseeing and take some wonderful pictures. Now tell me which of these shirts looks nice on me." Ankit took out two shirts from his closet.

I bawled at him, "I can't understand why you're not realizing the seriousness of this." I took a deep breath to calm down, but it didn't work. Ever since he started working with me, I've been tolerating his lax attitude, but it's high time now. "I've poured my heart and soul into this, I've sacrificed my job, my career, everything. I've cut off my social life, and it's nothing compared to the money I've borrowed from the bank. If this doesn't work out, I'm in deep trouble. So, if you still don't grasp the gravity of the situation, go and sit in your girlfriend's lap." I knew it was out of line, but I had no other choice.

Ankit looked at me, his face turning red with anger. "I know what this is all about. It's not about work or the project. It's about you being selfish. Since Seerat, I've tolerated your tantrums, but I know you envy our relationship. I've seen how you look at us when we're together."

His words hit me hard, and I felt a mix of anger and guilt. I had to set the record straight. "Give your thoughts a halt; they are flying too high. Don't forget that if it wasn't for me, you could have never met Kritika. I'm the one who introduced you to her. And here's a fun fact for you she used to love me. So, if I hadn't rejected her, she wouldn't have come to you. She settled for you because she couldn't get me."

Ankit's face turned even redder, and he pushed me out of the room, slamming the door shut. "Get out of my room! Didn't you hear me? Get out!"

I knew I had gone too far and regretted my harsh words. But I couldn't back down now. "Don't behave like a teenage girl. Come here and talk to me like a man. Oh, I forgot you don't have the guts for that. Tomorrow our flight is at 8, so don't be late. Otherwise, I'll leave you." I knew it was unbefitting, and I shouldn't have said it, but he called for it, and every word I said was accurate, as was nothing else.

He will find the truth one day or another, so let it be today.

I entered my room and immersed myself in perfecting the presentation. Tomorrow was the big day, and I couldn't afford to mess it up. Ever since Seerat left me, this project had become my sole focus. I had put everything on the line, and Tushar knew it too. Convincing him to invest in my company wasn't easy, but I managed it. Still, if I couldn't deliver as promised, I knew he wouldn't spare me, given his reputation.

As I stepped out of my room the following day, Ankit was already sitting on the sofa, ready to leave. Our last interaction had been tense, and I didn't want to ruin the vital day ahead with a silly argument. So, without saying anything to him, I went straight to the kitchen to prepare breakfast. Considering our lengthy journey, I thought Oats and smoothies would be a good choice. But I hesitated; I wasn't sure if he'd eat them. Nevertheless, I couldn't let my pride get in the way, so I prepared some for him and silently placed both dishes in front of him.

He looked at me and then at the food but didn't eat any. The tension between us was like adding fuel to the fire. We headed to the airport, and our flight was on time. The prospect of not talking to him during the entire journey felt daunting, especially when our seats were right next to each other.

Ankit and I had been inseparable since childhood. We had gone to school and college and even started a company together. While we had a few arguments in the past, this situation felt different. I might have drawn the line, but he crossed it, fully aware of Tushar's threat to our lives and careers. Tushar held more power over us than we could handle, and Ankit's carelessness and impulsiveness worried me.

I gazed out the window, greeted by pleasant weather outside. Over the past six months, I've journeyed extensively across India, making airplanes feel like a second home at times, given how frequently I've flown. Initially, the experience was suffocating; cramped legroom made me feel claustrophobic, sandwiched between two overweight passengers. But now, I find comfort easily, curling up and dozing off as if on a familiar couch.

The airplane feels like a cradle in the sky, signaling the start of another beautiful journey each time I board. Peering out the window brings tranquility, as if cruising through paradise, high above the clouds. The scattered clouds resemble pebbles on a beach, while thin mist above resembles a half-erased footprint. Fragments of cloud paint the ocean below, delicate strokes of white over blue. Shifting my gaze, I catch sight of the airplane's wing engine, a testament to human engineering roaring with power. Hoping to drift off to sleep, I close my eyes, but the hum of the engine keeps me tethered to wakefulness.

After an hour and twenty minutes, we reached Srinagar. I must have dozed off because I only woke when the air hostess approached to inform us about landing. I felt a bit disoriented momentarily, then quickly adjusted to the reality of being on an airplane.

"Please straighten your seat and fasten your seat belt," the air hostess reminded me, and I complied. Curiosity got the better of me, and I decided to ask her name, just to be polite.

"What's your name?" I glanced at my watch, realizing that we were about to land. Although it was a trivial question, I wanted to maintain a friendly demeanor.

"Navneet, Sir. It's Navneet," she replied a little louder the second time, probably thinking I was still half asleep.

"Yes, Navneet, could you please bring a glass of water for me? I need to take my medicine," I requested, and although Ankit looked

I Shouldn't Have Done This

at me strangely, he said nothing. I knew he must be wondering about the medicine I referred to.

"Sure, but please straighten your seat and fasten your seatbelt. We'll be landing any moment now," Navneet said as she headed to the pantry to fetch some water.

Returning with a glass, she handed it to me. "Sir, here's your water. Anything else I can help you with?"

"No," I replied, taking out a tablet to ease the constant headaches I've been having since I cut down on alcohol. I haven't quit altogether, but I prefer to stay sober these days.

As the plane descended, we left the cloud-filled paradise behind and returned to our everyday habitat. Peering downward, I couldn't help but feel this place was nothing short of paradise. Reciting a famous line by a Mughal Emperor, I thought, "Gar Firdaus Baar Roomee Zamee Est, Hamee Esto, Hamee Esto, Hamee Esto (If there is a heaven on earth, it's here, it's here, it's here)."

"I couldn't help but feel that this place was no less than a paradise. A gentle, divine smile came on my face, realizing that we were just going from one paradise to another."

A chilly breeze brushed against me as I stepped out of the airport. It was around 10 AM, and the sun was high up in the sky, but the clouds dominated the horizon. I had read that August temperatures in Kashmir could reach thirty-five degrees Celsius, but I'd bet it wasn't over 20 degrees.

I looked around, but no one was holding a name card. I pulled out my cell phone, remembering that Major Brar had warned us to get postpaid SIM cards as prepaid SIM don't work here due to safety reasons.

"I'm outside the airport; where are you?" I asked the driver who was supposed to pick us up.

"Come outside, Saab ji. Military folks won't let us in," the man replied in a Kashmiri accent, one I'd only heard in movies before.

"Look for a white Innova car," he added, providing the vehicle's details.

Our hotel wasn't far from the airport, so the ride was quick. I was too engrossed in the breathtaking valley to notice the time pass. We were to meet Major Brar at 2 PM, but he hadn't given us an exact address. His only instruction was to stay in our hotel room, where one of his soldiers would fetch us at 1 PM. "Don't be late," he emphasized before hanging up.

By 11 AM, we had checked into a luxurious hotel by the riverbank. With limited funds, we had to share a room despite our recent fight, which made the situation even more uncomfortable.

Feeling nervous and anxious about the meeting, I decided to take a hot bath to calm myself down. I changed into fresh clothes, determined to make a perfect first impression. After all, I'd meet a military professional trained to analyze people based on body language and attire. Though I wasn't professionally trained like them, I had done my homework.

At precisely 1 PM, we received a call from the hotel reception, notifying us that somebody was waiting for us. It felt like he had been there for a while, eagerly waiting for the clock to strike one.

We both got ready and left the room with our bags. A tall military personnel member, Pranav, stood near the reception area. He offered a handshake; I believed a firm handshake showed confidence. However, his grip made my hand feel lifeless.

Pranav urged us to get into the car without delay, as Major Brar had emphasized punctuality. I can't tell you how far the military base was from our hotel, but it felt like a giant castle with thick walls running across the road, crowned with galvanized razor-black barbed wire on top. Pranav stopped the car at the entrance, where they asked us to step out and present our identity cards. The guards stood there, their scary arms in hand. One wrong move, and you could find yourself lying lifeless on the ground. It felt as though the guard checking my identity card might declare it as fake, and the other guard would shoot me right there, but fortunately, nothing of the sort happened."

"They checked us and our bags. A guard pulled the drone from our bag, asking, 'What is this?'

'It's a drone. We're here to discuss this only,' I replied.

'You're not allowed to bring it inside.' His intimidating demeanor sent a chill down my spine. He mumbled something to another guard, speaking in a language I couldn't understand.

I glanced at Ankit. We had come solely to show the drone to Major Brar, and leaving it at the entrance wasn't an option. "There must be a misunderstanding. Please call Mr Brar to clarify," Ankit spoke, breaking his silence for the first time since morning.

"Okay, for now, wait in that room," the guard gestured towards a compact chamber on the other side of the gate. It felt like a detention facility with two guards standing watch. I muttered all the prayers I could remember while we sat on the wooden chairs, surrounded by the cold grey walls. The only noise came from the old ceiling fan.

After what felt like an eternity, another guard arrived. "You can go now." Relief washed over me, thanking God that he was allowing us to proceed.

Back inside the exact car we had arrived in, Pranav drove us to the visiting hall, where Major Saab would meet us. The base was much larger than I had imagined, covering several acres and resembling a city guarded by imposing walls.

Pranav dropped us off in front of a building and directed us to go straight. It was the first time they had left us alone since we entered the facility, and I must admit, I was a little scared.

"Sewa Parmo Dharma" (Service is our duty), Ankit read those words embossed at the primary entrance. A guard sitting at a table asked for our names and instructed us to sign in the register. He then told us to wait while he called Major Saab. In just a couple of minutes, Major Brar arrived. Standing tall at about 6 feet, with a

I Shouldn't Have Done This

broad chest and shoulders, he exuded an impeccable presence in his pristine uniform and turban.

"I am Major Kuldeep Singh Brar," he introduced himself. Standing next to him, Ankit and I felt like dwarfs. I had always known him as Major Brar and had never considered his actual name. "Colonel Shyam told me about you. He's my senior and your father's friend," he added.

Ankit nodded and offered a brief smile, but he remained quiet. I sensed he was as nervous as I was.

"How was your flight? Did you guys have lunch?" Major Brar's polite and friendly demeanor eased our discomfort.

"The flight was pleasant," Ankit replied, attempting a forced smile.

"What about lunch?"

"No, it's fine."

"Let's have something first," Major Brar suggested, looking at both of us. "Amit, just ask someone to take those bags to my office." With that, he walked away.

Ankit looked at me, silently asking what we were supposed to do. I raised my hands and shrugged, indicating that we should follow Major Brar. Ankit had no choice but to comply.

As I mentioned, the base was like a compact city fortified by enormous walls. It took us ten minutes to walk from the visiting hall to the Mess. The Mess resembled a grand monument, but when we entered, it appeared almost deserted, except for a few individuals who I assumed worked there. A staff member, who was mopping the floor, was called over by Major Brar to bring us some food.

"Please, have a seat," Major Brar invited us to sit at a table. These tables reminded me of the ones we had in our college hostel mess room, though these were undoubtedly in much better condition.

"So, whose idea was it to work on this technology?" Major Brar asked, taking a seat opposite us. His humility and efforts to make us comfortable were apparent. Unlike the stereotypical

142

military personnel, who were often solemn, we found Major Brar fun-loving and approachable. We opened up to him in just a few minutes, sharing incidents from our college life. In turn, he shared a mission story, recounting how he dressed as a milkman to infiltrate a suspected militant's house. Usually, sharing mission details was prohibited, but The tale occurred long ago, and the militants were no longer a threat.

"It's no simple job, not just our lives at stake. Every day, some of our fellow soldiers die while protecting our motherland. Imagine attending your friend's funeral when he got married just a month ago or knowing he's expecting a baby in just a month or two. It's agonizing, and you can't help but feel pity for them and their families. Your faith in God trembles, yet we must endure this pain almost daily."

Almost daily, our soldiers die fighting militants who live in our country, eat our food, and praise others. I could see the pain in his eyes. Kashmir is a wonderful place, perhaps the most beautiful in the world, but filled with constant melancholy.

After dinner, we wondered what would come next, but this time, it didn't feel as daunting as before. We were more comfortable now. "Show me what you have first, and then we'll talk about it in my office," Major Brar said.

He called someone to bring our bags. "Come with me; your bags will be here soon. In the meantime, tell me how you developed this technology."

It all came out smoothly. It felt more like a friendly discussion than a formal meeting. I explained everything to Major Brar, and he listened as if I were tutoring him before an exam, asking his doubts, and I happily provided explanations.

In a few minutes, a guy came with our bags. I recognized him as Pranav, who had picked us up earlier this morning.

The drone was disassembled since we couldn't bring it to the airplane. We reassembled it while Major Brar observed us. He didn't take any notes, but it seemed like he was assessing us at that moment. I became extra cautious, aiming to finish quickly without making any mistakes.

We demonstrated it to him, and then he tried it himself. He was intelligent and thorough, trying out everything we had told him without missing any points, and he didn't point out any issues either.

"Let's go to my office; we will talk there," he said, leading the way. Pranav was there to help us with our bags.

In Major Brar's office, he asked me basic questions about the design I had previously discussed, and I showed him the slides I had prepared for today's meeting. "Tell me the cost of setting up the production facility."

That was the question I hadn't prepared for, and I cursed myself for the oversight. I had been so focused on perfecting everything that I neglected the Production aspects. It was like an architect obsessed with building, a beautiful library but forgetting to consider the weight of the books. When the library was inaugurated, everyone praised its beauty, but soon, it started sinking into the ground due to the weight of the books. No one could figure out what went wrong until an architect from a foreign land asked about the weight of the books. The poor architect, so obsessed with beauty, forgot the practicality.

My doom was inevitable, and I had brought it upon myself. Should I bluff and give him estimated figures? Before I could speak, Ankit jumped in, "Sir, it depends on the production facility and various factors, such as the location – whether we set it up in Srinagar, a village, or Delhi." He took out his laptop and showed a presentation he had prepared for the day.

"He had prepared a meticulously detailed floor plan, with precise cost estimates for setting up the facility and the required capital for its operations. Additionally, he outlined the minimum number of personnel needed, each with a different background, along with their estimated salaries.

I Shouldn't Have Done This

Major Brar listened attentively as I observed him closely. He nodded and asked questions occasionally, and Ankit had all the answers. Unlike me, he didn't forget a thing. I thanked God and realized what a fool I had been for arguing with him yesterday. After all, people can enjoy life while being serious about their work.

"That is impressive. I will discuss this with my seniors today and let you know what we need to do next tomorrow. You two have done meticulous work. Email me your presentations; Pranav will drop you back to your hotel."

As we headed back to the hotel, I couldn't stop grinning. The meeting had been fruitful, and Major Brar seemed pleased with us. Overwhelming gratitude towards Ankit filled me; I would have been in trouble if he hadn't saved the day. I resisted the urge to hug him right there, not wanting to create a scene in front of Pranav.

When we reached our hotel room, I apologized, "I am sorry for everything I said yesterday. I didn't mean it.

I was just nervous about today's meeting."

He looked at me but said nothing.

"Now, don't give me the silent treatment like a teenage girl," I pleaded. I was genuinely sorry but didn't know how to make amends.

"No, you were right. I'm not serious about my work. You worked your ass off for this project, and I was just sitting around with Kritika." Although his words stung, I was glad he was finally talking to me.

"Come on, man. I knew I shouldn't have said it. I am sorry. Please let it go. Let's go out and buy some gifts. I want to get a Pashmina Shawl for my mother. You can buy something for Kritika if you want."

He said nothing, but his nod was enough. I knew him well. A high-spirited guy like Ankit couldn't stay mad at anyone for long.

After resting, we stepped out to explore the beauty of the place. It was love at first sight. Our hotel's location was perfect; on the backside, we could hear water burbling, enjoying its journey through the valley, and on the front side was the market. It wasn't too crowded, but you could spot a few tourists among the locals, who mainly wore traditional Pherans.

Across the road, lush green mountains stood tall. We wandered around the market for a bit.

"Would you like to try some Kahwa?" I asked Ankit when I spotted a vendor.

As usual, he said nothing but nodded. "Two kahwas, bhaiya (brother)," I requested the man, dressed in a Pheran.

"Are you guys from India?" Some kids standing nearby asked me.

The question sounded funny in our own country, but considering the sensitive political situation in Kashmir, I chose not to say anything hurtful. I smiled politely and replied, "Yes."

Kashmiri Kahwa tea is a unique green tea found and enjoyed by the Kashmiri people. I had heard a lot about it and was eager to try it. It had a delightful flavor, made from Kahwa tea leaves, green cardamoms, cinnamon, almonds, saffron, and sometimes honey. Sipping the piping hot tea, I felt its excellent taste. "Everything around here is serene. People here are blessed; I wish to spend my life here."

"I wish Kritika could be here with us today. She would love this place," he said, and then he looked at me, realizing that it might hurt. Life had always been a rollercoaster for me. Although I faced difficulties like everyone else, my life was filled with ups and downs. The girl I once loved more than myself had left me, and I was so lost in my emotions during college that I couldn't realize how time had passed. But now, I was over Seerat, and the past couple of days had been a financial struggle, but I was grateful for everything. I had a fantastic friend like Ankit, and everything was back to normal. We now owned a company, and hopefully, Major Brar would approve everything, allowing us to set up our plant.

I Shouldn't Have Done This

"Here, take my phone and call her," I offered my cell phone, hoping Ankit would reach out to Kritika and share our memorable experience in Kashmir.

"No, it's fine. She's probably swamped with work. I'll call her later," Ankit said, his eyes revealing a hint of sadness, perhaps missing Kritika already. We finished our Kahwas and returned the cups to the Shopkeeper. "Let's go; a little shopping might distract us."

Kashmir is renowned for its handicrafts, and the market was brimming with unique handmade souvenirs. Pashmina Shawls, in particular, were a specialty each a masterpiece crafted with love and care, no two alike. It was incredible to think we could carry a piece of this beautiful land with us, a reminder of its rich culture and heritage.

As we entered a shop, the Shopkeeper greeted us warmly. He must have been in his forties, his face etched with the struggles and joys of life, just like the beautiful shawls he sold.

"Show us some shawls," Ankit requested as he sat on a stool, his eyes filled with admiration for the exquisite craftsmanship. I wandered around, mesmerized by the array of colors and patterns, unable to decide which shawl to choose.

As I stepped outside to catch my breath, the atmosphere suddenly changed. Military vehicles filled the streets, and uniformed soldiers passed by with an air of urgency. I couldn't help but ask the Shopkeeper, "Where are these military people going? Is everything alright?"

"It's their daily drama," he replied indifferently, busy with the shawls. But his dismissive response didn't sit right with me, and I pressed further, "But they are here for your safety, aren't they?"

"We don't need their security. Take them with you," the Shopkeeper snapped, finally making eye contact. His eyes were darker than others, reflecting the depth of the pain he had endured.

"Why would you say that?" Ankit's voice carried both anger and concern, his emotions bubbling to the surface.

I Shouldn't Have Done This

"Because they have made our lives a living hell. They impose curfews at their whim, forcing us to shut our shops and rendering us unable to earn a living. The other day, they claimed to have killed ten militants in my village; tell me why a militant would sell eggs on the street; just assume he was a militant for a second, but why did they take away nine innocent lives along with him? How can they justify that?" He pulled out another shawl, but his eyes told a story of sorrow and loss.

That was the second side of the coin when Major Brar told us about the martyr soldiers earlier today; I felt terrible, and now, when this Shopkeeper said to me about the innocent people dying because of a handful of corrupt politicians. Life is tough for people living here. Nature has given them the chance to live in heaven, but people made it a living hell.

As I listened, my heart ached with empathy. The beauty of Kashmir's landscapes was overshadowed by the heart-wrenching stories of its people, caught in the crossfire of conflict. Nature's paradise had become a battleground, leaving behind suffering and anguish.

I was sad after hearing everything he told us, but I left thinking that's the part of life I couldn't do much about. We went to our hotel to rest. The next day was crucial in my life and changed my life.

* * * * *

Pranav was waiting downstairs. We greeted each other, ready to witness our dream come true. The roads looked different from yesterday, with armed and watchful soldiers stationed at every corner. Armored vehicles dotted the landscape, and military personnel barricaded and guarded some streets.

Upon reaching the base, the familiar routine eased our anxiety. Pranav led us directly to Major Brar's office. He was on a call but motioned for us to take a seat. Seeing him smile, I hoped our efforts had paid off.

I Shouldn't Have Done This

Once he concluded the call, Major Brar addressed us, "Guys, I liked your project, and I discussed it with my seniors. Unfortunately, they said no, and we can't proceed further."

His words struck me like a sledgehammer to the chest. The room seemed to spin, and a crushing weight settled upon my shoulders. It was as if all the air had been sucked out of the room, leaving me suffocating in despair. A lifetime of dreams and aspirations shattered in that single moment.

My heart sank to the depths of hopelessness, and I struggled to keep my composure. I glanced at Ankit, who looked as shattered as I felt. This rejection felt like the end of everything I had worked for - the end of my purpose, my passion, my identity.

"I... I don't understand," I stammered, trying to keep my voice steady despite the torrent of emotions threatening to consume me. "We worked so hard and put our hearts and souls into this project. How can they just say no?"

Major Brar's expression softened, revealing his empathy, but it offered no solace. "I understand your frustration, Meet. Sometimes, even when we pour everything into something we believe in, the outcome doesn't always align with our hopes. I'll see what I can do later, but I have other pressing matters to attend to for now."

A lump formed in my throat, choking back the tears that threatened to spill over. I wanted to scream, protest, and demand an explanation, but I couldn't find the strength. Defeated and broken, I felt like a ship adrift in an endless storm, with no harbor of hope in sight.

Ankit reached out, squeezing my hand, his eyes brimming with unspoken sorrow. At that moment, our dreams were torn apart, and it seemed like nothing was left to hold on to. We were lost, adrift, with no clear path forward.

As we left Major Brar's office, each step felt heavier than the last. The weight of the rejection weighed down on my shoulders like a burden too heavy to bear. The world around me blurred as tears clouded my vision. All I had hoped for, all I had fought for, it all felt futile now.

Walking back, profound sadness engulfed us. I felt hollow inside, unsure which was worse the shattered dreams or the unanswered questions. I tried to collect myself, but tears threatened to overflow. The spark ignited my dreams, which seemed to have faded, leaving only despair.

In the car, Ankit's teary eyes mirrored my own anguish. This time, both of us bore the weight of disappointment. Our hopes hinged on that opportunity, and now it had vanished. Once again, we were left wondering what went wrong. Ankit squeezed my hand, offering comfort, yet an eerie numbness enveloped me.

"Could you please go on ahead by yourselves? I need to return to the base immediately. Saab called with urgent news. Your hotel is just a kilometer down this road from here." With that, Pranav left us stranded on the deserted road, leaving us unable to protest.

Taking our belongings from the jeep, Pranav departed for the base. I exhaled deeply as we began the silent trek to the hotel.

"Did you catch anything?" Ankit squeezed my hand, but my heart weighed heavy with sorrow, and I hadn't noticed a thing.

"No," I replied, fear now replacing the grief in his eyes. A peculiar, blood-chilling sound emerged from the other side of the road. It resembled the low snarling of many voices, growing louder until it became a sullen, muttering roar.

A large mob armed with cricket bats, hockey sticks, and stones soon appeared. Fear gripped us as we watched the violence unfold. Desperation struck me as I attempted to call for help, but no signal bars appeared on my phone. A notification popped up with a message: "Article 370 Revoked."

"Today, the Modi government dropped a bombshell on Kashmir," the news flashed across media outlets. Home Minister Amit Shah had moved to revoke Article 370 and Article 35(A), vital constitutional provisions that granted Jammu & Kashmir special

I Shouldn't Have Done This

rights. While Article 370 had seen some dilution over time, Article 35(A) remained unchanged.

Amidst mounting tension, the government detained the top political leadership in a midnight swoop and imposed restrictions on their movement. Telecom and internet services were suspended, plunging the state into uncertainty."

The situation finally made sense, explaining the violent mob and the disrupted phone signals. We were left on our own in a volatile atmosphere. We waited until the mob moved away, trying to fathom the magnitude of the unfolding events.

Ankit scanned the surroundings and whispered, "No one is here. Let's hurry back to the hotel." Fear gripped us as we began to run, our hearts pounding in our chests. My legs trembled with terror, making each step an immense struggle. "We need to run, or we won't survive," Ankit urged, gripping my hand tightly as we raced forward.

As we sprinted towards the hotel, the sound of gunfire echoed through the air. The military personnel's warning shot scattered the mob, sending people in all directions, armed with stones. Some started advancing towards us, prompting Ankit to shout, "Faster, Meet!"

I tried my best, but the weight of the bags slowed me down. A stone hit my left shoulder, and I tumbled to the ground, twisting my right ankle in the process. I attempted to stand, but the pain was excruciating, leaving me certain that my ankle was fractured. Panic surged through me as I struggled to move. Ankit was already far ahead, having crossed the barricades.

Desperate for help, I shouted, but my pleas went unheard amidst the chaos. The person throwing the first stone approached me, hurling another in my direction. I saw it coming but couldn't evade it. Fear gripped my limbs, rendering them immobile. My mind played tricks, the world around me fading into oblivion. My heartbeat thundered in my ears as time seemed to slow down. The

I Shouldn't Have Done This

urge to run overwhelmed me, but my body refused to cooperate. Finally, the stone struck my head.

The world spun around me, voices becoming distant and blurred. Through the haze, I could see the man who had harmed me, and amidst the confusion, I caught a glimpse of someone I knew; I saw her; I saw Seerat.

Chapter 16

$\mathcal{A}$s I regained consciousness, an intense throbbing engulfed my head. I struggled to open my eyes, but the pitch darkness offered no solace. My forehead, where the stone had struck, seemed strangely untouched, devoid of bruises or injuries. Checking my ankle, I felt relieved that the pain had subsided. However, I realized that I was lying naked amid the forest, and panic set in as I desperately searched for my clothes, but the impenetrable darkness concealed them from my sight. Worries about Ankit flooded my mind. Why hadn't he come to my rescue? Was he safe? I feared for his well-being.

A distant voice broke the silence, asking, "How are you feeling now?"

My heart pounded, and I trembled with fear, uncertain who this person was. "Who is this?" I questioned, my voice quivering. The memory of being attacked by someone lingered, leaving me cautious of any stranger's intentions.

"I am your friend," the voice reassured, louder this time, as the person approached. I strained my eyes to see, but the absolute darkness rendered everything invisible.

"Ankit, is that you?" I asked, seeking reassurance. Despite my fear of dying, I dreaded being alone in this situation.

"No, your friend Ankit is back at the hotel, looking after you," the man replied calmly. He snapped his fingers before I could comprehend his words and was suddenly visible. An older man in his mid-forties stood before me, dressed in rags. His face bore the

153

wrinkles of experience, and his balding scalp framed a fringe of grey-white hair.

Embarrassed and vulnerable in my nakedness, I instinctively covered myself. This man was the one who had stripped me of my clothes. Anger surged, and I demanded, "What are you saying? Are you out of your mind?"

His smile seemed unsettling as if he found amusement in my discomfort. "Don't be shy; I have seen you like this before," he said, further fueling my anger and suspicions.

Confident that he was responsible for stealing my clothes, I demanded he return them. "Where are my clothes? Give them back to me!" I exclaimed furiously. This man had callously left me stranded in the woods, vulnerable and defenseless.

As my anger intensified, I was determined to make him understand the gravity of his actions. I wanted to teach him a lesson he would never forget, to show him the consequences of his cruelty.

"You don't need those clothes anymore. I didn't steal them, nor am I referring to the present day. I've seen you like this since you were born when you took those unusually long showers or even when you were with Seerat."

How did this guy know about Seerat? I was left confounded, and the throbbing in my head intensified. The pain became unbearable, and I couldn't take it any longer; I fell to my knees.

He approached me, attempting to place his hand on my head, but I instinctively backed away, dodging his touch. "Don't overthink it; it will only make it worse."

"Who are you? How do you know about Seerat? Where am I, and where is Ankit?" I cried, unable to comprehend anything. Everything seemed so muddled and bewildering.

"Come here, and I will show you," he said, grabbing my arm and helping me stand up. With a snap of his fingers, the ground beneath us vanished, and I could see through it to the other side. There I was, lying on a bed with bandages wrapped around my forehead

I Shouldn't Have Done This

and ankle. Ankit sat on a chair beside me, his eyes moist, looking at a picture of us in college on his mobile phone.

Goosebumps covered my skin, and instead of clarity, the situation became even more entangled. "Am I dead?" I speculated.

"No, not yet. You are still breathing," the mystery man replied with a smile.

Confusion still clouded my mind. "Why are we in these woods?"

"These aren't woods; it only seems that way because that was your last memory."

"Then where are we?"

With a flick of his arm, everything disappeared, and the trees in front of me vanished. Everything became brilliantly bright as if a powerful beam of light was coming from a distant source, but it was so intense that I couldn't discern its origin. It felt like we were standing in the ocean with nothing else around us.

The mysterious stranger had an aura of enigma about him, and I couldn't help but be drawn into his enigmatic world, where reality and memory intertwined. My mind was on a rollercoaster ride, trying to grasp the strange reality I found myself in.

"Are we in heaven?" I ventured another guess, as this place didn't fit my image of hell either.

"No, consider it a transfiguration zone," he replied calmly.

"What is it then? Is this where you decide whether I'll go to heaven or hell?" Fear crept into my voice; the last thing I wanted was to end up in hell.

"No, there's no physical place like heaven or hell. If they exist, they are on earth and are based on your deeds. The Almighty watches over an endless creation, preservation, and dissolution cycle. Souls are considered eternal, part of a spiritual realm, and reincarnated into new bodies in the physical realm. Each time a soul goes through this cycle, it learns new things and works through its karma," he explained patiently.

"So, I'll be reborn as a man again?" I sought clarification.

I Shouldn't Have Done This

"Your existence isn't limited to being born as a human. You might have lived past lives as animals, plants, or even as divine beings who govern part of nature. Any form of life is part of this cycle," he answered.

"But when will it all stop?"

"The ultimate purpose of every soul is to reunite with the prime soul from which it originated. It takes several lifetimes of learning and realization before this can happen. Once you achieve this realization, you will be reunited with the prime soul," he elaborated.

"Why haven't I reunited with the prime soul already? Why do I have to be reborn again?"

"Your essence carries the weight of many lifetimes," he assured me with a serene certainty. "In each incarnation, you've gathered the wisdom required for your journey towards ultimate unity with the prime soul. This current existence marks the culmination of your earthly experiences. After this, reunion is your destiny."

I felt a mix of happiness and confusion. If this was my last time on earth, why was I still waiting to be reborn?

"But you made some terrible mistakes that you must resolve before your soul can reunite," he gently revealed. "What have I done?" I searched my memories but couldn't pinpoint any actions that would taint my karmic cycle to the extent of being reborn as.

"You gave up," he responded instantly, and it felt as if he had wanted to say those words since we met.

"Is giving up a sin? I mean, it's not like I murdered someone or committed a heinous crime," I protested. I couldn't help but feel like he was akin to my mother, coming up with flimsy reasons when she wanted me to do something I didn't fancy.

"Giving up is not just about committing a crime; it's about losing hope and faith in yourself. It's about surrendering to the challenges instead of facing them head-on. Your character is defined by the decisions you make. You might have felt angry enough to strike someone, but choosing not to shows restraint and moral strength.

On the other hand, if you decide to resort to violence, you take a completely different path. Our actions shape who we are and what we will become. Giving up signifies a weak character, and you still have much to learn," he explained eloquently, and I had to admit he had a point.

Though I initially resisted, upon reflection, I realized he was right. I have always strived to achieve my goals and dreams. From getting into my desired college, completing my degree, and achieving good scores to securing a job and eventually starting my own company—I had fought for my aspirations.

"But today, you gave up when you wished to die," he said with that ever-present enigmatic smile.

There was something peculiar about him; he maintained that smile regardless of the gravity of the subject matter. He was correct again; I had given up in utter despair.

I gazed at the older man, and he was undeniably correct. Today wasn't the first time I had given up; I had surrendered my entire life. My dreams, my love for Seerat—I had let go of everything without realizing it.

"Yes, you were right. I've been giving up on things my whole life, and I never truly understood the gravity of my actions until now. You mentioned that I won't reunite with the prime soul and must be reborn to amend my deeds and learn the final lessons. So, is there any chance I could go back and rectify everything in this life?" I asked, hopeful for a chance to make amends.

He nodded, smiling reassuringly. With a flick of his arm, a wave of brilliant white luster rose from the ground, engulfing the entire space. I looked around for the other guy, but he had disappeared. The brightness surrounded me, and I was drowning in its intensity. The white fluid closed in, filling me with both trepidation and purpose.

Struggling to keep my composure, I saw Seerat shutting her door on me once again. This time, her words were even more piercing.

"You gave up on me," she said, and it was an undeniable truth. I couldn't distinguish whether my eyes were open or closed as I felt my heart pounding rapidly in panic. The need for air became urgent, but the brightness consumed everything. Eventually, everything turned black, and I closed my eyes.

Gasping for air, I finally opened my eyes and found myself lying on a bed. Ankit was sitting next to me, still awake, and the relief on his face was evident. He embraced me warmly, and I knew my spirit guide had given me one more chance. This time, I was determined to get her, to seize the opportunity that life had presented me with.

* * * * *

"Check on him, Dr. Something has happened to him. Maybe the stone affected his brain and damaged some vital parts. Now, he's speaking all rubbish," Ankit urgently called the doctor after I shared everything I had witnessed.

"He's perfectly fine, except for the injuries. It's entirely normal. Most people who have had near-death experiences aren't around to tell us how it feels, but some who have come back to life due to advancements in the medical field have shared their stories. I once met a patient in critical condition and performed CPR on him. When he regained consciousness, he described his experience. He saw a bright, white light that was incredibly calming and soothing. He wanted to move towards that light but heard voices calling his name. He was annoyed and angry at the person disturbing him from embracing that wonderful experience. It turns out that person was me, calling him back to his senses. Something similar happened to you, a bright white light. You know, there's a scientific explanation for this phenomenon. When our heart stops, the brain's oxygen supply is cut off, leading to hallucinations. It's the brain's last attempt to make everything right, and in your case, it succeeded," the doctor explained.

It was an exciting story, but I knew what I had seen regardless of the scientific reasoning. Whether it was my brain's last attempt to come back to life or my spirit guide, I was confident that I had lost Seerat once, and I couldn't bear to lose her again.

"I understand that you might not believe me, but I know what I saw," I told Ankit after the doctor left. He seemed skeptical of everything I had shared.

Getting off the bed, I changed my clothes. "Where are you going?" Ankit asked. He was angry and irritated with me, but I didn't care anymore. Worries about what others would think or say or societal expectations were ridiculous thoughts that held us back from achieving our true potential. I wondered if these were merely defense mechanisms we created, excuses to remain within our comfort zones, preventing us from going out and pursuing what we truly desire.

I had enough of it all; I flung the door open and walked away. "Where are you going?" Ankit inquired, "They've imposed restrictions under section 144, and nobody can go outside. If they catch you, they won't hesitate to arrest you and throw you behind bars." His anger had subsided, and his tone softened as he pleaded with me to stay. "Can't you see it was all a hallucination, your mind playing tricks on you? Look at your ankle; it still hasn't healed properly."

I acknowledged his concern but remained determined. "I have to find Seerat, no matter what," I replied, and without a second thought, I ventured out, ready to face whatever challenges lay ahead.

But I was adamant and wasn't going to back down this time. I knew my ankle was still hurting, but after everything I had been through in my life, I felt I could bear that pain. As I stepped outside, the sight was horrifying. Soldiers guarded every nook and corner of the city, armed to the teeth. It wouldn't take any time for a stray bullet to end my life. Yet, I had to find her, Seerat, but I had no clue about her whereabouts. What if Ankit was right, and all of this was just an illusion, a dream I had when that stone hit me?

Feeling lost and clueless, I asked myself, "Should I return to the hotel?" I felt hopeless once again in my life. I closed my eyes, trying to gather my thoughts, and there he was—the same man I had seen yesterday in my so-called dream. Fear washed over me, and I opened my eyes, wondering if I was hallucinating again or if I was still lying on the bed in my hotel room. Instead of clarity, my mind became more entangled. I was muddled, and even Ankit wasn't around to help me. But I took three deep breaths; sometimes, three deep breaths are enough to put things in place. And now, I knew what I had to do next—I walked straight to where that incident happened. It wasn't too far, but it wasn't an easy task with my injury. Moreover, I couldn't go straight there as soldiers patrolled everywhere, surveying the surroundings.

Finally, when I reached the spot, it was deserted. No civilians were around, only men in uniform. All the shops were closed. My brain seemed to stop working, and there wasn't anything I could think of. As the sun set and darkness descended, I returned to the hotel. I was fortunate that nobody spotted me wandering outside.

As I entered the hotel room, the door was open, and Ankit was brooding on the chair. "Do you have any idea that you jeopardized your life today?" he shouted at me. "If you don't care about your life, think about your mother and father. What would I tell them when they ask about you?"

The weight of his words sank in, and doubt crept into my mind for a moment. I knew he was angry, furious, and mad at me, but he had a point. It dawned on me that I had been behaving like a maniac lately. Perhaps it was because I couldn't accept that I was a loser. Nothing in life seemed to go my way, and all my dreams were falling apart without any control on my part. Unable to bear the weight of it all longer, tears burst forth like water from a dam streaming down my face. My muscles trembled, and I collapsed to my knees.

I Shouldn't Have Done This

I looked towards Ankit, hoping for some comfort. The throbbing in my head intensified—the side effect of living in constant fear and stress. A voice in my brain whispered, "You've given up again," and it grew louder and louder. But I hadn't given up; I had gone outside searching for Seerat, yet running around aimlessly felt futile. These conflicting arguments tore my soul apart, stealing my spirit and causing an unseen injury that no one else could perceive.

Ankit approached and helped me back to the bed. "Don't cry; I'm not asking you to give up. What I meant was that there's no point in roaming around and putting your life in danger," he said, offering me a glass of water to calm down.

"So, what should I do?" I asked Ankit after taking a sip.

"Just calm down, and let's think about what we can do," he replied, taking the glass from my hand and placing it on the table. "First of all, tell me what you want to eat. I'm starving."

I glanced at the menu, but Ankit intervened, "Don't bother looking. Due to restrictions, the hotel's kitchen is closed, and the waiter gave us only three limited options."

"Then why did you ask me? Just order something," I muttered, still feeling down.

We proceeded to the reception and ordered some Kashmiri Rogan Josh and a few Chapatis. "Do you want anything to drink?" Ankit asked.

"No, I'm fine," I replied, glancing at some local beverages the waiter offered. "Could you please bring the food to our room?" I asked him, as my swollen ankle made it challenging to move around.

"Have you managed to call your father?" I inquired as we returned to the room. Ankit was staring at his phone.

"No, I couldn't. There's no signal; the government has restricted phone and internet services for the local population to prevent rumors from spreading," he explained, displaying a sense of dejection.

I walked over to the chair where he sat and asked, "What's bothering you?"

161

I Shouldn't Have Done This

"I'm just worried about Kritika. What if something happens to me? She must be worried sick and these damn network issues," he said, looking at his phone and eventually throwing it away. His voice carried a tinge of anguish. It made me realize how self-centered I had been, only thinking about myself.

"Don't worry; everything will be fine. We'll get out of here soon, and you'll be back in Kritika's arms," I assured him, picking up his scattered phone. Just then, there was a knock on the door.

I opened it, and it was the waiter with our much-needed dinner. "Yes, everything is going to be alright. And you know, if Seerat is here in Kashmir, we will find her," Ankit said, his voice infused with determination.

As I handed the waiter a hundred rupee note as a tip, he said, "I couldn't help but overhear that you guys are looking for someone." He had the same accent as the shopkeeper I met on our first day in Kashmir, though he was a little shorter than the average local.

"Yes, but why does it matter to you?" Ankit couldn't comprehend why this stranger was interested in our conversation.

I felt his approach was inappropriate, but I intervened to avoid any unnecessary confrontation with the locals. "Yes, brother, we were indeed looking for someone. Can you help us?" I inquired politely.

The waiter replied, "Yes, I can. That's why I couldn't stop myself from asking. Even the other day, I noticed you were worried about someone. We Kashmiris understand the pain of losing our loved ones, and we never hesitate to lend a helping hand to others."

Ankit was unsure of how to proceed, and I wasn't entirely convinced, but I thought it was worth a shot if there was even a one percent chance of finding Seerat through his help. Without hesitation, I took a picture from my wallet, which I always kept with me, and handed it to the waiter.

"I don't know, man, how I'll ever repay you," I said, holding his hands, my eyes welling up with tears.

I Shouldn't Have Done This

The waiter reassured me, "I assure you, Sir Ji if she is in the Valley, we will find her. And you don't have to do anything special for me. I understand the pain of losing someone. I'm not doing this because I want something in return; I couldn't bear to see your pain."

After he left, my mind couldn't help but be consumed by thoughts of Seerat. Memories can be infectious; the real world seems nonsensical once you get obsessed with them. You drift from one memory to another, some evoking candid smiles while others remind you of the intense pain that makes you question your existence. Negative memories come at a price; they make you relive the pain you once endured, while positive memories bring a smile, assuring you that time has changed and what once belonged to you may no longer be yours.

"We should go now," Ankit said as he returned from the reception. With each passing day, surviving in the Valley was becoming increasingly challenging. We were trapped in the hotel and unable to venture outside due to the restrictions. Food supplies were dwindling, and our finances were running dry. Despite spending five days in the Valley, Hafiz couldn't locate Seerat, but he remained compassionate.

Throughout this ordeal, Major Brar had been a great support. He had arranged for a military van to take us back to Jammu, where we could return to Delhi. Perhaps Ankit's father had reached out to his friend, who happened to be Major Brar's senior, and that's how we received such assistance.

"Have you spoken to Hafiz?" I asked, reluctant to leave without finding Seerat.

"Yes, I asked him, and he said nobody has seen Seerat in the Valley," Ankit replied, packing some belongings. "Are you done with packing? He'll be here any moment to pick us up."

I Shouldn't Have Done This

"Yes, I'm almost done, but..." I hesitated. I didn't want to admit that I wasn't feeling right about leaving. Something inside me told me that Seerat was here, and I was on the verge of giving up on her.

"What's bothering you now?" Ankit sighed. Over the past five days, we had discussed every possibility of Seerat being in the Valley. Now, even Hafiz had given up, leaving me with no choice but to accept reality and leave.

"I don't know. Something feels off. I have this intuition that I'm not doing the right thing, that I should be out there fighting for Seerat instead of running away," I confessed.

Ankit moved closer, sitting next to me. "Listen, you've done everything a man could do, probably more than that. You risked entering the woods with your injured ankle when nobody else dared to leave their homes. You did all of that for her. Now, try to understand that you're not bailing on her. You have to accept the possibility that she's not here; it could have been a delusion or a simple misunderstanding."

His words brought a mix of emotions—relief and a tinge of disappointment. Part of me wanted to believe Seerat was safe and sound, not lost in the Valley. Yet, the lingering feeling that I should continue searching tugged at my heart.

"You're right," I finally said, trying to convince myself. "I must let go of this uncertainty and accept that Seerat might not be here. It's just so hard to accept."

Ankit placed a reassuring hand on my shoulder. "It's okay to feel this way. We'll keep her in our hearts; if destiny allows, we'll find her someday. For now, we need to leave and go back home. Our families must be worried sick, and we must assure them we're safe."

His words made sense, and reluctantly, I nodded in agreement. Deep down, I knew he was right, but the bond I shared with Seerat made it challenging to let go completely.

The military van arrived, and with a heavy heart, we bid farewell to the Valley and its mysteries. The journey back to Delhi felt long

I Shouldn't Have Done This

and arduous, and I couldn't help but replay the memories of our time in Kashmir, hoping that someday, somehow, we would find Seerat again.

Someone knocked on the door, and a new guy informed us that our van had arrived. I had been expecting Hafiz, with whom we had grown close during our time in the Valley. He had even treated us to a delightful Kashmiri gosht cooked by his wife, refusing any payment as he said, "We don't take money from our guests."

Curiosity got the better of me, and I inquired about Hafiz's whereabouts. The new guy replied uninterestedly, "He had to go to his village; his sister isn't doing well, so he left late at night."

Ankit and I gathered our bags and got into the van, accompanied by a guy around our age. He seemed eager to leave, reminding us we had to cross the border before 5 o'clock. But as I got into the van, I spotted Hafiz hurrying towards us, out of breath. I called him to express my gratitude for all he had done.

"Saab, Saab," Hafiz struggled to speak due to breathlessness. "I saw her, the girl you've been searching for. When I was returning from my sister's village, there was a group of protesters, and she was there with a camera. I believe she works for some news channel or newspaper."

His words stunned me, and I saw that Ankit was equally shocked. "Tell us where you saw her. We need to find her," I urged Hafiz.

"It's not far from here. I'll take you there," Hafiz said, happy to see a glimmer of hope in our eyes.

I pleaded with the van driver to drop us at Hafiz's village, but he refused, citing Major Brar's orders to take us to Jammu. Faced with a difficult decision, I left the van and searched for Seerat. Ankit was torn, understanding the gravity of our situation but also not willing to give up on the chance to find her.

"Meet. We've been stuck here for a week, and you know how much effort I put into arranging this opportunity. If we abandon it now, we might not get another chance. Major Brar helped us

I Shouldn't Have Done This

this time, but I doubt he'll do it again," Ankit reasoned, trying to persuade me to stay.

But I was resolute in my decision. "You go with this soldier then. I can't let this opportunity slip away. I have to find Seerat," I said, picking up my bag and heading out without looking back.

Upon reaching the location where Hafiz had seen Seerat, we found the area deserted, and everything appeared normal. Confusion engulfed me, and I asked Hafiz where she was. He, too, was at a loss, unsure of what had happened. "I don't know, Saabji. I swear I saw her speaking something in English with a microphone in her hand, but now everyone's gone. Maybe the military did something. They might have fired at the crowd. Let's go to my friend's place; he lives nearby. Maybe he knows what happened," Hafiz suggested.

I followed Hafiz to his friend's house, hoping to unravel the mystery of Seerat's sudden disappearance. The tension and uncertainty loomed significantly, and every passing moment felt like a lifetime. My heart raced with anticipation, wondering what fate had in store for us and whether we would ever find Seerat again.

We reached Hafiz's friend's house, and an eerie feeling crept over me as we approached. The place was secluded and surrounded by dense woods, giving off a strange vibe. Hafiz urged us to enter, and though I was anxious, I knew this might be my last chance to find Seerat.

With a heart filled with hope and trepidation, I followed Hafiz inside. My mind was racing with thoughts, and I silently prayed that this guy would have some information about Seerat's whereabouts. I couldn't afford to miss this opportunity; finding her was the only thing on my mind.

Upon entering the house, I was taken aback by what I saw. There, before me, stood Seerat. I couldn't believe my eyes; it was as if my heart had found its missing piece. Before I could utter a word, someone struck me with a stick, and everything went black as I fell unconscious.

Chapter 17

$\mathcal{A}$s I slowly regained consciousness, I found myself disoriented and unable to comprehend my surroundings. My vision was hazy, and it took some time for the blurry images to come into focus. As the dim light filtered through the cracks in the otherwise dark room, I could make out the figure of a man lying unconscious beside me. His battered and bruised face told a harrowing tale of the brutal treatment he had endured. A bloody split in his broken jaw added to the grimness of the scene, and I couldn't help but feel a surge of empathy for the man who shared this nightmarish fate with me.

The room itself was a sinister enigma, shrouded in darkness with no source of light, no windows, and no skylights. It felt like a malevolent void that had swallowed us whole, leaving us at the mercy of the unknown. My body was in excruciating pain, and I attempted to move, only to discover that my legs were tightly bound together. Every effort to free myself proved futile, and the pain in my hip was agonizing, making it clear that something was seriously wrong, perhaps even a broken hipbone. I was left immobilized, lying helplessly in that ominous room, wondering how I had ended up in this nightmarish situation.

My mind raced, trying to make sense of the events that had led me here. Hafiz, who had always been kind and helpful, had led me into this trap, and I couldn't comprehend why he would betray my trust in such a sinister way. It was hard to fathom that the person I had regarded as a friend had orchestrated this horrific ordeal.

With my body and mind grappling with the pain and confusion, I felt a sense of vulnerability like never before. The darkness around me seemed to embody the uncertainty and fear that had engulfed my world. I pondered what I could have done to deserve such a fate, but there were no answers, only an overwhelming sense of helplessness.

As I lay there, awaiting Hafiz's next move, I couldn't help but wonder what had driven him to commit such a sinister act. Was he under pressure from someone else, or had he concealed his true intentions all along? The questions swirled in my mind, but there was no one to provide answers, only the oppressive silence of the room.

In that moment of vulnerability, I realized the true nature of darkness – it wasn't merely the absence of light but a suffocating presence that seeped into every fiber of my being. I was at the mercy of forces beyond my control, and the fear of the unknown loomed.

Grappling with pain, confusion, and fear, I couldn't help but wish for a glimmer of hope, a chance to break free from the clutches of this malevolence. But in that dark room, hope felt like a distant dream, and I was left with nothing but the unsettling awareness that I was at the mercy of someone I had once trusted. My heart yearned for an escape, a way to unravel the mysteries of this grim situation, but for now, I was trapped in the darkness, with only my thoughts and fears for company.

Falling into the pit of unconsciousness, my thoughts swirled around the circumstances that had led me to this point. Suddenly, a voice pierced through the darkness, calling out my name. I immediately recognized that haunting voice – Seerat's voice, the one that had plagued my nights with its presence. At first, I questioned if I was hallucinating again, but the persistence of the voice dispelled any doubt. It sounded meek and filled with pain, leaving me with an unsettling feeling in the pit of my stomach.

Despite the darkness enveloping the room and my blurry vision, I could sense her presence nearby. Summoning all my remaining strength, I attempted to crawl towards her, desperate to find comfort in her familiar aura. However, my body refused to obey, and my limbs were too sore and uncooperative. I felt like a lifeless being, abandoned on the ground, waiting to fade into oblivion.

The pain surged through me, making it almost unbearable to endure. Gasping for breath, I attempted one last struggle to move, hoping against hope that I could somehow escape this fate. But it was in vain; I knew deep down that internal injuries were slowly claiming me, and my time was running out. The realization washed over me, and with a heavy heart, I accepted that my attempts to escape this plight were futile.

In the face of this cruel reality, I gave up. No matter how much I tried, I couldn't change the outcome. Resigned, I closed my eyes, hoping that with time, the pain would dull and I could find some semblance of peace before the end.

As she called my name again, her voice carried a sense of pain and hope that resonated deep within me. It was a hope that I could save her from this agony, that I had come here to find her, and that she would be free once more – much like the ray of light seeping through the crack in the door.

I longed to fulfill all her expectations, but the harsh reality was that I could not move. Opening my eyes, I shifted my gaze towards her. The rays of light had shifted, now falling upon her face. A purple and blue bruise covered her right cheek, and her eye had turned black and sunken into the socket. Blood still oozed from a swollen bruise near her eye.

Her eyes were closed, her hands tied to the chair, unconscious, and mumbling my name. She was the most beautiful girl I knew, and seeing her in this dreadful state tore at my soul. The lightning within me shook my body, and I struggled to rise to my feet, but I faltered and fell back to the floor. Determined, I crawled towards her and called out her name, but she remained unresponsive, lost in her own world.

I shook her leg gently, yet she still couldn't hear me, sitting there on the chair, unresponsive and unconscious. The rope that had bound her ankles to the chair had left red marks, evidence of her struggle. I knew she was braver than me, and she wouldn't have given in without putting up a fight.

I untied the rope from her ankles and wrists, and she slumped to the ground, still unconscious. I gazed at her face, her lower lip badly bruised and swollen. I recalled how she used to bite her lower lip, a gesture that always captivated me. Unable to resist, I gently touched her bruised cheek, and she groaned in pain.

I called her name, but she remained unresponsive, lost in her world. I used to call her "butterfly," a term of endearment that brought her joy. I vividly remembered the happiness on her face when I first called her that and the warmth of her embrace. I yearned for that moment again, for her to return to me.

Yet, now she lay lifeless in front of me, and I felt a wave of despair wash over me. I couldn't control myself and let out a howl of anguish. I had vowed to never lose her, but there I was, sitting helplessly beside her, feeling utterly defeated.

My hopes shattered, and I grumbled to the Almighty, questioning the fairness of it all. Gently, I cradled her lifeless body in my arms, and she whimpered and writhed in agony. I looked at her face, her eyes closed, and she murmured my name. "It's me, Meet. I am here with you. Everything will be fine; just open your eyes," I whispered, but she didn't respond, continuing to mumble my name. Gently, I cradled her head in my lap, ran my fingers through her hair, and spoke to her soothingly until she finally opened her eyes.

"Meet, is it you?" Her voice was weak, strained by the beating and pain she had endured.

"Yes, it's me." I held her hands and kissed them, and her whimpers transformed into sobs, then into heart-wrenching wails.

I was relieved that she had regained consciousness, but it pained me to see her in such a dreadful condition. My heart seethed with anger, wanting to exact revenge on those who had caused her harm.

After crying for what seemed like an eternity, she asked for water. In the darkness, I struggled to find anything. Crawling around, I managed to locate a pot in a corner. Though it had a little water, I could not carry it to her. With my legs tied, I had no choice but to crawl back to her with the pot in hand. As I reached her, ready to offer her the water, the door screeched open, and a man entered. He wore a long, ragged garment and carried a menacing gun. When he saw me near Seerat, he muttered something and kicked me in the gut. Without hesitation, he grabbed her by her hair and dragged her towards the door despite her desperate cries.

I couldn't bear to watch him treat her like this. Summoning my strength, I stood despite the rope around my ankles. Knowing I couldn't walk, I lunged towards the man to stop him. His eyes met mine for a split second – cold and devoid of fear. I tried to grab him, but my weakness was evident. He twisted my arm, causing excruciating pain to surge through my body. With a gut-wrenching punch to my stomach, I felt my strength waning. I collapsed to the ground, battered and breathless.

He glanced at Seerat, then at me, and coldly mumbled, "You are going to die," before spitting on my face. This would be the moment for me to fight back heroically in a movie, but this wasn't a movie. The pain was overwhelming, and I could barely think straight. Despite it all, one thing was clear: I couldn't let him take Seerat away from me. Summoning the last of my strength, I clenched onto his left foot.

"What the hell!" He cried, regaining his balance. "Do you also want to die?" His violent kick landed squarely on my face, breaking my nose. As I touched my nose, my hands were drenched in oozing scarlet liquid, but strangely, I felt no pain. It was as though I had become immune to the vicious blows raining upon me. He shouted

I Shouldn't Have Done This

something and two men rushed in to hold my arms, dragging me outside where other armed men stood guard.

The room we were taken to was small, yet more than ten men stood vigilantly, armed and ready. Curtains covered the windows, and I could see two guards stationed at the door, armed with automatic guns. On the other side of the room, trunks were stacked, and I feared they were filled with ammunition. They tied both of us to chairs at the center of the room.

A tall man descended from the staircase near the main entrance, and everyone present bowed before him, speaking words I couldn't comprehend. Though his face was masked, I could see his eyes burning with resentment and hatred.

"You have become conscious. I was waiting for that long," he taunted Seerat. She had regained consciousness, but the beating had left her too weak to say anything. Her head hung low, perhaps to avoid looking at the man, but primarily due to the excruciating pain she endured. He gripped her face, forcing her to look into his eyes.

"I don't have any enmity against you," he said to Seerat. "All I asked from you was a little favor, and you couldn't do it for me."

The confusion in the air was palpable as I struggled to make sense of the unfolding situation. Who were these people, and what was this favor they were referring to? It felt like a whirlwind of madness, spiraling out of control.

"Who is this guy?" one of them queried, glancing in my direction, prompting a surge of unease within me. If they didn't even recognize me, then what in the world was I doing there?

"Sahib, this man was searching everywhere for that reporter girl. We feared he might involve the police, so Hafiz brought him here. He even mentioned having connections with the Faujis," one of the men explained, shedding some light on the situation, though it only deepened my confusion.

"Hafiz, you've always been a dedicated soldier, prioritizing our mission above all else," their leader began, his tone shifting as he

I Shouldn't Have Done This

approached Hafiz, who stood nearby with a proud stance, basking in the praise. "But today, your actions have endangered our mission."

With a swift motion, their leader delivered a resounding slap to Hafiz, the sudden shift in the atmosphere leaving Hafiz visibly shaken, his earlier pride replaced by apprehension.

"You knew his connection to the Fauji, yet you brought him here. What if that Fauji had come looking for him?" Their leader's words were laced with tension as he leveled his gun at Hafiz, the gravity of the situation hitting him like a ton of bricks. Hafiz dropped to his knees, pleading for forgiveness in the face of his folly.

"The Fauji left for the airport with the other man," Hafiz muttered, his voice trembling with fear. "They won't find us here."

Their leader lowered his gun, a semblance of mercy evident in his actions. "You're a man of faith, Hafiz. Everyone makes mistakes, and even God forgives the first one. Who am I to punish you?" he remarked, his tone softer as Hafiz crawled towards him, kissing his feet in a display of remorse.

He turned to me and said, "But this guy here, he's no use to us, so there's no point keeping him around."

I was scared, realizing my time might be up. But this time, I didn't give in. I fought till the end. I had few regrets, except for not being able to live my life with Seerat. Maybe it was just my fate to be without her. Still, I felt grateful for the time we spent together. It was the best time of my life.

Before he could lift his gun, I heard Seerat speak up. "Don't do anything to him. I'll do whatever you want."

He looked at Seerat and laughed. "Look, the little girl can speak now," he sneered. I sensed something was happening but couldn't figure out what. What help could Seerat possibly be to them? "It's been three days," he continued, his tone harsh. "She hasn't said a word. I tried to warn her nicely that things would get rough if she didn't cooperate. But she was stubborn, only agreeing to talk now to save this guy." He laughed again.

I couldn't understand what this man was saying or what he wanted from Seerat. All I knew was that she still cared for me deeply, agreeing to something to save my life without hesitation. Something she clearly didn't want to do, enduring so much pain for my sake.

"Open her hands and make all the preparations," he barked.

"Sir, the other guy, he's still out cold," one of the men behind him replied.

"Then wake him up. I want everything ready by tomorrow," he commanded before leaving the room, followed by two other men.

Another masked man untied our hands, threw us back into the dark room, and locked the door. The darkness seemed even thicker this time, or perhaps our eyes just needed time to adjust. After all these years, I was finally with Seerat, but I couldn't see her. I had always imagined our reunion, but never in my wildest dreams like this. I used to think I'd have so many questions for her, but now, with her here, I had nothing to ask. Though I couldn't see her, I could feel her presence and crawled toward her, taking her hand. She started sobbing, in pain, and unable to move much due to her injuries, but she still reached out and hugged me.

At that moment, I realized that love was the most beautiful thing in the world. All the other pursuits seemed meaningless compared to the presence of your loved one. My eyes filled with tears, not from the pain I was enduring but from the sheer joy of being reunited with her. Soon, her sobs turned into heart-wrenching cries.

We lay on the ground, holding each other tightly, craving closeness as if fearing this moment was too good to be true, that it might vanish like a dream once we woke up. So we embraced it fully, sinking into a pool of memories. I remembered the first time I saw Seerat in her apartment, her sleepy eyes filled with dreams. Back then, I had no idea the power those beautiful eyes would hold over me. The first time our lips met, I knew I would wait a lifetime to feel that connection again. And the first time we made love, I realized I could spend eternity with her.

I Shouldn't Have Done This

Though death loomed over us, I found myself more afraid of living without her than of dying. The thought of losing her haunted me. So, after she quieted down, still cradled in my arms, I asked Seerat, "Who are these people, and what do they want from you?"

"They're just local thugs, calling themselves 'soldiers of freedom' under the name Tableegh-al-Mukhlasi. They claim they're fighting for Kashmir's independence from India, citing the loss of loved ones to Indian soldiers. But it's all nonsense. They're just pawns of local politicians vying for power in the valley. Since Kashmir became a union territory, these politicians and their lackeys are lost and desperate. Three days ago, while I was covering a protest against the government, they abducted me and my cameraman and brought us here," she explained, her voice tinged with pain yet steely determination. Now I understood their motives, and the other man lying nearby was our cameraman.

"They want me to report their message to the Indian population and government," she concluded.

"So, what's the problem with this?" I inquired, struggling to grasp the situation. After all, journalists often seize such opportunities to advance their careers.

"The issue lies in the manipulation of Kashmiri sentiments by this select group of individuals. For years, they've exploited the emotions of the Kashmiri people for their own gain. Countless lives have been lost due to their actions. They've instilled a deep-seated animosity towards their own country, convincing them that Indian soldiers and the government are their enemies. As the Indian government attempts to bring positive change, they seek to sow dissent again. If they manage to broadcast their message nationally, it will incite not only riots and protests in Kashmir but across India," Seerat explained.

"Why did you risk your life for this? You could have simply alerted your superiors and let them handle it. Why put yourself in danger?" I questioned.

I Shouldn't Have Done This

"Because I didn't want to live anymore. I tried, but living without you was unbearable. Not a night passed without thoughts of you consuming me. I thought I could cope, but I was wrong. So when these people captured me, I saw it as an opportunity to end the pain," she replied, her voice faltering, tears welling in her eyes.

"Why did you leave me?" The forbidden question slipped from my lips, a query I had long suppressed. Yet, as the words hung, I hesitated to hear her response. I had endured their physical torment, but I wasn't sure I could bear the agony of her answer.

"I..." Before she could say anything, a man in white clothes burst into the room accompanied by two others, his face contorted with anger as he shouted at the others. Another man arrived carrying a bucket of water, dousing the still unconscious cameraman on the floor. Frustrated by the lack of response, he kicked the prone figure in frustration. It seemed clear he bore responsibility for preparing everything, as their leader had instructed.

Upon noticing Seerat and me lying together, he stormed towards us, kicking me in the face and seizing my hair, dragging me forcibly from the room. Desperate to break free, I grasped his hand, but he showed no signs of relenting.

Glancing back, I saw Seerat's tear-streaked face, her pleas falling on deaf ears as she begged for our lives. With a grim finality, another man slammed the door shut, and the sharp crack of a gunshot pierced the air, freezing me in disbelief. Everything seemed to grind to a halt, the sound of a heavy thud reverberating through the room.

The man dragging me suddenly collapsed to the ground, blood pooling around his shattered skull. Shock coursed through me; I had never witnessed such a gruesome sight before. As the metallic tang of blood touched my skin, reality crashed down upon me. I staggered and bolted towards Seerat, still trapped in darkness.

The cacophony of gunshots outside intensified, and the room erupted into chaos as everyone scrambled for their weapons, taking up defensive positions at the windows.

I rushed into the room and swiftly closed the door, blocking the chaos beyond. Seerat remained sprawled on the ground, her strength depleted. Hurrying to her side, I attempted to help her up, but her injuries rendered her almost immobile. Despite my efforts, my broken ankle hindered any significant assistance I could provide.

"Seerat, we need to get out of here," I urged, even as the barrage of bullets continued to rain through the splintering wooden door.

Struggling to respond, she whispered, "I'm trying," her voice strained with pain and exhaustion. Her battered form seemed incapable of even the slightest movement. Desperately, I clasped both of her hands, endeavoring to pull her to safety. Though my injured ankle screamed in protest, there was no time to dwell on the pain. Summoning every ounce of strength I possessed, I managed to drag her to the side of the door.

The door now resembled a shredded barrier, offering little protection against the onslaught outside. Faint light streams illuminated the room through the bullet-riddled gaps, casting eerie shadows across the scene. I moved to reposition the still-unconscious man lying in harm's way, but Seerat's grip on my arm halted me. Though she uttered no words, her eyes spoke volumes.

Her silent plea was unmistakable at that moment amidst the chaos and danger.

But I couldn't leave the man lying there unconscious. Though I didn't know him, I couldn't shake the thought that he, too, must have a family. Someone anxiously awaiting his return, someone who loved him deeply, someone whose world would crumble if he didn't come home.

Reflecting on my imperfections and past mistakes, I realized our decisions shape who we are. Whether regrettable or not, each choice contributes to the person we become. I am but a culmination of every drink consumed, every cigarette smoked, every book devoured, every sleepless night sacrificed in pursuit of my dreams, and every excuse I've made.

I Shouldn't Have Done This

Throughout my life, I've made countless excuses and deceived myself about my mistakes. I was tired of the lies I told myself. Meeting Seerat's gaze, I nodded in determination, and she returned the look, her battered face unable to muster a smile.

At that moment, we both understood the weight of our decisions and the necessity of facing their consequences head-on.

As the cameraman lay unconscious and bullets continued to pierce through the door, I mustered every ounce of strength I had left to crawl toward him. Dragging a grown man with a broken ankle proved to be an agonizing task, the pain nearly unbearable. Despite the temptation to leave him behind, I pushed aside the thought when my eyes met Seerat's. Enough excuses; it was time to do what was right. With sheer determination, I pulled him away from the line of fire until he was safely out of harm's way.

Crawling back to Seerat, I took her hand and kissed her forehead, a silent reassurance amidst the chaos. Suddenly, the door was kicked open, flooding the room with blinding light. Instinctively, I shielded Seerat behind me, refusing to let them take her away.

As figures wielding guns entered the room, my vision blurred from the intensity of the light. Among them, I glimpsed a familiar face—Ankit. Relief washed over me at the sight of someone I could trust. Exhausted and drained, I closed my eyes, surrendering to the darkness with the unwavering belief that Ankit would save us.

Chapter 18

"Wake up and have your soup," Seerat said softly as she placed the bowl on the table beside my bed. Gently, she helped me sit up and adjusted the pillow behind my back. Her caring eyes met mine as she handed me the warm soup. She was dressed in a snug-fitting red Kurti that accentuated her beauty. A stray strand of hair fell across her face, and she casually tucked it behind her ear, letting her hair down from the messy bun she had worn while toiling away in the kitchen, which left her Kurti damp with sweat.

It had been over three months since the unfortunate incident that could have cost me my life. Strangely, the thought of death didn't scare me as much as the idea of living without Seerat. It might sound clichéd, considering how books and movies often depict love as some grand, dramatic gesture. But the truth is, love is a tender and beautiful feeling that blossoms in our hearts, and it doesn't require expressing grandiose acts. Sometimes, simple gestures, like holding hands or taking a leisurely walk together, can work magic.

People often say that when two individuals share a common destination, they make excellent companions. However, in their pursuit of reaching that destination, they usually forget to relish the journey. Life becomes a never-ending cycle of setting and achieving goals, each time reaching for something bigger and more challenging. The cycle continues perpetually, with no end in sight. It dawned on me that we should cherish the journey and savor every moment instead of focusing solely on the destination. We must learn to appreciate the beauty of life's unfolding chapters, for they are what truly matter.

I longed to walk beside Seerat during the enchanting sunsets, but circumstances had robbed me of that simple pleasure.

As I reminisce about our journey together, I cherish the subtlest moments we shared, unspoken words, and how our hearts connected. Love is a delicate thread woven into life's tapestry, binding us with an unbreakable bond.

For three long, challenging months, my ankle remained broken, rendering me unable to walk. Despite undergoing two surgeries, my recovery seemed frustratingly slow. Throughout this challenging period, Seerat, a caring soul, stood by my side, tending to my every need with unwavering support.

She gracefully took the empty soup bowl from my hands and gently helped me shift to the wheelchair. "Come on, let's go outside," she suggested, opening the door to let the cold Kashmiri winds brush against my face. As I looked around, I couldn't help but feel pity for the people of this land, who had endured hardships for decades due to the greed of a select few.

Our temporary residence in Kashmir was provided by Seerat's office, but I couldn't help but sense her inner struggle. Her face still bore some bruises from the past, serving as a reminder of the horrors she had faced. With a hint of sadness in her eyes, she brought a chair from inside and settled beside me.

"You should return to your office now; I'll be fine," I suggested, trying not to burden her further.

"Don't start that again," she replied, firm but tinged with love. "I've told you, I don't want to live or work here anymore. This place is a constant reminder of the horrors I've experienced. My boss understands, and he has granted me the time I need to recover from the trauma. Once I'm ready, we'll leave for Delhi together."

I couldn't help but marvel at Seerat's unwavering commitment to me, even in the face of her healing process. Yet, I couldn't shake

I Shouldn't Have Done This

the guilt for burdening her. She cared for everything, cooked, and managed household chores while supporting me wholeheartedly. I didn't want her to put her life on hold for me.

"Would you like to go inside, or would you prefer to stay here a little longer?" she asked, her concern evident.

"I'll sit here for a while," I replied.

"Tea?" she offered, already aware of my answer.

"Thank you, but I'm fine," I declined, not wanting to impose further.

"Don't be so formal; I'm making some anyway," she chuckled, her warmth filling the space around us.

Seerat's love and care enveloped me in a way I had never experienced before. These past three months had deepened our connection, making me realize how much I truly loved her. However, I couldn't let my emotions overshadow the reality. There was a chance I might never regain full mobility, and I couldn't bear the thought of holding Seerat back from her dreams and aspirations.

Seerat brought each steaming cup of tea and settled into the chair beside me. Nothing was better than a hot cup of tea on a winter morning, especially with the delightful aroma of cardamom and a hint of ginger that Seerat added. Her culinary skills were magical; every dish she made perfectly blended flavors and nutrition. Unlike my Punjabi mother, who believed that taste was directly proportional to the butter used, Seerat's cooking was a delight. I couldn't help but miss my mother, and it saddened me that we hadn't been able to meet since the incident due to travel restrictions. She had been distraught when she heard about my broken ankle, and we had decided not to burden her with the truth about the Tableegh-al-Mukhlasi and the kidnapping. Instead, I told her it happened during a trek, and she scolded me like a caring mother as if I were a five-year-old who had fallen from a bicycle.

"Any plans for today?" I asked Seerat, attempting to initiate a conversation. Ever since we started living together, she seemed quieter, and the spark that once defined us appeared to have faded. I understood that she was still healing from the trauma, so I tried my best to keep her distracted with conversations, even though most ended with one-word answers. I never liked one-word answers, not even when we first met, and we used to chat on the phone for hours, exchanging details about our lives. Now, living together in the same room, we seemed to have nothing to discuss.

"No, just the routines," she replied briefly, thwarting my efforts to engage her.

"How about watching a movie today?" I suggested, eager to spend more time with her.

"No, I'm not in the mood to waste time. I have a lot of work to do," she replied.

"No problem, I'll do it for you," I said, trying to bring some light to the moment. It earned a chuckle from her, and I couldn't help but smile.

Seerat fetched her laptop, and we decided to watch a movie. I wanted something light and enjoyable, a romantic comedy that could make us laugh. As I scrolled through the list of movies, I saw that it seemed like a collection of IMDb's top 50 films. While they were undoubtedly great choices, I yearned for something that could lift our spirits and bring back some of the joy we once shared. So, I chose a rom-com from the list.

"We'll put the laptop on the table in the living room," I said as we settled into the space. Though it wasn't the intimate movie-watching experience I envisioned, being beside Seerat comforted me. I reminisced about our moments together, lying on a bed, watching movies, laughing, and cuddling. I longed for those carefree days when our connection felt so strong.

As the movie began, I glanced at Seerat, who had already dozed off, looking like an innocent child who fell asleep anywhere after playtime. I wheeled myself over to her, fetched a blanket, and gently covered her without disturbing her slumber. Observing her peaceful

I Shouldn't Have Done This

state, I couldn't help but marvel at the unbreakable bond we shared. Even though life had thrown challenges our way, our connection remained solid and unwavering.

I decided to turn off the laptop; watching her sleep was more captivating than any film. At that moment, I realized that we may have been living together but not truly together. Still, the depth of our bond gave me hope that someday, we would reclaim the intimacy and joy we once had. Until then, I cherished each moment with Seerat and embraced the strength of our unbreakable love.

A few minutes later, my phone buzzed, and I saw it was Ankit calling. "Damn," I whispered, not wanting to disturb Seerat's sleep, so I hurriedly cut the call. I took my phone and Wheeled myself to the balcony. A moment later, it buzzed again, and I decided to answer this time.

"How are you, buddy?" Ankit's voice was filled with delight.

"I'm good. How about you?" It had been ages since we last met. The last time I saw him, I was almost dead, and we hadn't had a chance to catch up since then.

"Hey, listen. I talked to Major Brar, who has permitted us to meet you."

"That's great! So, what's the plan? When will you come?"

"Tomorrow," he replied.

A bit short notice, but it was still great news.

"I hope it's fine with you," he added when I didn't answer for a while.

"Yes, absolutely. If it wasn't for you, I would be dead."

"Now, don't get started again." His voice was humble. "I have to go and pack for tomorrow."

* * * * *

"He just called; he'll be here in an hour," I informed Seerat, who was busy preparing dinner. Though she wanted to do something special for him, I suggested she not worry about formalities. "If it wasn't for me, we wouldn't be alive," she replied, and her remark cracked me up.

"What?" she asked, slightly irritated.

"Nothing," I said, containing my laughter not to upset her.

As I was cutting vegetables, the doorbell rang. "It must be Ankit," I said confidently.

"I'll get it," Seerat offered, opening the door. And there he was, standing before us our hero, our savior. No, it wasn't Superman; it was Ankit.

He had changed since the last time I saw him, a beard and some extra weight. Dressed in a blue jacket and carrying a black backpack, he entered and warmly hugged Seerat. "How are you?" he asked, but someone else walked in Kritika before she could reply. What a surprise! Ankit hadn't mentioned her yesterday; even today, he kept quiet about her.

I glanced at Seerat; she didn't seem as happy as I expected. The colors on her beautiful face had momentarily faded. I couldn't understand; weren't they best friends?

"How's the surprise?" Ankit inquired, his smile reaching from ear to ear like a WhatsApp emoji.

Kritika came and hugged Seerat. "Everybody is hugging her; what's wrong with you people? I'm here too!"

We laughed, and I embraced Kritika as well. "How are you? It's been a long time since we met."

"Just four months," I said, inviting her to sit beside me on the sofa.

"Four months is a long time," she replied.

"Come with me, Kritika. Let me show you the bathroom. Freshen up, and then I'll serve dinner; you must be hungry." Seerat said, smiling oddly. Was something wrong that I couldn't understand? It seemed like she didn't like Kritika sitting beside me.

"Yes, and I want to chat with you too. So much to catch up on." Kritika stood up and followed Seerat to her room.

I Shouldn't Have Done This

"How are you, buddy?" Ankit came and sat beside me, taking Kritika's previous seat.

"I am good, bro. By the way, that's a nice surprise." I playfully punched him on the arm, making him blush.

"So?"

"So what?" I teased, knowing he wasn't good with social conventions.

"So, what did the doctor say?"

"About what?" I chuckled, leaving no chance to poke fun.

"About your ankle."

"Oh, yes. I have an appointment with him next week. He'll do some tests, and based on the progress, he'll tell us whether I need one more surgery or not. If things look good, he might recommend physiotherapy, and I could be on my feet again."

"That's great news." Ankit hugged me. He was genuinely a nice guy. Not many genuinely feel happy for others; people are becoming selfish and caring only about their money and themselves, but he wasn't one of them. He put his life at stake to save mine. "How are things between you and Seerat?" He glanced towards Seerat's room and whispered in my ear.

"Um..." That was a difficult question to answer. It felt like being in a viva, and the examiner asked a question I wasn't unprepared for. I struggled to find the right words to begin with.

Before I could respond, Seerat returned. "You should also go and freshen up in Meet's room."

"Oh yes, I'll show you where the bathroom is." I eagerly grabbed the opportunity to change the topic.

"That's fine. Just tell me where it is, and I'll go."

He left the room, leaving Seerat and me alone in the dining area.

"Food is delicious, I must say," Ankit complimented as he took another serving of Shahi Paneer and added it to his already-filled plate.

185

I Shouldn't Have Done This

"Thank you," Seerat responded warmly, helping him with chicken and chapatis. "I made it especially for you. I didn't get the chance to properly thank you for what you did for us."

"Yes," I said, "You left for Delhi before I regained consciousness."

"I did tell you guys the whole story," Ankit replied, still focused on the Shahi Paneer, "but are you still blaming me?"

"You didn't tell me the whole story," Kritika interjected, breaking her silence for the first time.

"What?" Ankit looked at her, seemingly annoyed by the interruption. "I told you before."

"Yes, your heroic saga. I don't want to hear that again. I want to know what actually happened," Kritika insisted.

"Alright," Ankit began to recount, "Meet and I came here to meet Major Brar for our project. As you know, the meeting didn't go well. On our way back to the hotel, the riots erupted due to the abrogation of article 370, but we were unaware as our phones weren't working. We got caught in the mob, and Meet was hit by a stone, leaving him unconscious near our hotel.

When he regained consciousness, he claimed to have seen Seerat. At first, I thought he had gone mad, talking about some spirit guide. Despite the chaos, we tried to find her, but all efforts were in vain.

Hafiz then approached us and said he had seen Seerat, so Meet went with him, and I headed back to the airport. However, I couldn't leave him alone, So after a few miles I asked the driver to take me back.

We went to the location Hafiz mentioned, but nobody was there. We spoke to a few soldiers on duty, who confirmed that there were no riots in that area. Something felt off, and I immediately called Major Brar to share everything.

I showed him a picture of Hafiz, and he informed me he had connections with a local militant group called Tableegh-al-Mukhlasi. Major Brar revealed that they were after the group's leader, Fakri, but his powerful connections made it difficult to take action.

I Shouldn't Have Done This

Following his leads and after finding you, he planned the rescue operation. He was determined to bring down Fakri, who was responsible for the deaths of hundreds of innocent lives.

After rescuing you, Major Brar made sure you received immediate medical help at the military hospital, and when you were out of danger, he approached me. Since outsiders weren't allowed in an army hospital, he asked me to leave, but he assured me he would take care of you and kept his promise."

Ankit recounted the entire incident to Kritika once more.

"I have some good news for you guys," Ankit announced with a smile.

My excitement grew; it had been ages since I'd heard any good news. I wondered what it could be, but instead of guessing, I asked, "What is it?"

Ankit began, "As you know, Major Brar is a good man, and he helped us a lot." He glanced at me for support, and I nodded, grateful for Major Brar's assistance when I was in the military hospital, unconscious. "I stayed in constant touch with him, checking on your well-being."

Curious, I listened intently, my eyes fixed on Ankit.

"And I persuaded him to consider our project. He spoke to his seniors, and they said yes. They will be funding us, and soon, we have to go and meet him again to sign the contract."

"Wow, that's the best news ever! I can't contain my excitement. I would have hugged you if I could stand up," I exclaimed.

"But there's more," Ankit said, raising both hands as if to ask for patience. My curiosity intensified.

"I also talked to Tushar about it, and he was willing to waive off our loan for a stake of five percent. Additionally, he's ready for technology transfer and could invest more if needed."

I had forgotten about that ruthless, inhuman creature. "I'm not sure about him. We can't give him a stake without consulting Major

Brar. And if Major Brar can help us pay back our loans, we don't need to give Tushar any stakes," I pointed out.

"Yes, you're right. We will discuss this with Major Brar. I will fix a meeting with him once you're feeling better."

"Sure, we have a lot of work to do before that."

"Of course, but there's one more good news before discussing work."

One more piece of good news? What could be better than this? Ankit had already made my day. It had been years since I heard good news, and here he was, sitting in front of me, delivering one news after another.

"Me and Kritika decided to get married," he dropped the bomb.

Seerat looked at Kritika, and they both shouted joyfully, hugging each other. "Why didn't you tell me this before?" Seerat congratulated both of them.

"Really, it's the best news ever! Both my best friends are getting married. What else could a man ask for?" I was genuinely happy for both of them. Ankit truly deserved all the happiness in the world. He saved my life, my company and didn't leave Kashmir without me.

He has changed so much. I still remember when he was a kid, he would get beaten up by teachers for not doing his homework. Everyone made fun of him in college for his perceived "dumbness," but he never let that affect him. Ankit was always a free-spirited soul. He has grown into a mature, sensible, and responsible man.

"When are you guys planning to get married?" Ankit asked Seerat.

"Mature my foot! Ankit holds a PhD in blabberology and a black belt in foot-in-mouth disease! He didn't even let me finish my view of him being mature and sensible before he proved me wrong!"

Seerat looked at me, and I looked down awkwardly. There was nothing between us since we got back together, and I hadn't brought up the topic because I was content with what we had. I didn't want to jeopardize things by rushing into marriage.

"We are not thinking about it. Our only priority is to get him back on his feet, and that's all we're working on," she replied calmly. I was relieved she didn't get upset or anything.

"It's getting late now, and you guys must be tired. You should go to bed. Both of you can sleep in my room, and I'll sleep on the couch," Seerat suggested.

"No need to sleep on the couch. We're not married yet, and we're not sharing a room," Kritika said firmly.

"But," before Ankit could finish his sentence, Kritika shot her sternly, and he stopped.

"So, you can sleep with me, and Ankit can sleep with Meet. After all, they are old roomies," Seerat said, and they both chuckled.

* * * * *

"Have you lost your mind?" I wanted to shout, but I managed to keep my voice under control. I confronted Ankit when he came to sleep in my room.

"What happened?" he asked innocently.

"What happened?" I repeated his words, struggling to find the right way to express my anger and annoyance without hurting his feelings. I didn't want to make the same mistake I made in the past, saying things that would cause harm. "You're asking me this? Tell me, what was the need to ask when you guys are going to get married?" I mimicked him, sounding like a nursery kid.

"Trust me, bro, I did it on purpose."

"Of course you did. You can't bear to see me happy and want to ruin my joy. Isn't that your purpose?"

"Don't be ridiculous," he said, rolling his eyes.

"I am being ridiculous." Why was I just echoing his lines? It's a common tendency when we don't know what to say next; we simply repeat the other person like a puppet.

I Shouldn't Have Done This

"Calm down and listen to me." He handed me a glass of water, and though I wasn't thirsty, I took a few sips to calm myself down. I took some deep breaths and focused on listening to what he had to say.

"I knew why she left you." Those were not the words I expected, and I felt my anger rising again. That question had haunted me, and my life was shattered trying to figure out why she left me. I wanted to punch him in the face, but I managed to restrain myself.

He continued, "A few days back, Kritika told me." Relief washed over me; he wasn't as big of a traitor as I thought. "You know that Kritika had feelings for you. You told me that yourself, remember?"

I remembered that night, just a day before we were supposed to go to Kashmir. We had a big fight, and I blurted out my feelings like a five-year-old in a moment of weakness. "Yes, and I already apologized for that."

"No, it's not about the apology. Let me finish first. You know that Seerat's father died when she was little." I couldn't fathom where he was going with this. "Kritika and Seerat's father were friends, and when Seerat's father died, he cared for everything. He paid for her school education, college education, and the rent of the room they used to live in. So, when she learned that Kritika loves you, she felt indebted and left you for her."

The revelation hit me like a ton of bricks. "What the fuck? She left me so that Kritika could have me? Who am I? A toy sacrificed for her friend?" The words left me speechless and seeped with hurt.

"Now, with Kritika and me getting married, there shouldn't be any issues for her returning to you. Go get her, bro."

I looked at him, still unable to process everything. How do I respond to this unexpected twist in my life? The emotions overwhelmed me, and I could only manage a feeble smile before lying on the bed, staring into the darkness.

The room was silent, and my mind was in turmoil as I tried to sort through my feelings and make sense of what had just been revealed.

Chapter 19

"What the heck are you doing? And why haven't you changed yet?" I shouted at Ankit as I entered his room, finding him still in his pajamas.

"Yes, yes, I know…" He replied, but not to me, but to someone he was talking to on his phone. I snatched the phone from his hand and saw Kritika's photo on the screen, saved as "Sweetheart."

"Hi, wait for some time; he's coming to bring you home once and for all," I said, ending the call. Ankit was getting married to Kritika, and we were already running late. "Why aren't you ready yet? Everyone is waiting for you!"

"I don't know, man. I'm nervous. I'm not sure if I'm ready to get married," he said, pacing around his room like a restless stallion. He lit a cigarette and took a long puff, adding to his agitation.

I couldn't fathom what was bothering him. They had been together for so many years and decided to get married six months ago. Last week, he was thrilled and busy shopping for the perfect Sherwani for his dream wedding. But now, on the wedding day, he had second thoughts.

"Calm down," I said, trying to get him to focus. "Come here and sit. Tell me, what's really bothering you?"

He took a deep breath and pondered for a moment. It seemed he didn't even know exactly what the problem was. "I don't know, man. Isn't it too soon to get married? Our company is still not making money and is still in debt. Shouldn't I wait to settle down first?" he blabbered.

I Shouldn't Have Done This

I couldn't help but wonder what was wrong with people these days. There was a time when some got married at the age of thirteen, and while I'm certainly against child marriage, now the pendulum has swung to the other extreme. The legal age for men to get married is now twenty-one, and yet most of my friends are in their late twenties or early thirties and still not married. They all want to settle down first and enjoy life before committing to marriage.

I don't have a problem with that, but I'm not a big fan of this culture. The average life expectancy of a human being is around sixty to seventy years, and the first half of it is often spent just getting settled. The last ten to fifteen years are often spent meeting doctors and battling diseases. So, we spent very few years with our life partner when we could enjoy life together.

Why do we have to achieve our dreams separately before marriage? Why can't we have shared dreams and goals where we nurture each other towards our aspirations? Two people working together to chase a shared dream is more accessible than working alone, just like a 400m relay is more manageable than running solo for 400m.

"Ankit's father urged us to hurry as we were already late. Following the plan, Ankit, two of our college friends, and I piled into Ankit's car while his parents accompanied his father's boss in another vehicle.

Uncle gave us directions to the assembly point, half a kilometer from the farmhouse. The wedding venue they booked was located in the far corner of the city, and considering the notorious Delhi traffic, reaching there in less than one and a half hours seemed improbable.

"Drive faster," Ankit said as he received a message. Though I didn't know who sent it, I was sure it was from Kritika, eagerly waiting for him.

I glanced at Ankit. "Even if we drive fast, we can't go to the venue without everyone else."

I Shouldn't Have Done This

He nodded and typed a response. As we reached the assembly point, a chariot and a dozen people stood there, holding lights. Eventually, his father and the rest of the group arrived, and the Baraat was ready to set off. The tradition of the groom travelling to the wedding venue on a mare, surrounded by relatives and friends, had evolved from a mere custom to a show of affluence. The road was alive with beautiful girls dancing in their resplendent attire, uncles discussing Indian politics with a glass of whiskey, and a few Aunts flaunting their opulent gold jewelry.

Upon arriving at the venue, we encountered some girls who stopped us at the gate, tying a red ribbon and demanding thirty-one thousand rupees for entry. It was another North Indian custom that didn't interest me much. The bride's sister typically performs this ritual, I encountered Nikita, who had blossomed into a stunning woman. The last time I saw her, she was merely a young girl accompanying Kritika. However, their ethereal presence didn't hold my attention; my eyes searched for Seerat, but she was nowhere to be found. Unable to wait for entry at the main gate, I opted for another entrance for workers.

Inside, the farmhouse exuded grandeur; Kritika's father had spared no expense. Adorned with lights and red flowers, it resembled a luxurious five-star lounge. The festivities were in full swing, with a DJ playing Bollywood beats on one side and guests indulging in complimentary snacks and drinks on the other.

Yet, Seerat remained elusive. I suspected she was with Kritika in the bridal room, but joining them amidst the swarm of relatives and friends seemed impossible. Instead, I sent her a WhatsApp message: "Where are you?"

After a minute, I noticed the two blue ticks, indicating that she had read my message but hadn't replied. Frustration mounted as I sent another text, "Come outside, I'm waiting for you, dying to meet you."

Again, she read the message without responding. What did she want? I felt exasperated, wondering what she thought of herself.

Seeking solace, I called a waiter and ordered some whiskey to calm my nerves. After some time, I began to feel more relaxed. I rechecked my WhatsApp, but there was still no reply. Before I could type anything else, they allowed the Baraat inside, and I spotted Ankit. I went to join him.

"Where were you?" he asked.

"Just having a few drinks," I replied, and he smiled.

Ankit proceeded to the stage, set on one corner of the farmhouse, and settled on the giant sofa specially decorated for the new couple. Photographers swarmed around him, capturing him in his Sherwani, resembling a character from Mughal-e-Azam. He was glowing with happiness, and why shouldn't he be? It was his big day. Lost in thought, I daydreamed about standing in his place, waiting for Seerat, who would be mine for the rest of our lives. "The bride is here!" someone shouted, pulling me back to reality.

The photographers left the groom to capture the bride's picture, as she was the center of attention. Kritika looked breathtaking in her red apparel, adorned with exquisite gold jewelry, exuding traditional elegance with a touch of modernity. Her hair was styled in a bun, with a few strands elegantly curled and colored brown, framing her face.

Walking gracefully beneath a red decorated scarf held up by her brothers, Kritika was accompanied by her cousins and friends. The photographers didn't miss a single angle while the DJ played a traditional folk song, adding to the mesmerizing atmosphere. My mind wandered again, and I imagined Seerat marrying me in the bride's place. The reality returned when someone bumped into me, and I saw her—Seerat walking beside Kritika.

Clad in a pink lehenga, Seerat looked like an angel. Unlike Kritika, she opted not to wear any jewelry, yet she outshone everyone in the crowd. Her long black hair cascaded loosely, partially concealing her bareback, revealing a glimpse of her amber skin beneath.

As I gazed at her, I remembered why I had longed for her all these years. No matter how much others advised me to move on, I couldn't. She was the one made for me, the one who completed me. Meeting anyone else wouldn't change that; I would always feel incomplete without her, and my life would never be the same.

I texted her again, "You look marvelous today."

Seerat glanced at her phone, and I saw her sensuous smile. It was the most beautiful thing I had seen in a while. Her smile was like sunshine; at that moment, I felt sunburned, entirely captivated by her.

She searched the crowd, and I stealthily slipped into a group of admirers, trying to hide from her in plain sight. Within moments, her message appeared on my phone: "Where are you?"

"Not far from you. Stop searching; you're spoiling the ceremony video," I replied.

She read the message, glanced around once more, and then spoke to Kritika, who was posing for photographers. Seerat moved away from the spotlight, and the DJ's lights cast a rainbow glow around her as she shifted her stance.

As she approached me, I skillfully moved deeper into the crowd, drawn in by the chatter about the breathtaking bride—Kritika's beauty was the talk of the town. Some boys snapped pictures, promising their future partners the same beauty, while a few girls gossiped about Kritika's hairstyle and her choice of jewelry.

My phone rang again, and it was Seerat's call. "Where are you?" she inquired.

"Not too far from you," I replied, a playful smile tugging at my lips.

"Come on, stop playing games," she chuckled, scanning the area for me.

I Shouldn't Have Done This

On the stage, Kritika and Ankit stood together, the picture-perfect couple. Their unwavering support had been my anchor through difficult times, and I couldn't help but feel grateful.

After scanning the perimeter fruitlessly for me, she turned and made her way toward the bar.

"If you're heading to the bar, pour a drink for me too," I called out to her.

Pausing again, she glanced around, unable to locate me amidst the bustling guests. "So, you're in the mood for games?" she teased, her big brown eyes sparkling with amusement.

"Yes, I want to play with you tonight," I confessed without much thought.

She struggled to maintain her composure, pursing her lips tightly, but eventually, her resistance crumbled, and a mischievous smile danced across her lips. "Well then, you'll have to come to me for that," she challenged, now fully engaged in our playful exchange.

With a mischievous glint, I teased Seerat, "Or, how about you come to me?"

She responded quickly, "What must I do for that?"

"You have to follow my instructions," I said, my heart pounding.

"What are they?" she inquired, her curiosity piqued.

I pointed to the bar on her left, "Look towards your left. Ask the bartender to make a cocktail for you."

Her witty retort came instantly, "So, you want me drunk to take advantage of me?"

I playfully replied, "Do I need to get you drunk for that?"

Her cheeks flushed, and I could tell she was blushing, even from a distance.

"Touché," she laughed and had her cocktail.

"How is it?" I asked

"Sweet" she replied. "Who makes sweet cocktails."

"In that case, ask him for a vodka shot; you will like it."

I Shouldn't Have Done This

She ordered a vodka shot and downed it without a moment's hesitation.

"Good, now have one more," I encouraged her.

"One second," she paused to chew on a lemon slice, and I couldn't help but grin at her playfulness.

Seerat signaled the barkeeper for another shot, her gaze sweeping across the venue as she confidently downed it. After repeating the process, a gentle flush of pink colored her cheeks, a testament to the vodka's effect. Half a minute later, she rejoined the call, her voice tinged with amusement, "Now what?"

"Look to your right," I directed. Seerat complied, and I continued, "Can you spot the sweet stall?"

"Yes," she replied, scanning her surroundings.

"Head over there and indulge," I suggested.

A playful spark ignited in her eyes, and she chuckled, "I know what you're up to. You want me to have some sweets to quicken the pace."

"Well done, Ms Holmes, but you're mistaken," I replied, enjoying our banter.

"Then what is it?" she inquired, her voice brimming with curiosity.

"I just want to taste something sweet while savoring you tonight," I confessed.

Her smile revealed understanding, and she savored a Gulabjamun. I pictured the sweetness melting in her mouth, a moment that intensified my desire to hold her close and share a passionate kiss. Suppressing my urges, I shifted my position, ensuring my presence remained a secret.

"What else? Don't ask me to eat or drink anything else. I'm telling you, I won't do it," she asserted.

"That's all, I promise," I assured her.

"Now tell me, where are you?" she inquired eagerly.

I Shouldn't Have Done This

"Don't rush; wait for a few more moments. But first, go on stage and take a picture with Kritika and Ankit," I suggested.

"Why?" she questioned, intrigued by my request.

"I don't want your best friend to be upset with you for missing her wedding. Having a picture together will prove that you were here," I explained.

Without a second thought, she joined Kritika and Ankit for a photograph, positioning herself between them. While Kritika exuded radiance, my attention gravitated toward Seerat, who effortlessly outshone everyone with her undeniable allure.

"Do you see the empty table on your left?" I directed her. It was secluded at the far end of the farmhouse, away from the bustling crowd. "Go and sit there."

Without uttering a word, she nodded, her awareness of my watchful eyes evident. As she walked towards the table, the crowd gradually thinned. Just as she passed the last door of the front facade, I acted swiftly, seizing her arm and pulling her closer. A muffled exclamation escaped her lips, and I swiftly covered her mouth with my hand. Our eyes locked for a fleeting second, and the proximity allowed me to truly appreciate her beauty. Her large, kohl-lined eyes were captivating, holding a mesmerizing power capable of ensnaring anyone. Though I couldn't fathom how ancient Egyptians controlled their slaves, I was certain Seerat possessed a similar ability, with a glance capable of making anyone willingly devoted to her.

As I led Seerat to the terrace, I maintained my grip on her arm. The main building was deserted, with everyone outside, immersed in the wedding celebrations and relishing warm food on that chilly winter night. I quietly shut the terrace door, creating an intimate space for us.

"Why did you bring me here?" Seerat's breaths were deep from our hasty ascent.

"Marry me," I declared with unwavering resolve.

I Shouldn't Have Done This

The terrace was dimly lit, its faint glow emanating from the decorative lights on the front facade. Though I couldn't see her face clearly, her evident surprise intrigued me. Before she could react, I continued, "I know why you left me."

Confusion etched across her features as she asked, "Why?"

"Ankit shared all the details with me," her eyebrows furrowed with curiosity. Quickly, I chimed in, "Kritika filled her in." Her puzzled expression softened into a smirk, her head tilting.

As Ankit and Kritika exchanged their first vows (PHERA) with the Panditji chanting mantras, I elaborated, "Your fathers were close friends, and after your parents' demise, her father supported your studies and expenses. When you discovered Kritika's feelings for me, you distanced yourself, feeling indebted to her."

"Why would I feel indebted to her?" Seerat questioned, seeking clarity.

"Because her father supposedly paid for your education," I explained, summarizing the story.

"That's utter nonsense!" Seerat's attention returned to the wedding ceremony. Ankit and Kritika were taking their third phera. "For the record, her father didn't finance my education. My father was a successful businessman who left ample funds for my studies. In fact, I often treated Kritika to meals at the canteen," she clarified, offering an unexpected revelation.

Feeling foolish for jeopardizing this magical night, I glanced at Ankit, now taking his sixth vow with his parents standing proudly near the Mandap. My emotions swung between happiness and anger; I doubted Ankit despite his unwavering support.

"He said it because Kritika told him this story," Seerat replied, as if she had read my mind or perhaps sensed my inner turmoil.

"But—" Before I could utter a word, she interjected, "Because she wanted to see how Ankit would react when he found out she has feelings for you. She knew sooner or later it would come out,

I Shouldn't Have Done This

potentially ruining their relationship and your friendship. She didn't want that, so she concocted this story before getting married to him."

In that moment, I felt a mix of emotions—happy yet foolish. How could I have doubted him? He always wished the best for me.

"But Ankit already knew," I blurted out.

"But Kritika didn't know. If she had known, she wouldn't have concocted this stupid story," Seerat remarked, still gazing toward the ongoing ceremony.

"Tell me, then. Why did you leave me?" I persisted, eager for her answer despite her warning not to ask.

"I told you never to ask me that question, If only it were that straightforward; if I could divulge, I would have done so long ago," Seerat replied firmly, her eyes unyielding as they remained fixed on Ankit and Kritika.

My voice trembled with sorrow as I realized I might never know her true feelings. After waiting so long for Seerat, I only got uncertainty and disappointment. The night had not unfolded as I had hoped, yet, even in the face of rejection, I knew I could never stop loving her—she was my first and only love, and my heart belonged to her alone.

With a heavy heart and nothing left to say, I turned away, ready to leave the terrace.

"But I never said I wouldn't marry you," her voice broke through the silence, filling me with hope, "and one day, when I feel the time is right, I will tell you."

I turned back, my eyes meeting hers. I could see a glimmer of joy in her eyes in the dim light.

Overwhelmed with emotion, I couldn't contain myself any longer. I pulled Seerat into my arms and kissed her passionately, pouring all my love and longing into that moment. As Ankit and Kritika completed their last vow, the sky erupted with dazzling fireworks, illuminating the night with a breathtaking display of celebration and love.

Chapter 20

"Are you serious?" Kritika's voice thundered, leaving us all clueless and bewildered. Just a week ago, we had admired their perfect love and how well they complemented each other, and now she was yelling at him.

To be fair, it wasn't entirely her fault either. Confused? Let me take you back to the beginning of this tale. Ankit had promised Kritika a wonderful honeymoon—a romantic getaway to New Zealand, complete with skydiving, stargazing, and scenic hikes that every couple dreams of. They had meticulously planned and booked everything, all set for the perfect adventure. But here comes the twist. Just two days before their flight, Major Brar called Ankit and arranged a meeting with his senior to discuss some critical matters. Ankit couldn't say no to him, knowing that Major Brar had been instrumental in making everything possible for them.

Ankit was in a dilemma about how to break this news to Kritika, so he called me for help, and I asked Seerat to come along. He thought Kritika might not get angry if we were there to support him, but to his surprise, he was mistaken.

"Don't yell at me," Ankit mumbled, looking like a poor, embarrassed soul before us. I had always known Kritika as soft-hearted, and I couldn't have imagined in my wildest dreams that she could have this side to her.

"I am not yelling at you," she tried to control her pitch, offering us a smile that seemed more for show than genuine.

I Shouldn't Have Done This

"If that wasn't shouting, then what is?" Ankit managed to utter, still a mix of terror and embarrassment.

"You'll know when I shout," she retorted, locking her fierce gaze with his, each word emphasized with a power that sent shivers down his spine. It scared him to the core, and I could tell by the pallor of his skin and the beads of sweat forming on his forehead that he felt like he was in a chemical imbalance.

"It wasn't his fault. Mr Brar set the meeting suddenly, and I would've gladly substituted for him, but it was about the financial aspect that Ankit is in charge of," I intervened, coming to his rescue, well aware that this shield-maiden could behead me with a single mighty blow. But what kind of friend would I be if I didn't stand up for him?

"You stay out of it," Kritika exclaimed, not wanting to hear me. It seemed Ankit would have to face the consequences alone.

Seerat spoke up for the first time, trying to console Kritika, "I can understand why you're so upset. I would also be devastated if I were you, but it's not his fault. Look at him."

Ankit stood there with a puppy face, though he would have looked more convincing without that wild beard.

"Don't be mad at him; instead, make him pay for it. Maybe spend more time in New Zealand or even go to Australia along with New Zealand. I've heard Australia is fantastic this time of year," Seerat suggested, trying to ease the situation.

Ankit looked at me perplexed, wondering if Seerat was saving her or throwing herself under the bus. I told him to stay calm and understand Seerat's strategy. Kritika was too upset to listen to anyone, so Seerat calmed her down, comforted her, and validated her feelings. Later, when Kritika was better, Ankit could explain his situation and discuss things.

"Hey, you moron, when is this stupid meeting scheduled?" Seerat asked Ankit, her tone still gentle but with a hint of playfulness to lighten the mood.

I Shouldn't Have Done This

"Day after tomorrow," Ankit replied instantly, relieved someone stood up for him.

"And where is it?" She inquired, maintaining the same tone.

"Ladakh," he responded.

"That's perfect. Why don't you also go with Ankit? I've heard Ladakh is a beautiful place, and once you two return, you can go on your honeymoon," Seerat suggested, trying to be helpful.

"Yes, that's a superb idea. You should come with us," Ankit seized the opportunity, moving closer to Kritika and holding her hands. "Any place will be beautiful if you're with me."

While I admired his courage, I couldn't help but cringe at the cheesy line he picked.

"Why don't you also come with us?" I chimed in, eager to spend some quality time with Seerat. "The meeting with Major Brar will only take a few hours; after that, we'll be free. We could go to Pangong Lake the next day."

"I don't know if I can go back there after all I've been through," she hesitated, her voice tinged with uncertainty. The mention of Kashmir brought back many memories, and the pain we both endured resurfaced. I remembered those dark days when I couldn't walk for five months, and the trauma was etched in my mind.

"Come on, Ladakh is different, and you can't keep brooding over the past forever," Ankit interjected, trying to convince her.

All eyes were on Seerat, waiting for her to speak. The room was filled with profound silence, and it felt like the anticipation before our prime minister addressed the nation. We all held our breath, anxiously waiting for her response. Finally, she smiled, and she nodded, saying, "Okay, I'll go."

The moment was met with ecstatic cheers from all of us. It was a tense moment, but her decision brought relief and happiness to each one of us.

* * * * *

The air hostess announced we were approaching Leh airport, and the captain had turned on the fasten seat belt sign. As I eagerly glanced outside, the enormous barren desert came into view.

"Where is my jacket?" Seerat looked around for her jacket when we landed at Ladakh airport. As soon as we stepped out, Ladakh's chilly air and speckled sunrays welcomed us. Ladakh, which was a part of Jammu and Kashmir a year ago, is now an independent union territory.

Ladakh is a land of high mountain passes and the coldest desert in the world. It is famous for its culture, monasteries, and scenic beauty. Nature has rendered a marvelous, incredible, and implausible landscape. Situated at 10,000 feet above sea level, the amount of oxygen is less compared to plain areas. Since we had taken a direct flight, we didn't have time to acclimate ourselves, so I was a little worried about Seerat. However, it seemed she wasn't affected at all.

Ladakh Airport is a military airport, and we could see a lot of soldiers around. If it were my first time, I would have been scared, but now Ankit and I were constantly working with them, and we had been to military cantonments many times before.

After the security check, our driver was waiting outside when we came out of the airport. He dropped us at our hotel. Ankit and I freshened up and left to meet Major Brar while the girls decided to lie down and relax in their hotel rooms. The military base in Ladakh was similar to the one we saw when we first met Major Brar, but this time, we knew the drill, and things didn't seem as scary. We were familiar with the code of conduct and felt proud to be around. When the soldier asked us to sit and wait, instead of sitting quietly and worrying about what would happen next, we engaged in small talk with him. His name was Kamal Jeet Singh, and he hailed from the Moga district in Punjab. He shared some little adventures he had while serving the Indian military and also advised us on local places to roam around.

I Shouldn't Have Done This

When permission was granted, they let us inside, where we met Major Brar and two fellow officers looking after our project funding. They were clear and specific about their wants and laid a detailed plan for the next quarter. We promised them we would deliver what they wanted. The meeting went well, and soon, we were back in our hotel, ready to explore the blissful city of Ladakh.

As I stepped into the room, Seerat lay still, deep in sleep, and I hesitated to disturb her peaceful slumber. Soft lamplight cascaded over her hair, casting a gentle glow. She appeared so innocent, like a child lost in dreams. I settled beside her, planting a tender kiss on her forehead. Though she seemed asleep, a smile danced on her lips, betraying her awareness of my presence. Yet, she chose to feign sleep, turning onto her stomach.

Captivated by her serene expression, I could have lingered indefinitely. However, the weight of recent events hung heavy on my mind, sending shivers down my spine. Unwilling to disrupt her tranquil facade, I played along. I brushed aside her glossy black locks with delicate care, kissing a small heart-shaped birthmark, longing to convey the unspoken words between us.

Seerat remained motionless, masking her emotions, a skill she wielded masterfully. Yet, I sensed the tremor that coursed through her body. Beneath her surface, a tender gentleness awaited. Gently tracing letters upon her bare back, I felt her resistance wane, replaced by a longing embrace. Her heart beat against mine in that moment, a rhythmic cadence of affection.

As our lips met, it was more than a kiss; it was a promise, a culmination of longing and patience. In that embrace, love and desire intertwined, transcending even the most enchanting tales. The evening passed swiftly in her embrace, but duty called when Ankit knocked on the door.

"Aren't you guys ready yet? We have to go out. I told you to get ready and meet in an hour," he said.

I Shouldn't Have Done This

I glanced at my watch; time had slipped by unnoticed. "Just give us a moment, and we'll be ready," I replied with a forced smile.

"We'll be waiting for you guys at the reception."

As I closed the door, Seerat and I shared a laugh. Time truly flies when you're with someone you love.

"So, where are we heading?" I asked Ankit as we joined them at the reception. Kritika and Ankit sat on a sofa, engrossed in their cell phones. It was their first outing together after marriage, though not their honeymoon.

"Bro, you won't believe it. I spoke to the manager, and he arranged rental bikes for us. So I got two bikes instead of booking a cab and a driver." Ankit's excitement was contagious, and Seerat was thrilled, too.

Two marvelous metal steeds awaited us outside the hotel – one white and the other military green.

"That one's mine," Ankit claimed the military green bike before I could object. Not that it mattered; any bike would do as long as I had Seerat with me. "Let's go, don't want to miss the highlights."

"Where are we headed?" I asked as I hopped on my bike.

"Follow me," Ankit shouted over the roaring engine as we sped out of the hotel premises.

The fresh country air invigorated me, and I felt a surge of energy as we rode through Leh's narrow, hilly streets. Children played in front of their humble abodes, and I realized that this part of India hadn't fully embraced urbanization yet. Soon, we hit the main road, where the bustling market of Leh mesmerized me. But Ankit had other plans, and I was eager to see what awaited us.

We left the concrete buildings behind and ventured into a wide road winding through the barren mountains. Ankit slowed and yelled, "Ride faster, or we'll miss it!"

I didn't know where we were headed, but the thrill of the unknown propelled me forward. The rugged terrain eventually gave way to a breathtaking sight – a magnificent white-domed monument.

We stood at the doorstep of the Great Buddhist Monument, Shanti Stupa, perched atop a steep hill at a dizzying height. The place held immense religious significance for Buddhists, as it enshrined the relics of Buddha, consecrated by the 14th Dalai Lama himself. When we reached the summit, the sweeping view of Changspa village left us mesmerized. The stupa's architectural beauty drew a crowd of people, all captivated by its charm.

It felt like the gateway to a tranquil world, far removed from the chaotic lands we inhabit. I instinctively grabbed Seerat's arm, and we slipped away from the bustling crowd, finding solace in the quieter corners. Ankit and Kritika were busy taking selfies and creating memories, just like everyone else. We, too, were enjoying the moment, sitting together and witnessing the sun setting behind the majestic mountain range. The sky transformed from the blazing yellow of the sun to the warm auburn of a hearth, finally settling into a serene azure hue. The beauty of the place overwhelmed us, and it felt like we had discovered a gateway to heaven, where heaven itself embraced the heart.

As we were lost in the magical moment, Ankit's call interrupted us, "Where are you guys? We've been looking for you."

"We're coming," I replied reluctantly.

Looking at Seerat, I knew she didn't want to leave, nor did I. However, reality tugged at us, and we couldn't stay forever. We returned to the parking lot with heavy hearts, where Ankit and Kritika were waiting for us.

As they eagerly showed us the pictures they had clicked, I realized we had none to share. Our time atop the stupa was etched only in our minds as blissful memories. In the rush of today's world, we often get lost in capturing moments for our social media profiles and fail to appreciate the true essence and beauty of our surroundings.

I Shouldn't Have Done This

Perhaps we should spend more time soaking in the splendor rather than focusing solely on clicking pictures.

Next, we headed to the Leh market, which came alive as the sunset. Tourists thronged the busy market, offering an array of souvenirs, woolen clothes, Pashmina shawls, silk scarves, and local beaded jewelry.

Everything around us was so enticing that I wanted to buy it all. Seerat and I entered a shop that specialized in local beaded jewelry. The shopkeeper displayed a hundred designs, each more enchanting than the last, leaving her pondering which one to choose. However, I spotted the perfect piece—a simple silver chain with a pendant. As she adorned it, I couldn't help but adore her even more.

Our hunger pangs finally caught up, and we found a charming restaurant. Unlike traditional establishments, this one had no tables and chairs. Instead, they served food on wooden logs, each about a foot long, and we sat comfortably on the floor. Since we were a group of four, they brought two logs closer and placed a wooden plank on them. The ambience exuded a unique charm reminiscent of the monastery we had visited earlier, with red-colored paper chandeliers casting a soft glow and a subtle aroma filling the air.

The restaurant had quite an extensive menu, but to our surprise, most recipes were just variations of momo, noodles, and soup. Of course, we couldn't forget to order kahwa as well. Our hunger pangs compelled us to try a little bit of everything. To our delight, the dishes here tasted better than we had experienced in Delhi, where they infused a desi twist into every preparation. Here, the taste remained authentic, true to its original flavors, and I firmly believe that some things are best enjoyed in their pure form.

As I sipped the kahwa, memories of my time in Kashmir flooded. This version of the aromatic drink had a unique taste, distinctly different from what I had tasted before. Its mildness was complemented by a subtle hint of jaggery, which lent a delightful sweetness to the soothing blend.

I Shouldn't Have Done This

After a bustling day, we finally returned to the hotel. All I wanted was a relaxing bath and a cozy bed, as the plans for the next day were even more exhilarating.

Chapter 21

I awoke with unbridled excitement well before the alarm had a chance to ring. The anticipation of the day's adventure had kept me from sleep, yet surprisingly, I felt wide awake and energized. As the alarm finally chimed, I quietly slipped out of bed, glancing at Seerat, who still appeared peacefully asleep. With time to spare, I decided not to disturb her and headed to the hotel garden for some yoga. The fresh morning air filled my lungs as though on automatic refill, a stark contrast to the polluted air I was used to in Delhi, often called the "gas chamber."

The yoga session invigorated my body and mind, leaving me feeling refreshed and connected to nature. Afterwards, I settled in the park, enjoying the serene beauty of the slowly brightening world. The sun had yet to rise, casting a mesmerizing blend of navy and black hues across the sky. Graceful trees swayed harmoniously with the gentle breeze, seemingly performing their own ballet. It was a moment of tranquil bliss, but underlying it all was a tinge of anxiety. Our plans to visit Pangong Lake hung in the balance; rain could easily ruin our chances. The winding road through the mountains to the lake was already perilous, and with the weather turning ominous, the risks multiplied exponentially, putting our journey in jeopardy.

As I sat, yearning for the sun to rise, my phone's ring interrupted my thoughts. Our travel companion, Ankit, cheerfully greeted me, oblivious to my preoccupations. "Wake-up call, bro! Good morning," he exclaimed.

I Shouldn't Have Done This

"Good morning, thanks, but I'm already wide awake," I replied, trying to hide the concern in my voice.

"Great. Can you meet me in the garden?" Ankit asked, seemingly eager to start the day.

Curious about our contingency plans in case of bad weather, I joined Ankit in the garden. However, his shivering and inappropriate clothing for the cold winds told me he was not fully prepared for the sudden change in weather.

"I was doing some yoga," I said, attempting to explain my delay, but before I could continue, he interrupted, "I'm not in the mood for yoga. Get ready quickly; we can't afford to be late."

My apprehension finally surfaced, "We can't go anywhere in this weather."

Confused, Ankit looked around, the severity of the situation dawning on him. The once joyous dance of the trees had transformed into a struggle against the forceful winds.

Retreating to our rooms, we found Seerat and the other girl ready and waiting for us. Ankit conveyed the disappointing news, "We can't go in this weather; it's too risky."

They exchanged silent nods, knowing waiting in the hotel was safer than braving the wild weather outside. Seeking solace in Ankit's room for its better view, he slid open the balcony door, and a gust of chilly air swept in. Breakfast was promptly ordered, and I grasped the cup of tea, holding it with both palms to warm my chilled fingers. The simple milk tea, reminiscent of what we have back home, offered an unexpected comfort despite my usual indifference towards tea.

As the relentless rain persisted, our hopes dwindled, and Ankit eventually confirmed the cancellation of our Pangong Lake bookings. Disappointment hung in the air, casting a shadow over an eagerly anticipated trip.

Returning to our room with Seerat, the disappointment lingered, but the rain's charisma couldn't be denied. The weather thwarting our plans had also woven an undeniable charm, igniting a different kind of warmth between us. Cuddling and caressing, we found solace in each other amidst the cold and dreary ambience.

Lost in our intimate cocoon, a knock on the door startled us. "Who is it?" I called out, secretly hoping someone else would answer the door.

"It's Ankit," came the reply.

Sighing, I reluctantly left the warmth of the bed and quickly got dressed. "Coming," I muttered as I approached the door.

"What now?" I asked, feigning annoyance at the disruption.

"The rain has finally stopped; we can go now," Ankit declared, excitement brimming in his voice.

Checking the time, it was already ten. "We're already late; I don't think it's a good idea," I expressed my concerns honestly, yet the allure of the adventure stirred within me.

"We might not have another chance tomorrow since we've rented the bikes for only three days," Ankit explained.

"Why not extend it?" I suggested, considering the possibilities.

"No, the guy who rented us the bikes already reminded me three times that he has them booked for another group, and…" Ankit hesitated.

"And what?" I pressed for more information.

"And you can finish what you had started at Pangong Lake. I have booked separate tents for us," Ankit said, a hint of mischief in his eyes.

I looked at Seerat; she blushed, her gaze shifting towards the window.

With our adrenaline pumping, we got ready in a mere ten minutes and geared up to embark on our journey. The rain had finally ceased, but the clouds hung ominously in the sky, and the air remained cold and damp. The slippery roads presented a concern, and I couldn't help but harbor reservations about driving on such

I Shouldn't Have Done This

dangerous terrain. Yet, the die had been cast, and there was no turning back.

Seated on our bikes, Seerat and I eagerly anticipated the adventure that lay ahead. The hotel manager rushed towards us, holding out a helmet. "Sir, you forgot this," he said, breathless from his haste.

"I don't need it, but thanks," I replied, my heart pounding excitedly as I ignited the 350CC beast. Its mighty roar echoed, signifying the raw strength that would conquer Leh's unforgiving terrain.

"But sir, it's against the rules," the manager persisted, concern on his face.

"Rules are meant to be broken," I retorted playfully, engaging the gears and thundering through the driveway.

Reaching the last petrol pump before the hilly terrain, we filled both bikes' tanks and an extra can for backup. Despite its unpleasant odor, I suggested Seerat use the loo at the petrol pump, knowing there might not be any sheltered bathrooms ahead.

As we journeyed, the city's concrete jungle faded into oblivion, replaced by a desolate and captivating landscape. These roads, crafted by the remarkable efforts of the Border Roads Organization (BRO), were a testament to their relentless dedication. Skillfully navigating the treacherous curves, we occasionally encountered military convoy trucks occupying most narrow roads. However, they graciously made way for us to overtake them.

As time passed, the black clouds surrendered to the relentless sun. Ladakh's desert nature unfolded as harsh sun rays pierced our skin. Grateful for Seerat's sunscreen, we evaded the fate of Ladakhi women with their telltale red faces.

Scaling new heights, we reveled in the breathtaking landscapes that surrounded us. The majestic mountains stood tall, their silhouettes resembling erratic graphs on a doctor's monitor - a poignant reminder of life's uncertainties. I once dreamt of escaping

213

I Shouldn't Have Done This

to these mountains, seeking solace amidst their tranquility. But today, amidst their harsh grandeur, I realized we couldn't escape our realities; they would inevitably find us wherever we sought refuge.

After a challenging journey, we finally reached Chang-La Pass, a soaring milestone claimed to be the second-highest motorable road in the world at an astounding 5360 meters. Other bikers were already there, capturing the moment with pride.

"HIMANK welcomes you to the mighty CHANGLA," the milestone's inscription greeted us alongside the Indian tricolor. We, too, snapped some pictures, taking in the overwhelming beauty that surrounded us. As we refueled ourselves with a simple meal of Maggi noodles and hot coffee, we realized that this journey had already gifted us with unforgettable experiences.

In awe of the vastness and grandeur of Chang-La, we felt gratitude in our hearts, knowing that there was still so much to explore on our way to Pangong Lake.

"I'll be back in a minute," I announced cheerfully, eager to utilize the waiting time for our order to arrive by visiting the shared washroom.

The washroom experience turned out to be less than pleasant, to say the least. I gingerly entered with a heightened sense of caution, hesitating to touch anything within. Deciding not to lock the door, I hoped for a quick and uneventful visit. But fate had other plans. Midway through my business, a sudden knock on the door startled me. Reacting swiftly, I used my left foot to prevent the door from swinging open fully, averting an awkward encounter with a fellow tourist.

Stepping out of the washroom, I found myself face to face with Kritika, her expression somewhat stern. "You should have locked the door," she admonished in a slightly chilly tone.

With a sheepish grin, I retorted, "You should have knocked."

After washing my hands, I returned to our table, where Seerat and Ankit had already dug into their meals, apparently too

I Shouldn't Have Done This

famished to wait for me. Hoping Kritika would kindly refrain from mentioning the washroom incident, I took my seat and focused on the upcoming journey.

A few minutes later, Kritika reappeared, her demeanor surprisingly composed, choosing not to bring up the awkward mishap. The episode was soon forgotten as we readied ourselves to continue our thrilling adventure.

The descent from Chang-La led us into a breathtaking landscape enveloped in lush greenery, starkly contrasting the chilly and barren mountains we had left behind. Tall, majestic trees stood like silent guardians, their verdant leaves swaying gently in the mountain breeze.

The grandeur of the mountains was awe-inspiring. Their peaks seemed to stretch endlessly, reaching for the heavens as if striving to kiss the sky. Glacial streams cascaded down the slopes, their glistening waters converging to form playful rivers that meandered through the valleys, creating a mesmerizing tableau of nature's artistry. It was an enchanting spectacle that left us speechless, our eyes feasting upon the picturesque panorama.

As we rode together, we encountered a military convoy, prompting us to cautiously navigate the narrow road. The considerate soldiers allowed us to pass, and I took the lead, my heart swelling with gratitude and pride for our brave military forces.

However, after riding for a while, a feeling of unease crept over me. Ankit was nowhere in sight, and I couldn't shake off the worry that gnawed at my heart. Deciding not to ignore my gut feeling, I slowed down and waited, hoping he would catch up.

Minutes passed, each one feeling like an eternity, until a soldier from the convoy approached us with a concerned expression. He informed us of an accident that had occurred behind us. My heart sank, and without hesitation, I turned my bike around and rushed back to the site.

As I approached the scene, a wave of relief washed over me when I saw Ankit sitting on a nearby rock, accompanied by Kritika. Despite the minor scratches on his palm, he seemed relatively unharmed. Grateful for his safety, I rushed to his side, concern still etched on my face.

"Hey buddy, are you alright?" I asked, genuinely concerned for Ankit's well-being after the accident.

"Yeah, I'm fine," he replied, attempting to downplay the pain he must have been experiencing.

Turning my attention to Kritika, I gently inquired, "And you, Kritika? Are you feeling alright?" Despite not showing any visible scratches, her discomfort was apparent.

She managed a weak nod and whispered, "Yes."

"Thanks a lot, brother," I expressed my gratitude to the kind stranger who had lent a helping hand in lifting the fallen bike. The left side of the motorcycle bore some scratches, and the rear-view mirror shattered during the fall. Curiosity getting the better of me, I asked Ankit, "What happened, buddy?"

"After I overtook the military trucks, I was returning to my lane when I overlooked the gravel and loose sand on the road. My bike slipped on it," Ankit explained, still assessing his injuries. He rolled up his tight jeans to reveal a bruise on his knee.

"I think we should go back to the hotel. Let me call for some help," I suggested, reaching for my mobile to inform the hotel manager and arrange assistance.

"No, it's fine. Just give me ten minutes," Ankit insisted, walking towards the other side of the road.

"Where are you going?" I called out to him.

"To wash this sand off my hands," he replied, descending the narrow track leading to the nearby river. Intrigued, the rest of us followed suit.

As we approached the riverbank, I was taken aback by the pristine beauty of the water, untouched by human interference. The pebbles underneath appeared smooth, inviting me to dip my feet into the cold water. Unable to resist, I removed my shoes and waded into the river. The initial chill sent shivers down my spine, but soon, a soothing sensation engulfed me as I settled on a large rock within the river, submerging my feet in the gentle flow.

Gazing at the towering mountains that had stood for centuries, the river flowing like a majestic serpent between them, and the fiery sun nestled between the peaks, I felt a sense of tranquility. It reminded me of the scenery I used to sketch as a child.

We sat there in peaceful silence, our connection with nature transcending words and selfies. It wasn't an overwhelming or euphoric emotion but rather a warm, comforting one, as if I had stumbled upon a path leading to eternal contentment.

After some time, Ankit felt better, and we resumed our journey towards Pangong Lake, now just an hour away. Nature's splendor unfolded before us, presenting its mesmerizing forms in all their glory. As we continued our ride, we witnessed lush green lands and a flock of sheep grazing peacefully by the riverbank we had just experienced.

By the time we arrived at Pangong Lake, darkness had descended upon the landscape. Amidst the numerous camps, we struggled to find our designated spot. Seeking assistance, we showed our slip to a caretaker at one of the camps. He directed us to a nearby tent, but it turned out to be wrong. Our actual camp was another half-mile away.

A person awaited our arrival, holding a list of names to guide us. He instructed us to follow him on his bike, leading us to our campsite.

We were exhausted and desperate to reach the tent as soon as possible, but it seemed fate had other plans to test our determination. The road was pitch dark, with only our bike's headlight illuminating a small section ahead. As we rode, we encountered a small waterfall, something we had dealt with before on this trip. Slowing down and

I Shouldn't Have Done This

gearing down, we carefully maneuvered through the water to avoid getting drenched. However, just as we thought we had overcome this obstacle, a more significant challenge awaited us.

I spotted a massive crater in the road and slammed on the brakes, narrowly avoiding a mishap. We got off our bikes and stepped into the cold water that seeped into our shoes, numbing our feet within minutes. The Caretaker had warned us about common landslides during the rainy season in this area, but we hadn't anticipated this. I used my mobile torch to search for a relatively intact part of the road, and we found a tiny section that seemed safe to proceed on.

I signaled Ankit and the Caretaker to follow me, and we carefully pushed our bikes through the narrow passage, crossing to the other side of the crater. But that wasn't the end of our challenges. When I tried to start my bike, it refused to come to life; the water had likely affected the engine. We tried tirelessly to kick-start it for almost half an hour, but nothing worked. Exhausted and hopeless, we sat on the roadside, pondering our next move. No one was around to help, and the lack of a mobile signal made the situation even more difficult.

As I contemplated our options, an idea struck me. I sat on my bike, put it in second gear, and asked Ankit to push it. When the piston gained momentum, I quickly closed the clutch, and to our immense relief, the engine roared back to life. Thanking our lucky stars, we continued towards our camp, utterly drained from the day's events.

Upon reaching the camp, the Caretaker informed us that dinner would be ready in half an hour. Before indulging in a delicious meal, I wanted to freshen up and requested a bucket of hot water from him. Upon entering our tent, I was astonished by the setup; it felt no less than a hotel room. A comfortable double bed with a cozy mattress on one side and a small sofa on the other. A wooden shelf provided space to keep our belongings, and even a well-equipped attached bathroom with a curtain. Seeing how a temporary tent could offer such luxurious amenities was incredible.

I Shouldn't Have Done This

After a refreshing bath, we headed to the main tent for dinner, where yet another surprise awaited us. The dining tables were elegantly set, and the food was served in fancy crockery. The Caretaker then informed us about a campfire they had arranged outside, adding to the magical ambience. We were in awe of the splendid seating arrangement they had made, using sand sacks covered with plastic tarpaulin. Comfy cushions and blankets awaited us around the campfire, creating a truly out-of-this-world experience.

As we settled into our seats, the Caretaker mentioned that he would retire to his tent and that we could call him if we needed anything. He also informed us that they had to switch off all the lights after ten o'clock due to regulations. Initially, I was worried about not having access to lights to charge our cell phones, but little did I know that what lay ahead would reveal the authentic charm of our off-grid adventure.

As the clock struck ten, all the lights went out one after another, and the surroundings turned pitch dark, except for the bonfire Caretaker had set up for us. He cheekily charged us an extra three hundred bucks for it, but at that moment, I realized it was a blessing in disguise. The absence of city lights allowed the stars to shine brightly above us, an awe-inspiring sight. Coming from Delhi, where light pollution was a norm, I had never seen so many stars. It felt like someone had spilled a million diamonds in the sky, and they would twinkle there for eternity.

Seerat, sitting in the warm glow of the bonfire, looked absolutely stunning in the beige hue of the flickering flames. I admired her without blinking until she noticed and frowned at me playfully. I quickly averted my gaze, not wanting to break the magical aura around us. Instead, I laid my head on her lap as we lounged on the makeshift sofa, gazing at the glittering stars. It reminded me of the time I gifted her fireflies on the night we first made love to each other. The memory brought a sense of nostalgia and contentment.

I Shouldn't Have Done This

But as the night wore on, the temperature dropped, and I started shivering from the cold. Seerat noticed my discomfort and quickly covered me with a blanket. Her every gesture was filled with immense love, and I felt truly blessed to have her in my life. Listening to her and Ankit reminiscing about the times when Seerat wasn't around, I couldn't help but admire our bond.

Eventually, it was time to retire to our tents. Inside, it was pitch dark, and I reached for my phone to use its flashlight. However, Seerat playfully snatched it from my hand, switched off the flashlight, and tossed it away. She then moved closer, wrapped her arms around my neck, stood on her toes, and kissed my lips softly. I loved her sweet gestures and how she compensated for her short height with such affection.

Before I could respond, she broke the kiss and said, "First, go and get changed." Considering what I had in mind, it was a strange request, but I didn't want to upset her. I complied and went to the bathroom to change my clothes.

Overall, the evening had been enchanting, surrounded by nature's beauty and in the company of the one I loved most. Seerat's presence made everything perfect, and I couldn't be more grateful for the love and warmth she brought into my life.

As I stepped back into the room, she was sprawled out seductively underneath the bed's covers.

"Hey you..." I managed to mumble, my heart pounding in anticipation.

She didn't say anything but gave me a playful smirk. I paused momentarily, taking in the sight of her clothes scattered on the ground, the soft glow of a candle she had lit casting a captivating ambiance.

She gracefully got out of bed and walked over to me, her presence sending shivers down my spine. "We had some unfinished business to attend to," she said with a mischievous glint in her eyes.

I Shouldn't Have Done This

I leaned in to kiss her, but she stopped me with a teasing finger to my lips. "Not yet," she whispered, her breath warm against my skin. With a playful grin, she removed my t-shirt, pulling it over my head. Then, with a firm push, she gently forced me down onto the bed.

I tried to sit up, but she firmly held me in place. "Seerat-" I began, but she silenced me with a sensuous kiss, leaving me breathless and longing for more. She clarified she was in control, and I willingly surrendered to her desires. She wanted to take things slowly, relishing every moment of our intimate encounter.

Her lips trailed down my neck, grazing my collarbone and exploring my chest. I struggled to keep my hands in check, knowing she wanted to savor the anticipation. Her knees still pinned my hands to the bed, preventing any touch.

"Seerat," I whispered her name, the struggle evident in my eyes. Understanding my inner turmoil, she released her hold on my hands and guided them along her back. She kissed my chest, moving with tantalizing slowness, sending me electric waves. She whispered, "Your turn," and playfully nibbled my earlobe.

In one swift motion, I flipped her body onto the bed, my desire for her overwhelming. I couldn't get enough of her; my hands explored every inch of her, craving all of her. Her moans of pleasure fueled my passion, and I buried my face in her neck, biting gently until she whimpered with ecstasy.

As I looked into her eyes, I whispered, "Oh, Seerat, you drive me wild."

Chapter 22

"Give it back to me," she demanded, her face flushed from the copious amount of wine she had consumed. We sat together near the crackling fireplace in our cozy rented apartment. It had been an eventful day; her office had urged her to cover a story on a Kashmiri terror group, and despite having little choice, she bravely accepted the assignment.

When her story aired on television, it sent shockwaves through the nation and caught the attention of influential politicians. News channels buzzed with discussions about her report, hosting experts to analyze the current situation of Kashmiris. The heated debates surrounding the revelations she had uncovered dominated prime time slots. Newspapers overflowed with editorials applauding her fearless journalism, and she even received an award for her audacity. Her life had transformed, and she was now constantly on the move, covering stories across India, a bonafide celebrity in her own right.

Amid her demanding schedule, I cherished every moment spent with her whenever she was home. Navigating Delhi's traffic to travel between our homes and workplaces seemed like an unnecessary hassle, so we decided to move in together to fully revel in each other's company.

"No more wine for you," I gently confiscated the bottle, setting it on the table beside me. "You've already had enough."

In response, she playfully hurled a pillow at me. "I need more," she slurred.

I Shouldn't Have Done This

Her childlike hesitance and stumbling amused me, reminding me of a spirited little girl. Despite struggling to maintain her balance, she collapsed back onto the sofa. I offered my assistance, but she was determined to manage independently.

"You think..." she began, but a hiccup cut her off. Without hesitation, I fetched a glass of water, only for her to be interrupted by another hiccup.

I loved witnessing her like this, accessible from her usual composed exterior. Amidst the challenges of the past few years, she had dedicated herself to taking care of me and, in the process, had momentarily lost some of her carefree and mischievous essence. Now, I delighted in seeing it resurface again, for it was that very side of her that I fell in love with repeatedly.

I cherished every one of her idiosyncrasies and playful antics. They constantly reminded me why I had fallen for her in the first place.

"Come with me; let's get you to bed. Tomorrow is a big day," I suggested, extending my hand to help her. However, she couldn't manage a single step independently, so I scooped her up and tucked her into bed. The clock had already struck 1 AM, and she had a journey to Agra ahead in less than six hours.

In the stillness of the night, I gazed at her lying there, appreciating the multifaceted woman she was—strong, independent, and daring, yet with a tender and playful side that only a select few had the privilege of experiencing. These moments made our relationship extraordinary, and I treasured them.

A smile tugged at my lips as I prepared to join her in bed. No matter what life threw our way, we had each other to lean on, love, and find solace amidst the world's chaos.

* * * * *

"Good morning, sleepyhead! Wake up; you have to leave for Agra. Wake up and get ready," I said, attempting to rouse Seerat

I Shouldn't Have Done This

from her slumber. But she didn't respond. So, I moved closer, and she grabbed my arm, pulling me onto the bed. She hugged me with her eyes still closed and messy hair.

In college, I dreamed of getting married and having my wife wake me up. I imagined pulling her into bed and hugging her, just like in Bollywood dramas. Today, the situation was reversed, and she pulled me in, and surprisingly, I loved it even more. Seerat was different from anyone I had ever known.

"Come on, wake up, it's already seven," I lied.

Startled, she jumped out of bed and checked her mobile. It was still 5:30.

"Now, shower; I will make breakfast for you."

Reluctantly, she walked to the bathroom and took a shower. She emerged with only a towel wrapped around her, water droplets from her wet hair trickling down her bare shoulders, making her look divine.

I couldn't take my eyes off her. She sat on a chair near the kitchen counter, rubbing her head in pain.

"My head is still hurting," she groaned, resting her head on the counter.

"Have this lemonade; it will help," I said, placing the glass on the table. "What do you want for breakfast?"

"I don't know," she replied.

"Have some cereals."

I made a bowl of cereal for her. "When will you come back?"

"Three days. It's the last election rally in Agra, and after that, there will be no action until the day of UP elections."

"Have you given any thought about the marriage date?"

"Yes, I was thinking about it, and we will discuss it once I'm back."

She looked at the clock; the hands indicated 6:32, and she realized she was already running late. She quickly slurped her bowl of cereal and hurried to the bedroom to get dressed.

224

I Shouldn't Have Done This

"Bye honey, I'll come back soon," she kissed me and left for Agra.

With her gone, I had no idea how to spend those three days. Every moment without her felt like an eternity. Missing her already, I took out my cell phone and started looking at her pictures when a message from Ankit popped up. "Hi, how are you?"

"I am good," I typed, but another message came in before I could hit send.

"Can you come to the plant today? Major Brar wants to discuss the plant's progress."

I didn't have much work to do, so I said yes.

We were setting up our plant in Dehradun, with Ankit overseeing it closely in coordination with Major Brar. Major Brar had suggested the location, saying, "You can set up your plant in Dehradun, and I can help you whenever you need." He facilitated getting government land on lease, and we could hire labor from nearby villages at reasonable wages. However, we faced a challenge finding engineers willing to relocate to a distant town, so we established our R&D office near Delhi.

Since we were working with a government organization, we were barred from collaborating with any private entity for at least three years, extendable up to five years if necessary. Though we tried negotiating, most of the funding came from the government, making it more of a grant than an investment, as Major Brar often reminded us. He believed "it was not the government's business to do business."

This venture was a kind of experiment for Major Brar; existing technology in the market wasn't suitable for military use. While the government entity responsible for research did a commendable job, they lacked the production capacity and rate needed. So, they decided to fund and help us develop the technology for mass production to support the defense services.

225

I Shouldn't Have Done This

We had already made significant progress, developing drones with high-definition cameras that could fly into enemy areas and send live footage to the base. Additionally, we created drones with high payload capacity to supply medicines and other essentials to our soldiers in remote locations. Another invention was a small drone capable of flying into enemy territory and exploding like a grenade.

When I arrived at the plant, I met with Major Brar and the other senior members from the engineering wing. Surprisingly, they listened to us very carefully and attentively. The meeting went much smoother than anticipated; it felt more like a friendly discussion than a formal one. They displayed a keen sense of observation and possessed sound technical knowledge. They had doubts about our technology and production setup, which we had planned earlier. Fortunately, we managed to address their concerns, and the meeting ended positively well past seven in the evening. Since it was too late to return to Delhi and Seerat wasn't home, I decided to stay at the guesthouse.

Ankit invited me over for dinner at his house. After getting married, Ankit and Kritika rented an apartment near the production facility in Dehradun. Initially, Kritika was hesitant, but after some convincing, she agreed, and now she had fallen in love with the place. During her last visit to our house, she talked for an hour with Seerat, expressing how much she liked the weather and couldn't even imagine returning to Delhi.

Before heading to dinner, I decided to call Seerat. It was just the first day, and I already missed her terribly. "Hi baby, how are you?" I asked.

"Can I call you back? I am in the middle of something," she replied and hung up.

I admired her sincerity and enthusiasm about her work, but sometimes it broke my heart when she couldn't spare some time for me.

I Shouldn't Have Done This

Ankit's home wasn't far from the guesthouse, so I walked over. Kritika had already prepared dinner for us and was a brilliant cook. Ankit poured some whiskey and wine for Kritika and us before dinner. It was a fantastic night, except for the fact that I missed Seerat terribly, and she didn't even seem to be thinking about me. I kept checking my cellphone occasionally, hoping for a call or message from her, but there was nothing.

Eventually, the friendly dinner turned into a business meeting when Ankit asked about the feedback Major Brar had given. Kritika didn't seem interested in the discussion and made it clear with a stern look at Ankit.

"Why don't we discuss this over a coffee tomorrow in the office?" Ankit proposed, and I quickly diverted the conversation to a more casual topic.

The next day, we thoroughly discussed all the topics at the office, and after the discussion concluded, I left for Delhi. Unfortunately, there was a massive traffic jam on the way home, so I made a few phone calls. I contacted Roy, who worked in our Delhi office, and explained the changes in design, asking him to incorporate them into the model. I also called a few vendors. As the traffic continued slowly, I called Mr. Sharma, the real estate agent helping us find a house after our marriage.

"Hi, Mr. Sharma, how are you? I was waiting for your call," I said.

"I am good," he replied, with his thick accent, explaining that he was caught up with work and couldn't call earlier.

"What about our home? Haven't you found anything suitable for us yet?"

"I have an apartment in Punjabi Bagh, so if you are interested, I can arrange a meeting," he said.

"Yes, sure. When can we meet?" I was excited about the prospect.

"Come at 5 in the evening. The house owner is leaving for Bangalore tomorrow," he informed me.

I Shouldn't Have Done This

Though I wished to go there with Seerat, I didn't want to miss this opportunity. "I will be there," I assured him.

I tried to reach Seerat again, but she didn't pick up. She is probably still busy with the election coverage. Disappointed, I honked the car horn and vented my frustration at other cars.

* * * * *

I reached the location approximately 15 minutes before the agreed-upon time, debating whether to call Mr. Sharma to confirm the address. Deciding to wait five more minutes, I pulled out my phone, disappointed to find no messages or calls from Seerat. "She could have at least left a message," I muttered, my heart sinking.

"Perhaps she's caught up with work. You know how competitive it is out there," the sensible part of me reasoned, attempting to console the restless thoughts within. Before the internal debate could continue, Mr. Sharma arrived.

After exchanging pleasantries, Mr. Sharma led me to the apartment, and immediately, I felt a surge of excitement—it was love at first sight. The place was perfect for both of us, but I refrained from showing my enthusiasm to Mr Sharma, employing an essential bargaining tactic that might save me some money.

"How do you like it?" Mr. Sharma inquired.

"It's nice, but I'm not entirely sure," I replied, attempting to conceal my genuine interest. I asked a few more questions, then took my leave.

Spending the night without Seerat weighed heavily on my heart. I longed to meet her again and share the excitement of the house I had seen—a place we could finally call our own, where we could begin building our new family together. As I lay in bed, memories of how we first met and how our love blossomed flooded my mind. Despite knowing how deeply we cared for each other, there was still a lingering question from the past, Why had she left me?

I Shouldn't Have Done This

Sleep eventually claimed me, and my mind wandered into the realm of dreams, where our journey continued.

* * * * *

I woke up late the next day, and upon checking the time, it was already fifteen past ten. However, my heart was brimming with joy because Seerat was coming back. As I glanced at my phone, disappointment washed over me as there were no messages from her. I felt Mixed fury and sadness, but I couldn't wait any longer. I dialed her number, and she cut my call.

Frustration surged, and I called her repeatedly until she finally picked up. "What?" she curtly said.

After three days of trying, she had only one word for me— "What."

"Where are you, and what are you doing?" I inquired.

"I am driving, baba. I will call you later."

"That's what you said yesterday and the day before yesterday."

"I was busy, but now I have finished all my work and am coming home. Once I reach, we can talk all day."

Suddenly, my annoyance dissipated upon hearing she was on her way back home. "Really, you're coming back?"

"Yes, now can I hang up?"

"What's the hurry? I called you for the last three days, and you didn't pick up, and now, when you do, you want to end the call. It feels like you don't love me anymore," I teased playfully.

"I love you, but I was busy, and now I am driving. It's not safe, and it goes against the rules."

"Rules are meant to be broken," I replied with a hint of mischief.

"Fine, tell me what it is."

"I have good news."

"What? Are you pregnant?" She giggled at her own joke.

"No," I replied, slightly irritated.

"Then?"

I had exciting news to share about the perfect house I found, but I decided to make it more fun. "First, give me a kiss."

"I'll kiss you once I reach home. Now, tell me what the good news is."

"No, I need it right now. I can't wait any longer."

"Fine," she agreed, and with anticipation, I heard her voice, "Uuummm...." Then, a loud sound and her scream interrupted the moment.

"Seerat, Seerat, what happened? Are you alright?" I asked worriedly, but she didn't say anything

My heart raced as I redialed Seerat's number repeatedly, but each attempt ended in frustration as the call went unanswered. Fear gripped me, and I imagined all sorts of terrible scenarios, making my anxiety soar.

Unable to sit still, I grabbed my car keys and rushed to the door. I needed to ensure she was safe, no matter what it took. With my mind clouded by worry, I fumbled with the keys and finally started the car. The engine roared to life, and I sped off towards the direction Seerat was supposed to be coming from.

The sun dipped below the horizon, casting elongated shadows upon the desolate road as I drove with increasing urgency, each beat of my heart syncing with the passing seconds. An avalanche of terrifying thoughts cascaded through my mind. What if she had been in an accident? What if she lay injured on the roadside, awaiting aid that might never arrive?

I redialed Seerat's number, fervently hoping for her answer, but was met with a disheartening voicemail tone. Panic surged, threatening to overwhelm my senses. Clutching the steering wheel tighter, I pressed the accelerator, urging my car to propel faster to reach her before it was too late.

As I advanced along the route Seerat was expected to take, each mile felt like a hammer blow to my chest. The road unfurled endlessly before me, a sinuous ribbon of asphalt leading only to the

I Shouldn't Have Done This

depths of my apprehension. With every twist and turn, I prayed for a glimpse of her car, a sign that she remained safe and unharmed.

Unable to bear the burden of uncertainty alone, I dialed Ankit's number, my fingers trembling as I awaited his response. When he finally answered, I poured out my fears, my voice cracking as tears filled my eyes.

"I don't know what to do," I confessed.

After a pause, he said, "Do you know where she was when she called you?"

"No," I replied, my voice strained with worry.

"No problem. I'll contact my father to retrieve her cell phone location. Send me your location as well. Kritika and I are on our way. If you find her, call me immediately," he instructed before ending the call.

My mind whirled with a tempest of anxiety and dread, each moment without her stretching into an eternity. Memories of our laughter shared dreams, and the warmth of her touch flooded my thoughts, intensifying the ache of her absence. I replayed our last conversation, her voice now a haunting melody, a stark reminder of what I stood to lose.

I snapped out of my reverie as my phone rang, an unknown number flashing on the screen. With bated breath, I answered, hoping it was Ankit's father.

"Hello, this is Constable Sumit Mishra from the general hospital," the voice on the other end said. "Your number is listed as Seerat ji's emergency contact. What is your relationship with her?"

"I am her fiancé. How is she? Is she okay? What happened?" I queried urgently.

"She has been in an accident and has been admitted to Agra General Hospital. Please come here," the constable informed me.

My heart plummeted at those words, though a part of me still denied their reality. It was my fault. I had pressured Seerat to talk to

I Shouldn't Have Done This

me while she was driving. If something happened to her, I wouldn't be able to forgive myself.

Arriving at the hospital, I raced through the sterile corridors, my footsteps echoing in the empty hallways. The scent of antiseptic hung heavy in the air, mingling with the sharp tang of my fear. I demanded information about Seerat's condition, my voice strained with desperation, "Where is Seerat?" I inquired

"She's in the operating theatre. The doctors have informed us that her condition is critical. Please complete the formalities at the counter," the policeman directed.

"How did this happen?" I sobbed uncontrollably, my emotions overwhelming me. "Her car collided with a truck. We're still investigating the details," he explained gently.

I knew how it had happened. I was the one who had called her despite her reluctance. I was the reason she was in this critical condition.

Sitting in front of the operating theatre, consumed by worry for her well-being, was the only action left to me. I had weathered tough times before but never felt such profound helplessness. Unable to contain my frustration any longer, I turned to the nurse and inquired about the expected duration of the procedure. Just as despair threatened to overwhelm me completely, Ankit and Kritika arrived.

When I caught sight of Ankit, I could no longer hold back my tears. He approached and enveloped me in a comforting embrace, sensing my anguish and helplessness. With a nod to Kritika, he directed her to escort me to the waiting area while he took charge, engaging with the nurse and constable to gather information.

Each ticking second stretched into an agonizing eternity, the weight of uncertainty crushing my spirit. When the operating theatre doors finally parted, granting me a fleeting glimpse of her, I couldn't trust my eyes. There she lay, once the epitome of beauty and vitality, now reduced to a fragile figure adorned with bruises and

I Shouldn't Have Done This

swathed in plaster. My heart shattered at the sight, tears welling in my eyes as I beheld her lifeless form surrounded by a labyrinth of medical apparatus.

"How is she, Doctor?" Ankit's voice trembled with concern, mirroring the turmoil within my soul.

"We've done everything we can," the doctor's somber tone conveyed the gravity of the situation. "But her condition remains precarious. The next 24 hours will be critical. She has sustained multiple fractures and injuries."

My chest tightened with an unbearable ache, the weight of uncertainty pressing me like a leaden cloak. Each word from the doctor was a dagger to my heart, plunging me further into the depths of despair.

My legs gave way beneath me, and I collapsed onto the chair I had occupied just moments before. Ankit rushed to my side, offering support, but his presence couldn't alleviate the suffocating weight of guilt and anguish that consumed me. I cursed myself inwardly, knowing that my mistake had caused her suffering.

After what felt like an eternity, they transferred her from the operating theatre to the ICU, granting me permission to see her. She lay there, unconscious and vulnerable, a bruise marring her delicate features and plaster encasing her injured leg. A tube protruded from her mouth, a drip attached to her trembling hand. Every ounce of her pain resonated within me, a relentless ache that tore at my soul.

I wished fervently that I could trade places with her, to bear her suffering in her stead. If granted a single wish by a merciful god, I would willingly exchange my existence for hers in an instant. I longed to reach out, to caress her cheek, to press my lips to hers, to envelop her in a tender embrace, and whisper reassurances that everything would be alright.

As I reached out to touch her hand, trembling with hope and fear, a miracle unfolded before my eyes – her fingers twitched in response. A surge of euphoria swept over me, and in that moment,

I Shouldn't Have Done This

I knew she could feel my presence. Gratitude overwhelmed me, a cascade of prayers answered by a benevolent higher power.

Excitedly, I beckoned the nurse, my voice trembling with anticipation, as I shared the miraculous movement of her hand. Could this be a sign that she was finally out of danger?

But reality crashed down like a tidal wave as the nurse gently explained that it was merely a reflex, a response to the agony coursing through her injured body. With her words, my elation dissolved into a suffocating sorrow. How could I have caused her such agony? The weight of guilt pressed down on me, crushing my spirit.

Ankit and Kritika, ever supportive, urged me to eat, but my appetite and happiness vanished. I declined their offer and retreated to the floor outside the ICU, consumed by remorse. They joined me, their presence a comfort amidst the silent chaos of the sleeping hospital.

As the world around me slipped into slumber, I remained restless, unable to find solace in sleep. Instead, I whispered fragments of prayers learned in childhood, seeking solace in their familiar cadence, even as tears silently trailed down my cheeks.

When I saw a familiar figure, I had seen this man before, yes I remember he was the one I saw when I was in Kashmere and got stuck during stone pelting and a stone hit my head and fell in the forest and asked me not to give up on Seerat.

"What happened? Someone told me that you were looking for me." That man came closer to me, this time I knew that it wasn't a madman from the forest, a doctor told me that my mind was hallucinating the last time I saw him due to the interrupted blood supply to my brain but this time I was okay I knew that he was god, but he denied it.

"Please, god help me; please save Seerat." I kneeled in front of him and bagged.

"I am no god, and this is not in my hand; her fate is already destined, and nobody can change it."

I Shouldn't Have Done This

"Why are you doing this to me?"

"Why would I do anything to you or anyone in this universe? You are a being of free will. You lived all your life with your choice, and when the result of your choices comes, you blame god for this."

"What choices are you talking about? I lived all my life with dignity; I did nothing wrong, always helped others, and never harmed anyone. Yes, I gave up a few times, and the last time you pointed this out, I realized this was my mistake and rectified it; then why is all this happening to me."

"This is just the result of your Karmas; you will reap what you saw." He smiled

"What Karmas are you talking about." His habit of not coming straight to the point frustrated me.

"Rules are meant to be broken; you have used these words a thousand times all your life. You have broken rules millions of times, and people have suffered because of it. Karma has given you chances, but there is a limit to everything; even Lord Krishna forgave Shishupal for 100 mistakes and even had to punish him for his 101st mistake. Karma gives you chances to rectify your mistakes, but when you don't understand, it gives you a warning and finally punishes when the person does not understand."

"But I never had any chances or warnings, so why am I being punished?" I questioned, my voice tinged with frustration and confusion.

"Karma operates by its own laws, unaffected by exceptions," came the solemn reply. "Throughout your life, you've flouted rules and been granted numerous opportunities. Even when faced with near-death in Kashmir, it served as a warning, yet you failed to heed it. Now, what you face is the consequence."

A wave of anguish coursed through me as memories of my past flashed before my eyes, tears welling up involuntarily. "Then punish me if you must, but why Seerat?" I pleaded.

I Shouldn't Have Done This

"I am no deity, and who am I to mete out punishment?" the voice responded calmly. "Your lives are intertwined; sometimes, one person's Karma can affect another. Just as a father's hard work can bring wealth and prosperity to his children, so too can one's actions impact those around them. Your Karma has inevitably influenced her life."

At that moment, the weight of my actions and their repercussions reverberated within me, leaving me grappling with the profound interconnectedness of our fates. "Please, forgive me. I'll do anything to make things right. Just save her," I begged, desperation choking me.

He smiled gently. "Then dedicate your life to guiding others away from the mistakes that you made. Seerat will live, but your journey isn't over. One day, when your karmic slate is clean, you'll be reunited."

AFTER 18 MONTHS

EPILOGUE

I glanced at my phone; the glowing display read 05:30. I anticipated the alarm's chime, though I no longer relied on it to rouse me. Sleep had become a rare visitor, evading my grasp through most of the night. Instead, I often found myself gazing into the abyss of darkness that enveloped my surroundings—an echo of the shadows that seemed to pervade my life.

I still recall my dream on my first day of college—an interview scenario, now a reality. It was the dream of becoming an entrepreneur, of instigating societal change. Today, I am hailed as a successful businessman, yet the fulfilment of this dream has not bestowed the happiness I once craved.

When the alarm eventually sounded, I rose from the bed and drew open the curtains, welcoming the morning light that illuminated the room. Yes, this was the house I had envisioned sharing with Seerat. It was another dream that became a reality, but not how I envisioned it.

The man I saw in the hospital, I don't know whether he was god, an angel or a manifestation of my mind, said that he would let the Seerat live with me, but that doesn't mean I will not be punished. It has been eighteen months since that incident, but there hasn't been a single day when I didn't curse myself for what I did to her.

I took a thermometer, checked her temperature, and noted her vitals. Her condition was stable, but she was still in the Coma. I spent most of my time beside her, refused to leave Seerat's side, and determined to be there when she woke up.

But that man told me one more important detail that became the basis of my life: if and when my Karmic slate was clean, we would be together again, which became my life's mission. Now,

238

Epilogue

wherever I go, whoever I talk to, I tell everyone not to make the same mistakes that I did.

"Good morning, Sir," greeted Ms. Anita, who cared for Seerat in my absence.

"Good morning. I've checked Seerat's vitals and made note of them. Please tend to her and change her clothes."

"Today is a special day," Anita remarked, fetching fresh attire for Seerat.

Indeed, it was a significant day. I had been invited as the chief guest to the college where I once studied. Assisting Anita in attending to Seerat, I instructed her, "You look after her. I'll prepare and leave. If anything arises, don't hesitate to call me."

* * * * *

When I reached college, many people were standing there to welcome me, and I could not recognize them except for Mr Shastri, who used to teach us thermodynamics. The college has changed a lot; the water fountain that amused me when I came here first was missing, the admin block has been shifted, and so has the auditorium. In the auditorium, I met Ankit, who was sitting beside me. We cherished a few moments in this college before the program started.

Engaged in conversation about our current project, I was interrupted by the announcement of my name and an invitation to the stage.

"Please, sir, share some of your life experiences with us and inspire the students," the program's host urged.

Unaware of what to do next, I stepped on the stage and poured my heart out.

My dear friends, esteemed guests,

As I stand before you today, I am humbled by the opportunity to share a piece of my heart with you. My journey has been a

Epilogue

winding road, fraught with missteps and mistakes, but it has also been illuminated by moments of profound clarity and grace.

There was a time when I thought breaking the rules was cool, and it was the only key to unlocking my dreams, oblivious to the toll it would take on those I held most dear. My fiancé, the anchor of my soul, stood by me with unwavering love and support. Yet, in my relentless pursuit of success, I lost sight of what mattered.

The pain of that loss, my friends, is a daily burden. It is a wound that refuses to heal, a reminder of the depths of my fallibility. But it is also a testament to the power of love—love that endures even in the face of our gravest mistakes.

And I'm sure that each of you gathered in this room is familiar with the karmic cycle and the principle of reincarnation—a fundamental concept found in many faiths. It's the belief that our actions in this life shape our destiny in the next and that this cycle of birth and rebirth continues until our karmic debts are balanced, leading us back to the source of our existence.

Some may believe in a different cosmology, one that includes notions of heaven, hell, angels, or demons. But regardless of our individual beliefs, one thing remains constant: the unseen forces surrounding us. They are not distant entities lurking in the heavens or beneath the earth's surface. No, they are right here, among us, behind every wall, every window, observing our every action, recording every deed.

I cannot say whether reincarnation is governed by karma, but I am sure of one thing: when we depart from this life, our karmic debts are settled. We reap what we sow in this lifetime alone. And if, indeed, we are granted another chance at life, our karmic slate is wiped clean. We are given a fresh start, a blank page to inscribe our new destiny. Such is karma's profound simplicity and significance— an elemental force as fundamental as the atom itself. The accident had happened because of me. I had insisted on talking to her while she was driving, and she had tried to reason with me, saying she

Epilogue

would call me back later. But I was adamant and selfish, wanting to hear her voice, oblivious to the dangers of the road.

That moment replayed in my mind a million times, tormented by regret and guilt. If only I had waited, if only I had understood the risks, perhaps she wouldn't be lying here, fighting for her life. The weight of responsibility crushed my spirit, and I couldn't forgive myself for putting her in harm's way.

Weeks turned into months, and Seerat's condition remained critical. Every day was a rollercoaster of emotions as we witnessed minor improvements followed by setbacks. It was a painful journey, and every moment felt like an eternity.

I immersed myself in Seerat's favourite books—their pages worn, their stories etched into my consciousness. I sought solace in the rhythm of her heartbeat monitor, hoping it would sync with mine once more. The nurses, their eyes kind yet knowing, became my confidantes. They understood the silent battles raging within me—the guilt, the longing, the desperate plea for forgiveness.

I whispered secrets to Seerat, secrets I had never shared before— the childhood fears, the dreams unfulfilled, the fragility of my own mortality.

I stood by her, sharing memories of happier times and telling her how much I loved her. I pleaded with her to wake up, to forgive me for my recklessness, and to give me a chance to make things right.

But Seerat didn't wake up, breaking my heart into a million pieces. The pain of seeing her lying there, unresponsive, was unbearable. Our dream house became my sanctuary and prison as I clung to the hope that she would someday open her eyes and smile at me again.

In the quiet moments of solitude, I have realized the actual cost of my mistake. It was not the accolades or achievements that left me hollow; it was the absence of the one who loved me unconditionally despite my flaws.

Epilogue

And so, I stand before you not as a success story but as a humble pilgrim on a journey of redemption. My past mistakes are a stark reminder that true fulfillment is not found in the pursuit of glory but in the bonds of love and compassion that binds us together.

So, my dear friends, I implore you to heed my words. Do not make the same mistakes that I made. Cherish every moment, every embrace, every whispered "I love you." For it is in these simple acts of love that we find the true essence of our humanity.

Every night when I sleep, I see her. I talk to her, love her, and then I hear her scream, and wake up shouting, "I shouldn't have done this". May this story be a testament to the power of love, forgiveness, and redemption. And may it serve as a beacon of hope for all those who have stumbled along the way.

Thank you from the depths of my heart.

www.ingramcontent.com/pod-product-compliance
Lightning Source LLC
LaVergne TN
LVHW061542070526
838199LV00077B/6869